The Legal Career Guide:
From Law Student to Lawyer

Gary A. Munneke
Associate Professor of Law
Pace University School of Law

American Bar Association
Career Series

The Legal Career Guide
Copyright © 1992 by the American Bar Association.
All rights reserved.
Printed in the United States of America.

Library of Congress Catalog Card Number: 92-071306
ISBN: 0-89707-763-6

American Bar Association
750 North Lake Shore Drive
Chicago, Illinois 60611

2 3 4 5 6 7 96 95

About the Author

Gary A. Munneke is an Associate Professor of Law at Pace University School of Law where he teaches Torts, Professional Responsibility, and Law Practice Management. A 1973 graduate of the University of Texas School of Law, Professor Munneke is a member of the Texas and Pennsylvania bars. He is an active member of the American Bar Association, serving as Chair of the Law Practice Management Section Publishing Board, and the President's Coordinating Committee on Legal Education. Previously he served the ABA as Chair of the Standing Committee on Professional Utilization and Career Development, a member of the editorial boards of *Barrister* and *Legal Economics* magazines, and the Task Force on the Role of the Lawyer in the 1980s. Professor Munneke has engaged in career counseling for law students since 1973 and has served as Research Chair and President of the National Association for Law Placement. He conducts LawStart seminars for students entering law school and has spoken extensively on the topic of careers in law.

Professor Munneke's other books include: *Materials and Cases on Law Practice Management* (West, 1991); *Careers in Law,* VGM Professional Career Series (1992); *Barron's Guide to Law Schools;* 9th ed. (Barron's, 1990); *How to Succeed in Law School* (Barron's, 1989); *National Association for Law Placement 1985 Employment Report and Salary Survey* (NALP, 1986); *Opportunities in Law Careers* (VGM Career Horizons, 1981, 1986); *Non-Legal Careers for Lawyers: In the Private Sector,* with Frances Utley (ABA, 1984): *Your New Lawyer: The Legal Employer's Complete Guide to Recruitment, Management, and Development,* ed. (ABA, 1984); and *The Report of the Task Force on the Role of the Lawyer in the 1980s.* (ABA, 1981).

Contents

Acknowledgments

This manual was influenced by *From Law Student to Lawyer,* the first book in the Career Series of the American Bar Association. The Series is designed to provide law students and lawyers with information on the practice of law and its alternatives through books and monographs that cover not only general information applicable to all who seek to use their legal training for maximum professional achievement and in the service of others but also information on specialized practice for those who wish to direct their energies into particular areas of law.

A project of this scope is not, nor could it ever be, undertaken by one person or a small group of individuals. It was conceived and is being carried through by the American Bar Association Law Student Division.

The Board of Governors and Standing Committee on Association Communications have reviewed the concept of the Series and the program and have given it their unanimous approval.

The author expresses particular thanks to Frances Utley, former staff director for the ABA Standing Committee on Professional Utilization and Career Development who served as author of two earlier ABA books on career planning, *Where Do I Go From Here?* (1973) and *From Law Student to Lawyer* (1984). Indeed, many of Ms. Utley's ideas and words are incorporated in this text. As the voice of the ABA on matters involving career development for over two decades before her retirement she has made a lasting contribution to the career planning field that is evidenced in this work.

In addition, the author thanks former Dean W. Page Keeton for his support at the University of Texas School of Law, as well as Alice Scull Kirkendall, Rachel Treichler and Adrienne Diehr, also from Texas, who contributed to *The Placement Handbook,* portions of which are incorporated herein.

Several people contributed to the author's professional growth. Law school classmate, Diana Marshall, who is now a partner at Baker and Botts in Houston, was a constant sounding board for ideas from 1973 to 1980. Remarks from a 1975 speech by Julie Johnson, then placement director at Stanford Law School, added insight into the role of the law placement director. She said that our emphasis ought to be on career counseling, because if students did not know what they were looking for, they could make serious mistakes and become dissatisfied personally and professionally. She was one of the first to suggest that placement directors spend more time helping people and less time scheduling them.

Gratitude is due also to the speakers at a February, 1984 program called "Salvation for the Solo Practitioner," J. Harris Morgan, Roberta Ramo, Sam Smith, Jimmy Brill, and Bernard Sternin. They suggested that lawyers should run their practice in a business-like way, and proclaimed that if lawyers did not get organized, develop systems, and implement sound business practices, they would not prosper. The idea that law students need to understand how law firms operate in order to make sound career decisions as well as to succeed in those organizations evolved from this program.

The author thanks Cullen Smith, managing partner of the Waco, Texas firm of Naman, Howell for initiating my American Bar Association involvement, and Ann Kendrick of Lewis and Clark Law School who persuaded the author to become actively involved in the leadership at the National Association for Law Placement (NALP). I would also like to thank Lujanna Wolfe Treadwell, executive director of NALP, Professor Peter Kutulakis of Dickinson School of Law, and Kathleen Carlisle, Associate Director of Career Planning and Placement at Widener University School of Law.

Finally, the author expresses appreciation to many colleagues and friends from the NALP who have shared their ideas, opinions and information over the years.

Professor Gary A. Munneke
March, 1992

Part I

Career Planning

Most gulls don't bother to learn more than the simplest facts of flight – how to get from shore to food and back again. For most gulls, it is not flying that matters, but eating. For this gull, though, it was not eating that mattered, but flight. More than anything else, Jonathan Livingston Seagull loved to fly.

Richard Bach

1
Choosing a Career vs. Finding a Job

The legal profession occupies a unique and enviable place in the American social order. Ever since our colonial forbearers booted out the British, and de Tocqueville proclaimed lawyers as the new American aristocracy, lawyers have enjoyed a certain mystique in this country.

It is not that attorneys did not exist before the American revolution, or that they have not exerted influence in other societies. And it is not simply that the Declaration of Independence, the Constitution, and the American Revolution were in large measure the product of legal thinking. The truth is that a nation built upon the rule of law places lawyers at the focal point of many transactions that govern the daily lives of its people. For over 200 years lawyers have carried this mantle.

The popular television series *L.A. Law* epitomizes the current public fascination with lawyers just as Perry Mason did a generation before. Even before television, lawyering was seen as the avenue to prestige and security for countless aspiring immigrants, generations of aspiring politicians, and innumerable blue bloods following in the footsteps of their fathers. The bottom line is that lawyers possess tremendous prestige, if not always respect, in this country.

Lawyers are well off economically; they do not make as much money as doctors, but they do not starve either. A family lawyer, the late George Red of Houston, said to me while I was in law school, "You'll never get rich practicing law. You can make a comfortable living, but the only rich lawyers were born that way or went into business with their clients."

People go to law school for a number of reasons other than money and status. Many students choose law in order to influence

3

the outcome of events or to persuade others. Many come to law school because of the intellectual challenge or because they are attracted by the problem-solving aspect of legal studies. Because the legal profession is diverse, and because law schools seek diversity when they recruit students, there are many other reasons why people pursue legal careers.

Although it is probably futile to generalize about the psychological attributes of law students and lawyers as a group, all of us have chosen law. We contemplate a career in law. We take the LSAT. We endure three or four years of law school. We survive a grueling bar examination. And we embark upon a career with great hopes for the future. Most of us find jobs as lawyers, and many of those who do not were pursuing alternative careers from the beginning.

By all accounts, we lawyers have it all. Perhaps no other field offers a comparable combination of monetary rewards, prestige, and potential satisfaction as does the law. Certainly, no other career offers as wide an array of options.

Why, then, are we not happy? Despite the advantages of being a lawyer, a number of studies confirm that there is a high level of dissatisfaction within the legal profession. This troubling conclusion was reached in surveys produced by the ABA Young Lawyer's Division in 1979, 1985, and 1990, and by the Maryland State Bar Association in 1988.

I am haunted to this day by the suicides of two classmates, Boyd and Louise. Boyd was a brilliant law review editor, a pleasant personality and a dedicated lawyer. Although he could have practiced anywhere, he chose a career in public interest law representing migrant workers in South Texas.

Boyd came by my office at the University of Texas once to talk about changing jobs. He was frustrated and discouraged by the work, but determined to move on. About two weeks later, I was shocked to learn that he had taken a different way out.

Louise was strikingly beautiful, articulate, and talented. She came from money and dressed immaculately. She married well and seemed to be happy. In her professional life, Louise prospered so well in her law firm that she was appointed to a judgeship. But somehow, all this was not enough. Before she reached the age of 30, Louise took her own life.

I am not recounting these stories to depress you, but rather to share with you my perplexity. How could these two people with so much going for them decide that life did not offer enough to merit going on? And, while Boyd and Louise may be extreme examples, why are there so many lawyers who are unhappy with their lives?

The key question for law students contemplating the future should not be "How do I find a job?" but "How can I find satisfaction in a legal career?" Many lawyers do find happiness in their careers. They use the law as a vehicle to develop and sustain the lifestyle they have chosen. Most lawyers would not give up their jobs to go work on the assembly line. Thus, the central questions for anyone entering the legal profession should be, "How do I locate the road to happiness?" and "How can I avoid treading the road that leads to dissatisfaction?" This book starts with the assumption that you want to know more than simply how to get a job. You want to know how to find satisfaction in this career you have chosen.

Look at the terms *job* and *career.* A job is the sale of your skills, time, and energy to someone for a fee. Even if you are self-employed, you sell your skills to yourself. A job is work for pay, and work is not always fun. A job implies that it is something you do out of necessity, for reasons like keeping food on the table and a roof overhead.

A career, however, is an identity—a series of jobs connected by a common theme. With a job, you can leave it behind when the five o'clock whistle blows. With a career, you maintain the identity whether you are on the job or not.

When someone asks a corporate lawyer who works for an auto company what she does, her answer is not "I work for Chrysler." She says, "I'm a lawyer." Artistic types have probably mastered this better than anyone. If you ask the waiter in a restaurant down in Greenwich Village what he does, he will tell you "I'm an actor." If you ask the clerk in the antique bookstore what she does, she will answer, "I'm a writer."

Law school does an excellent job of imparting an identity as a lawyer. No matter what you do after you graduate, you will always be a lawyer. You can never go back to being a *nonlawyer,* the pejorative term we use to describe all those who are not members of our elite club.

Taking this thought a step further, there are many careers within the legal profession. That is, there are countless alternative identities as lawyers.

Increasingly, lawyers are not just the generic brand, but some subspecies of the more general identity. Part of the process of finding happiness is discovering the unique identity within the legal profession that is particularly yours.

Richard Bolles, in his book *The Three Boxes of Life* suggests that our lives are made up of three "boxes"— working, playing, and learning. At different times in our lives, we spend more time in one of the boxes than the others. While we are in school, we are in the learning box. At our jobs, we are working. When we retire, we devote ourselves to play. Bolles suggests that for our lives to be most satisfying, they should always incorporate elements of all these boxes.

You should strive to meld work and play. Find jobs where work is play. Get paid to have fun. If Michael Jordan can do it, so can you. Too often, we are either unable or unwilling to free ourselves to enjoy what we do. Or we are so driven that we do not allow ourselves to find an ounce of pleasure in our work.

Wake up, people! Life is too short to spend it being miserable. And the answer is not to assume a Panglossian view of the world, refusing to accept reality. Life is full of pain, disappointment, drudgery, and frustration. Happiness is not as much constant bliss as it is success in overcoming adversity.

It is hard to imagine any type of training that offers the individual a range of career choices greater than legal education does. That very availability of choice dictates the importance for each law student to develop at least a broad outline of the goals he or she hopes to achieve, both professionally and personally.

This book will aid you in making your decision by providing information that is as accurate and up-to-date as possible. It will refer you to reliable sources for checking information and updating your career plans. And since the value of mentors in career education cannot be overestimated, the experiences and perceptions of practicing lawyers are offered to help you develop a career plan.

But career planning is not something that can be accomplished in a single session. It is an ongoing process that permits you to evaluate opportunities as they arise, reflect on changes in your personal situation affecting your career, and assess new trends within the profession that impact on your practice.

Your initial career plan should start from where you are this minute and project what you perceive to be reasonable goals for yourself for the next five to ten years. Keep in mind, however, that an average professional life spans forty years. Because changes are inevitable, concentration on the shorter distances is a more practical approach.

Think of your career plan as a road map to be used on a trip. You have plotted your general destination, but along the way you may receive word of worthwhile side trips, problem road conditions, detours, or new highways. Just as trusty road map enables you to make changes with a minimum of inconvenience, your career plan should do the same for your professional life.

2
Lawyers and the Practice of Law Today

The practice of law has changed dramatically in the past decade. As you prepare to enter the profession, it is critical to be aware of the changes within and outside the legal field and how lawyers and firms are responding to these new developments.

Demographics

Although there is surprisingly little empirical research on lawyers and the legal profession, a number of studies provide insights into what the profession is like today. The most significant of these is the decennial *Lawyer Statistical Report* prepared by the American Bar Foundation (ABF).

The most recent *Statistical Report* is a 1982 census identifying 649,000 lawyers in the United States. Extrapolating from that figure, it is estimated that there were over 750,000 lawyers in 1990, and that the number will grow to one million by the year 2000.

Other developments are having an impact on the profession. The percentage of lawyers who are solo practitioners has decreased from nearly 60% in 1950 to less than 40% in 1982. Interestingly, the number of solo practitioners has remained fairly stable, pointing to an increase in the number of lawyers practicing in firms with other lawyers as a cause for the change in percentage.

The number of lawyers practicing in large firms is also increasing, although only 5% of all lawyers practiced in firms over 50 lawyers in 1982. That percentage may have doubled by now, but the typical lawyer still practices in a small firm or alone. Legal periodicals, such as the *American Lawyer,* often give a skewed picture of the profession, suggesting that large firms make up a larger portion of the profession than they do.

Over the years, the percentage of lawyers engaged in the private practice of law has remained fairly stable. About 30% of all lawyers practice outside of law firms. This includes 10% in corporations, 9% in government service, 4% in the judiciary, and 9% in a variety of other positions, including military law offices, public interest law offices, and related activities.

These figures do not reflect many of the large number of lawyers who have "defected" from the profession. The ABF surveys rely upon data supplied by the Martindale-Hubbell Legal Directory, which is primarily a directory of private practitioners. There is probably some under-reporting for those lawyers not engaged in private practice, especially those who work in jobs outside the legal profession.

The lawyers in these nonlegal jobs include those who never practiced law after law school as well as those who left the practice of law after some period of time, frequently to go to work for clients. Some lawyers move in and out of the legal profession periodically.

Work and Lifestyle

Given the complexity and diversity in the legal profession, is it possible to make any generalizations about the work and lifestyles of lawyers? Perhaps.

For one thing, a high concentration of lawyers live and work in urban areas. In rural areas, there may be fewer than one lawyer for every 1,000 people, but the ratio is one lawyer for every 100 people in many of the largest cities. Perhaps it was this ratio that prompted a cartoon showing one person saying to another at a cocktail party, "How did I know you're a lawyer? Everybody's a lawyer!"

The odds are two to three that you will live and work in a metropolitan area of one million people or more when you graduate, according to the National Association for Law Placement Employment Report and Salary Survey for 1990.

Another observation about the legal profession is that the majority of lawyers are relatively young. Because the number of law school graduates increased significantly in the 1970s and 1980s compared to earlier years, two-thirds of all lawyers have less than 20 years of experience.

The median age of all lawyers is less than 40, reflecting this youthfulness. Demographers project a "greying" of the profession over the next 30-40 years as the baby boom generation grows older.

Various surveys have pegged average lawyer income at anywhere between $50,000 to over $100,000 per year. Such wide differences imply different sampling and collection methods. Surveys that focus on smaller towns are likely to indicate lower salaries. Surveys that include lawyers in government and public interest legal work produce lower figures than surveys of private practitioners alone. Surveys reflecting the relative youth of the profession also indicate lower levels of income.

The range of starting salaries for law graduates is from $15,000 to over $80,000. Ironically, the highest starting salaries may be higher than the median for lawyers generally. The overall salary range for lawyers is much greater, from less than $15,000 to over $1 million per year. The average small law firm partner can expect an annual income of slightly more than $100,000.

In recent years, the advent of the two-career family has resulted in a doubling of income for many couples. Two 1990 law school graduates conceivably could earn combined salaries of over $160,000 per year. The pressures and the burdens on a relationship from such a commitment may be staggering. The lifestyle considerations facing two-career couples impose additional career planning problems for both the short- and long-term.

Young women, whether their partners are lawyers or not, must make difficult decisions about career and family. Do you wait to have children until after you win the partnership sweepstakes? Do you take time out before starting work? Can you schedule your work on a part time basis?

Despite the fact that the percentage of women in the legal profession has increased dramatically, the profession as a whole has done little to make these choices easy. And although men and women graduating from law school in the 1990's consider lifestyle issues important, sensitivity to these issues remains embryonic among the practicing bar.

For example, very few firms provide day care facilities for employees although an increasing number of business enterprises outside of law do. And many firms do not have formal parental leave policies—until someone actual requests such leave.

Practice Concentration

Another trend that is having a wide-ranging impact on the legal profession is specialization. Increasingly, lawyers are utilizing their legal skills in combination with the skills they have acquired in other disciplines. Specialization includes not only formal recognition as a specialist under a jurisdiction's Code of Professional Responsibility or Rules of Professional Conduct, but also de facto specialization in the form of practice concentration or limitation.

As society has become increasingly complex, the number of areas where legal representation is needed have increased. In many cases, lawyers have developed expertise in a single area (e.g., tax, EEO). An increase in the willingness of clients to sue their lawyers if they are not satisfied with the outcome of a case has made many lawyers reluctant to take cases if they lack experience in the area.

In short, the renaissance lawyer is dead. The demise of the lawyer as generalist and the evolution of the lawyer as specialist have profound implications for those who are entering the practice of law today.

The concept of specialization has become a term of art within the professional responsibility context. The Model Rules of Professional Conduct define the circumstances under which a lawyer may hold himself or herself out as a specialist. Traditionally, only patent lawyers and admiralty lawyers, due to the uniqueness of those practice areas, were allowed to call themselves specialists. In recent years various state bars have promulgated rules governing the certification of specialists. Those jurisdictions now allow lawyers certified under procedures established in their jurisdictions call themselves specialists. The original comments to Model Rule 7.4 suggested that it would be improper to use of the terms "concentrated" or "limited to" when referring to uncertified specialization. In February, 1988, however, the ABA House of Delegates amended Rule 7.4 by eliminating reference to the terms "concentrated" or "limited to", an action confirmed by the U.S. Supreme Court in *Peel v. Attorney Registration and Discipline Commission of Illinois,* 495 U.S., 110 S.Ct. 2281, 110 L. Ed. 2d 83 (1990), invalidating an Illinois disciplinary rule restricting communication of specialty. Thus, presently, a lawyer may utilize such expressions without implying specialist status. This discussion will use the term "practice concentration" to denote expertise in a substantive area of law.

Although it may be clear that patterns of de facto specialization have emerged in the legal profession, such practice concentration should not be confused with officially sanctioned legal specialization. Many jurisdictions provide for the certification of specialists in certain areas of practice, but no state has taken the next step of restricting certain areas of practice to specialists in those areas. It is not clear at this time what the future holds for specialization in the legal profession. Will we move closer to a medical model where practice areas are carved up and reserved for particular subgroups within the profession and where advanced specialized training becomes a barrier to entrance into the specialty practice? Or will lawyers adopt a free market approach to the designation of specialization?

The potential for malpractice drives many lawyers to avoid cases outside their particular field of expertise. There is also some evidence that lawyers who hold themselves out as possessing greater expertise than the average lawyer can charge and collect higher fees for their services. The prospect of greater income may offset the risk of greater liability for malpractice resulting from a higher standard of care.

What does this trend toward practice concentration mean for you, the law student? Just as the generic lawyer is giving way to the specialist, the generic law student is finding it increasingly difficult to compete with classmates who possess special skills and abilities. There are increased pressures to make longer term career decisions at an earlier stage in your legal career. The consequences of poor career decisions can have more impact on the direction of a legal career than in simpler times. The trend towards specialization means students must recognize that they cannot keep all of their options open forever. When you cross a particular bridge, you frequently burn other bridges behind you.

When there were generic law graduates, factors such as class rank, law review status, and law school attended were often the only distinguishing characteristics among candidates for jobs. The trend toward practice concentration tends to impel employers to consider more diverse criteria than in the past. Thus, there is greater emphasis on credentials related to many areas of practice concentration, including not only practical experience in the field during law school, but also educational and pre-law work experience. Law graduates today are simply not fungible.

The corollary of this movement towards specialization has been the development of a cottage industry in legal consulting and support services. An increasing number of organizations provide expertise, specialized technical services, and other assistance to law firms.

Usually, these services have grown up in areas where the firm either lacks expertise (e.g., computers) or cannot provide the service in-house as cheaply as it can buy it outside (e.g., legal research services). The service companies tend to be small entrepreneurial ventures doing highly specialized work. Many of the practitioners in these support services are lawyers, frequently individuals with training in both law and some other discipline.

Competition

A final trend that affects everyone getting out of law school and entering the profession today is competition. The large number of law school graduates has increased competition for jobs. The large number of lawyers has increased competition for legal work. The large number of large law firms has increased the competition for institutional clients that hire such firms. This competition is all within the legal profession.

Outside the profession, many other organizations from banks to title companies to psychologists provide the same services as lawyers, frequently cheaper and sometimes better. There are fewer and fewer activities from which lawyers can exclude individuals not licensed to practice law.

This, in turn, has blurred the lines between what is the practice of law and what is not. Lawyers have reacted by expanding the scope of their professional services into areas that would have been taboo even a decade ago. In addition, as formerly nonlegal work becomes "legalized," more lawyers go to work for organizations in direct competition with law firms.

The line between which services fall within the domain of the legal profession and which do not is not at all clear. As the number of institutions and individuals providing services in competition with legal services increases, the grey area between law practice and nonlegal work expands.

In many states, title companies have taken most of the real estate closings from private practitioners. These companies are nonlegal business entities, yet many lawyers work for title companies or own them. Are these lawyers practicing law or engaging in extra-legal business? Should work that is considered "legal" when performed by a lawyer become "nonlegal" just because a nonlawyer does the very same thing?

Representing sports or entertainment figures as an agent is another good example. Both lawyers and nonlawyers may be involved in negotiating contracts representing clients' interests, and making financial decisions.

Lawyers provide advice and representation to clients concerning legal problems. Significantly, almost no problem is exclusively legal in nature; and almost every problem has a legal component.

Lawyers who are licensed to practice in one or more jurisdictions may represent clients in court. Many lawyers, including a large number of private practitioners, never see the inside of a courtroom.

Lawyers represent both individuals and institutions (e.g., corporations, government agencies, etc.). Lawyers who work for institutions have a single client, the organization that employs them. Lawyers in private practice, on the other hand, sell their services on the open market to people and organizations who will hire them.

In short, whether you accept a position in private practice or go to work for someone else, you will probably be giving legal advice to clients. In either case, you may or may not be involved in litigation as an advocate for your clients' interests.

For those embarking on a legal career, the permutations of positions are infinite. Although there may be some totally nonlegal jobs, this book proceeds on the assumption that most of the jobs that lawyers accept involve some legal component.

Economic Realities

During the past 20 years in the legal profession, the idea that law is a business has evolved. Law firms today, more often than not, consider themselves as business organizations that provide legal services to clients for a profit. A quick look at the economic realities firms face will help the law student understand future employers better.

In a service business like law, income is limited by time. If there are 8,710 hours in a year, and a lawyer spends 3,650 of them eating, sleeping and commuting, only 4,060 hours are left to spend in the office, assuming that the lawyer does absolutely nothing else! And if that lawyer could manage to spend two-thirds of his or her time on client matters, it would be possible to charge 2,707 hours to clients for work.

In reality, it is nearly impossible to attain this level of productivity. A number of surveys have confirmed that the average number of billable hours for lawyers in the United States is around 1,600. The surveys show that associates bill over 1,700 hours annually, slightly more than partners. A law firm that expects its associates to bill over 2,000 hours per year is actually expecting 3,000-3,500 hours of work annually, which translates into 60–70 hours per week.

Since there is a natural limit on the amount of time available to provide legal services, there is a cap on the income a lawyer can generate as well. There are basically three ways that partners, the owners of the legal business, can make more money:

1. They can charge more (e.g., $200 per hour instead of $100 per hour) or they can repackage the fee so that it does not look like an hourly bill (e.g., $2,000 for a contract that took two hours of work, thanks to automated document processing; or a one-third contingency fee that produces a $600,000 settlement for 20 hours of work). Or they can unbundle their charges, that is, bill the client for the secretary, the paralegal, the photocopying, and other charges as well as the time of the lawyer.

2. They can practice law more efficiently. With computer and management systems, lawyers can increase the bottom line by reducing the cost of the production of the legal service while keeping the cost of the service to the consumer the same. One way to accomplish this is to practice in larger organizations. Economies of scale disadvantage the small law firm just as they do the Mom and Pop grocery store, the tailor, or the home builder.

3. Finally, lawyers can make money off the work of other lawyers. The idea is simple. If lawyer A has enough clients to keep two lawyers busy, lawyer A could hire lawyer B at a salary low enough to allow A to make a profit from B's work. The alternative would be for A to refer excess business to B and let B profit directly, or to share the profit with B in which case A and B would be partners. The concept by which the A's of the world hire and make a profit from the B's is called leveraging.

To make the game more interesting, the A's usually hang out a carrot for the B's ("We'll make you one of us in seven years, if you'll let us make a profit on your work in the interim. And when you're one of us, we'll get more like you. There are plenty more where you came from.") There are ominous signs that in the decade of the 90's many lawyers will skip the carrot step, and go directly from making a profit to "there's more where you came from."

These economic realities are changing the makeup of law firms and law practices. More importantly, these changes are altering the career opportunities available to law school graduates. In this environment, some of the assumptions of yesterday must be reexamined in light of new evidence. And old answers will not necessarily be the best ones to the questions raised in tomorrow's job market.

3
The Law School Experience

For better or worse law school leaves an indelible imprint on your psyche, your analytical approach to problems, and your public image. You can never be a "nonlawyer" again. Part of becoming a lawyer involves learning the legal culture: the language, the customs, the professional ethos. Directly or indirectly, much of the legal education process involves assimilating you into the profession.

Legal Skills

Beyond indoctrination into professional values, law school imparts a number of skills. Some of the most obvious skills law students develop include: oral advocacy, legal analysis, legal research and writing, reading critically, spotting issues, analyzing problems, articulating positions, defending statements, identifying and distinguishing relationships, drafting documents, editing, and many others.

The Socratic method, designed to "teach you to think like a lawyer," involves not one, but an array of skills that you can use in solving problems as a lawyer. At the same time, law school subtly develops other skills that ultimately may be just as important to success in the legal profession: coping with pressure, meeting deadlines, juggling diverse and sometimes conflicting responsibilities, competing civilly, organizing tasks, managing time, and creating innovative arguments.

Law students may gain an understanding of the substantive law in areas of the core curriculum. Many law students are exposed to lawyering skills through clinical education programs, simulation courses, and co-curricular activities such as moot court and law review. Students who serve on a law journal develop specialized editorial skills.

Students who work in clinics enhance a number of practice-oriented skills including client interviewing and counseling, negotiation, instrument drafting, and problem solving. These students may also learn related skills involving office management, timekeeping and time management, and other organizational skills. It is possible to develop some of these practice-oriented skills in other law school courses, i.e., simulation classes and even some traditional law school classes.

Unfortunately, not every law school student will be exposed to a full range of these experiences. Although there may be a set of fundamental skills that virtually all law students develop to one degree or another, there are certainly other elective skills that essentially make each law student unique.

A positive aspect of this educational divergence is that law graduates truly can market themselves as unique individuals. There was a time when law school graduates were perceived as essentially fungible. Although this myth is sometimes perpetuated by legal employers, the best strategy is to distinguish yourself from the crowd.

Personal Strengths As Skills

Law school imparts a number of personal strengths or skills that do not appear in any law school catalog. In fact, many students do not even recognize them as skills. While it is probably the case that all law students develop these personal strengths to some degree, different students will develop a different mix of skills.

The first skill is persistence or determination. Not surprisingly, skills analysis interviews with law students frequently bring out this personal strength. ("I was the first person in my family to go to law school." "Everything always came easy to me before law school. Suddenly, it was a struggle just to stay in the middle of the class." "I had to work my way through school. I really wanted this.")

Another skill is the ability to depersonalize arguments, ("When you said that my argument was stupid, I know you did not mean to say that I am stupid. You meant to say that you disagreed with me and on that much we agree. As for your specious argument that....")

And, of course, there is the ability to hold your ground under fire. ("Prof: "That's your answer?" You: "Yes." Prof: "Did you actually read this case?" You: "Yes" Prof.: "If I told you that no court in any American jurisdiction has ever taken your position, what would you say?" You: "I would say that the courts had not really looked at the underlying policy.")

You have learned to deal with pressure. ("I know you said that if I did not make it home over this weekend, the engagement is off. But I have 500 pages of reading due for Monday, a brief due in the clinic, and two job interviews on Friday.")

You learned an ethos of professionalism. Such concepts as due process, constructive notice, confidentiality, conflicting interest, and burden of proof become ingrained in your psyche. Certain ideas such as the notion that you do not have to agree with your client in order to represent her, and that you do not have to believe in your client's innocence in order to require the state to make its case will seem perfectly logical to you. These attitudes are not imparted solely through your professional responsibility course. Rather they are inculcated through the entire educational process from orientation through graduation.

You will master an entire new language called legalese. This specialized vocabulary, with its arcane terms of art and linguistic constructions, will forever set you apart from lay people.

Whatever else it may be, law school is clearly more than simply learning a set of black letter rules we call substantive law. Too often, students focus on the substantive side of their education (e.g., "I've taken evidence, environmental law, regulated industries, and a seminar on toxic torts.") rather than the underlying skills that set them apart from classmates and those who do not possess a legal education.

What You Don't Learn In Law School

Ask any practicing lawyer: "Is a new law school graduate ready to practice law?" The answer will invariably be an emphatic "No!"

Most of us readily accept the seeming inconsistency between the notion that when we take the bar examination, we know more law than we have ever known before or will know again, and that we know frightfully little about being a lawyer.

Some people begin to develop practical lawyering skills by working in law offices before and during law school. Others receive an inkling of what to expect through some of the more practical courses in law. Still others may have grown up around legal families where they have learned about the practice of law first hand.

'For the most part, however, we have learned how to become matadors by reading books on bull fighting. And suddenly, we are standing in the middle of the ring.

Although the array of skills that you develop during law school is formidable, and probably far more extensive than you might have imagined, there are many career skills that are commonly not developed during the education process. Many law practice skills cannot be learned before you actually begin to practice law. You can develop some of these skills through part-time and summer work while in law school, but true legal proficiency is a product of experience. Additionally, although your law school placement office may help teach career development skills, learning how to make career decisions and look for a job involves an entire set of skills that the formal educational process frequently does not address.

Another set of skills that law school almost always ignores includes personal management: finances, relationships, drugs and alcohol, and coping with stress. Both in law school and in the legal profession we tend to hold forth the shibboleth that if we can get the job done, it does not matter what we did the night before. And yet, while serving on a law school academic standards committee, I saw a high correlation between the inability to manage one's personal problems and the inability to perform in law school. Increasingly, bar associations, courts, and lawyers are recognizing that this principle applies to practice as well, and it is not uncommon to discover that a lawyer whose law practice is in shambles has a personal life of similar quality.

In the medical model for education, aspiring doctors go through an internship and residency after medical school. In Canada, through a process known as articling, law graduates must submit to the same kind of on-the-job training. These programs teach novitiates much of the knowledge that is not or cannot be taught in a classroom.

In the United States, training is left to legal employers, who often employ a sink or swim philosophy. A law school friend of mine went to work for the district attorney in a major metropolitan area. When he arrived for work the first day, he found a stack of files sitting on his new desk. When he opened the top file, he noted that he was due in court to prosecute a case at 10:00 that morning. At 10:21, he had lost his first case. Many graduates enter law practice only to discover that they are forced to teach themselves how to practice law.

This whole matter is complicated by the fact that there are many ways to practice law. The criminal defense lawyer's practice is not at all like the insurance defense lawyer's. Practice in a small town may be totally unlike working as an associate in a Manhattan mega-firm.

Despite all of this, new lawyers master their craft in the first five to seven years after law school. Because the legal profession has not developed efficient mechanisms for providing this post graduate education, many inexperienced lawyers feel frustrated, incompetent, and confused.

Although studies show that this kind of dissatisfaction tends to diminish over time as the inexperienced lawyer develops competence as a practitioner, many lawyers actually leave the profession during this period. Ironically, and despite new lawyers' fears, the vast majority of malpractice awards are against lawyers who have been out of school more than ten years.

The problem of defining competence has been a difficult one. Bar association committees, law review writers, courts, and observers of the legal profession have grappled with this question.

The American Bar Association Task Force on Professional Competence in 1983 defined competence this way:

Although it may be difficult to determine what makes a lawyer competent, it should be obvious that the process of obtaining competence extends far beyond law school graduation. Even though the process begins in law school it does not end there. In a larger sense, however, competence may be viewed as a constantly receding goal, a status which is never quite attained, or, perhaps, as a series of plateaus each higher than the last, with no true summit at which to rest.

If the ABA is willing to view competence as a "constantly receding goal," you should be able to accept that your level of performance may not be perfect upon graduation. As you proceed through this book, and as you pursue your legal career in the years to come, keep in mind these ideas about developing professional competence. Remember that a career is more than a series of jobs; it is a collection of unique, interlocking skills that can be brought into play in a variety of different settings.

Viewed in this light, job hunting involves identifying the situation where your skill set can be applied most effectively. If you can identify your unique pattern of skills you will always have work, and you will find satisfaction in what you do. If you fail to grasp this fundamental principle, you will always be a round peg trying to fit into some square hole, always passing time in some boring job, waiting and hoping for the "right thing" to come along.

The Bar Exam

As if law school finals were not enough, the bar exam stands as one last hurdle you must pass before you are licensed to practice law. Bar examination requirements may be relevant to career decisions in a number of different ways.

If you want to practice law in the traditional sense, you must pass the bar in the jurisdiction where you plan to practice. For some positions, such as practicing corporate law or teaching, you may not need to be licensed in the jurisdiction where you work, but you must be licensed in one or more other jurisdictions. Some positions (e.g., hearing examiners in state government) do not include bar passage as a prerequisite to being hired. Even in such areas, however, many law school graduates believe that bar membership is useful to them, and at a minimum affords the option to go into traditional law practice at some point and time.

For whatever reasons, the vast majority of all law graduates sit for the bar. In fact, the number of new bar admissions exceeds the number of law school graduates annually. This is because most states allow candidates to sit for the bar more than once, so every year the number of people who graduate from law school and sit for the bar is supplemented by a group of second, third, and fourth time test-takers from prior years. Nationally, most applicants eventually pass at least one bar exam.

Since the requirements for admission are slightly different in every jurisdiction, you must apply for the bar in the jurisdiction(s) where you plan to practice. If you get a job early, you will be locked into taking the bar and meeting the requirements in that jurisdiction. If you pass the bar in a particular state, your job search, at least as far as law practice jobs are concerned, will be limited to that state. Also, the passage rate varies considerably from state to state.

The biggest question, then, is not whether you will pass the bar, but where? Most states offer the bar examination only twice annually, and some (e.g., Delaware, Nevada) only once. Most bar exams are offered at approximately the same time (late July and mid-February).

The scheduling problems mean that you probably can not sit for more than two examinations during one examination season. Some states coordinate examination dates so that applicants can take the examination in neighboring jurisdictions. Others afford applicants no such luxury.

Furthermore, although all but four jurisdictions now require the multistate bar examination (MBE), there are different rules as to passing scores and acceptance of an MBE score administered in a different jurisdiction. You should investigate carefully the rules and procedures for taking the bar exam in all jurisdictions where you are considering applying for jobs.

Since the United States Supreme Court decision in *Supreme Court of New Hampshire v. Piper,* 470 U.S. 274, 105 S.Ct. 1271, 84 L. Ed.2d 205 (1985), residency requirements for bar admission have been eliminated for the most part. Jurisdictions that have attempted to restrict non-resident admission, however, may still present a few snares for the unwary.

For instance, you may be required to attend a personal interview with the character and fitness committee—a task much easier for the resident than the non-resident. Or you maybe required to obtain letters of recommendation from attorneys licensed to practice in the jurisdiction. At least one state (Delaware) requires applicants to serve in apprenticeship before being licensed.

The ability to move from one jurisdiction to another is also a factor. Some states, through reciprocity arrangements, allow attorneys with experience to be admitted on motion, while other states require experienced attorneys to sit for the full bar examination along with recent law school graduates.

Because of the high degree of career mobility these days, the chances are very good that you will not your spend entire career living and working in one jurisdiction, and even if you do, it is likely that you will have handled cases in several states. Looking down the road a bit, is it possible that you and your family may move? If you acquire a high degree of specialization, is it possible that new and more rewarding opportunities have developed in other areas of the country?

While you may never have to face those or similar questions, this is still a good time to think about potential answers. Many students find it is possible to take more than one bar examination and to qualify for entry into the bar of several states. If you can do so, be one of those students. Bar exams are far easier to take now than later, and taking more than one would be a good hedge for your future. Although you cannot determine the future, it is wise to take preventive measures against factors that could seriously impair your career development.

There is, however, an even more immediate concern; to find out what the exact bar admission requirements are for the state(s) in which you are currently interested. As long as bar admission standards remain under the jurisdiction of the individual states and territories of the United States, it is wise to know exactly what the specific standards are and how they will be interpreted in your own situation in the states where you may wish to practice.

Decisions about where to sit for the bar, and when, are important ones. They should not be taken lightly. You will save yourself a whole lot of grief if you check out these matters before you make major career decisions.

Many legal jobs are contingent upon bar passage. You cannot afford to fail the bar after a successful educational career and job search. Only a few jurisdictions provide a "diploma privilege" (automatic admission for grads of state law schools). In addition, a student's youthful brushes with the law or other problems may present complications with the character and fitness committee in some states.

Many law students do not think about potential problems until it is time for them to graduate and they apply to take the bar. Because information is easily accessible, it makes more sense to deal with the bar exam much earlier in the career planning process than is common.

A Mixture of Clear-Cut Choices and Serendipity

The whole job search can be faintly reminiscent of a medieval allegory in which the protagonist sets out on a quest for some noble ideal and encounters unbelievable trials and temptations along the way. Snares and pitfalls abound; false guides lead him astray; nothing is what it seems to be. The entire journey is like a surrealistic nightmare. But armed with a workable plan, your own modern quest for a job can be quite different.

Put another way, there are many planned and unplanned events that punctuate the lives of all law students. Because no one can control every aspect of their life, it becomes that much more important to act on sound information when the need to make decisions arise.

Many law students express uncertainty about when to undertake various activities in the career choice and the job search processes. Lack of sophistication about nuances in the job market and the hiring cycle of legal employers may deprive some students of opportunities that otherwise would be available to them.

Some students simply avoid dealing with career issues because the stress involved in job hunting makes it easy to procrastinate. Perhaps because of the many demands placed upon their time, many law students have a tendency to deal only with problems that need immediate attention. These students often look for jobs when they absolutely, positively have to do it.

The basic premise here is that if you act on information in a timely manner throughout your law school career, not just when approaching graduation, you will maximize your options. The corollary, of course, is that if you fail to act on information in a timely manner, you will reduce your options. It all sounds pretty simple, right?

The truth is that nothing is ever as simple as it seems (just as nothing is ever as complicated as you were led to believe). There are many variables in this equation. You should understand, however, a few basic principles. Some of these include the law school you attended, the geographic area of the country, the hiring patterns of the specific segments of the job market you are approaching, the timetable and the demands of your spouse or special friend, your outlook on life and long term career objectives, your individual marketability based on special skills and credentials, as well as many other factors. Although it is difficult today to call any law student typical, let's look at two fairly representative law students, Sally Jones and Bob Smith.

Profiles of Two Typical Law Students

Sally just graduated from a solid state-supported law school after completing a full time 3-year J.D. program. She was active in a number of different student organizations, including the editorial board of the school's second "law review". Sally is 27, having spent three years working as an aide to a congressman before coming to law school. She is single and flexible as to where she is willing to live.

During her first year of law school, she attended a placement orientation for first year students conducted by her law school placement director. She spent some time in the placement office after final exams that semester, meeting with the placement director to put together a resume and cover letter and get ideas about law firms that might interview first year students.

She sent out about twenty letters to local law firms, none of which panned out. Several of the firms, however, interviewed her, and she was able to collect valuable information that she would use later. Through a friend, she heard about a judge who needed a clerk for the summer.

It turned out that the judge wanted her to work for free, so she finally decided to take courses through one of the law summer abroad programs advertised on the placement bulletin board. This not only allowed her to get away from the law school itself, but also permitted her to take some credits that would let her lighten her load during the next year.

Sally did not dally overseas but returned to school in time to complete a writing competition for the school's law reviews. She also spent some more time in the placement office, researching employers, meeting with the placement director to clarify some of her objectives, to revise her resume, and to do a practice interview in anticipation of the real thing.

That fall was crazy. Even with the lighter course load, school was just as demanding as the first year. Her commitments to student organizations, especially required hours in the law review office, left her with no time for a personal life. She broke up with her boyfriend of four years, an accountant who announced that she just didn't know how to make a commitment. Sally responded that her commitment at this time of her life was to law school. Having made that decision, many other choices in Sally's life became simpler.

To top it off, Sally's car died; the car had been with her longer than the accountant. In order to finance a new automobile, Sally had to find a part-time job. She went to work for an eight-lawyer general practice firm that said she could work there full time the next summer. This was fortunate, because although she went to a number of on-campus interviews that semester she didn't receive any offers.

The spring went better than the fall, as her work kept her occupied. During the summer, the only time she set foot in the law school was when she had to go for law review, having been elected to the editorial board during the spring.

Towards the end of the summer, Sally updated her resume again, listing experience gained from her job at the firm. Instead of conducting a mass mailing like some of her friends, she sent it to selected firms she had contact with over the past two years, or that had been recommended to her by individual lawyers. The notes she had kept came in handy. She took a week before school started to do some interviewing resulting from her letters.

Despite what seemed to be some definite signs of interest by some of these employers, everyone seemed to hedge about making her an offer. Sally talked to the placement director who suggested that those firms with formal summer clerkship programs were waiting until they made offers to their summer clerks while the smaller firms that did not have such programs were probably uncertain about their hiring needs.

The director asked if Sally might expect a permanent offer from her present employer. Surprisingly, Sally did not know, but she made a note to find out. The director urged Sally to go through fall on campus interviews again, which she did. Her trouble got her on the wait list for three firms, but, alas, no offer.

She did take a semester leave from her clerking job to work for her congressman in a re-election campaign. At the victory party, the congressman told her that if she wanted a job on the Hill after graduation, there was always room for her. When she went back to work at the law firm, she had a long meeting with the managing partner who told her that firm really liked her work, and would like to hire her, but would not know until after the second quarter of the fiscal year (June 30) whether it would be possible to do so.

During her last semester, while she was trying to tie up all the loose ends from law school and apply for the bar exam, Sally continued to follow up on those employers that had expressed some interest in her. She also answered several ads on the placement bulletin board and in the local law journal. No luck.

At graduation Sally's dad asked why she did not have a job. Her mom wondered why she was not married. She wondered to herself if she needed all this grief. But she should not complain, she thought, since she did have one job offer, even if it was the same position that she had before she went to law school.

In the ensuing weeks she did not have time to think about much of anything except for bar review lectures. She was surprised to receive a letter from one of the firms with whom she had interviewed the previous August, indicating that their needs had changed and making her an offer. Then on June 30, right on schedule, she got a call from the senior partner at her old law firm offering her a job. Things were definitely looking up.

While classmates thought Sally was lucky, the fact was that she had been working towards getting a job throughout her law school career, not just at the last minute. She took advantage of her school's placement program and turned minor set-backs (like the car dying) into opportunities (a part-time job that led to full-time employment).

Unlike Sally, Bob was 35 years old and had family obligations. He had always wanted to go to law school, but with a wife and family on the way after college, law school was just not in the cards.

Bob got a job in the executive training program of a local company and moved up the corporate ladder to become a vice president. He worked with the company's general counsel on an almost daily basis, negotiated contracts, and was frequently involved in the legal affairs of the company.

Despite his success, Bob increasingly felt the need for a new challenge. His old interest in law was rekindled through his law-related activities at work. On the home front, everyone seemed to be absorbed in their own worlds. The kids, now teenagers, had their friends and activities at school. His wife had started her own business several years ago and was busy with that.

Bob took the LSAT and, to his surprise, did quite well. This was fortunate since he had never been in contention for a Rhodes Scholarship when he was in college. He met with his boss at work and told him about his plans for law school. Bob's boss agreed not to dump any new assignments on him, but made it quite clear that when push came to shove Bob's responsibilities at work took precedence over law school. Bob agreed, inasmuch as his company was footing the bill for law school tuition.

Nothing happened as planned. Bob worked five days a week and went to school four nights a week. Studying took up all of the available time during weekends. Then, as if some pernicious god wanted to test his mettle, the house needed major repairs which took precious hours away from studying. Just when Bob got the house repaired, he learned that his company was being taken over and reorganized. Bob was beginning to wonder if he had made the right choice.

The first year of law school was pretty much of a disaster. The highlight of the year was the miracle that Bob did not flunk out. Even when things settled down at work, Bob found that he was so far behind in school that he had to struggle to catch up. Fortunately, his business experience coping with high pressure crises helped him survive the first year.

The second year was much like the first in terms of workload, but not punctuated with the near disasters of the year before. Bob's grades and mental health improved considerably.

During his third year, he was offered a law-related position at work reviewing contracts directly with outside counsel in cooperation with the general counsel. The GC discussed career options with him and indicated that since Bob was presently a VP, a lateral move to legal was not possible.

Bob weighed his current position with an entry level legal job, and had decided to stay put when he was asked by a partner in the firm that handled most of his company's business if he would like to join the firm as "of counsel" after graduation. He could continue to work with his company, but develop other legal clients as well.

This arrangement suited management, particularly the general counsel. Bob received a generous early retirement settlement which more than offset the differential in salary.

The fourth year at law school was great. To smooth his transition, the company allowed Bob time off to enroll in the law school's clinical program. Bob saw much more of his family, which pleased everyone, and was doing interesting challenging work.

Although Bob never set foot in the placement office or prepared a resume, he was working on making career choices throughout his law school years. Like Sally, he made conscious decisions when he approached a crossroad and tried to maximize his objectives.

Of course, these fictionalized accounts do not reflect the exact experiences of any two law school graduates. They do represent some of the planned and unplanned events that happen to all law students.

The serendipity of opportunity is always interwoven with aspirations and plans for the future. You may not be able to exercise control over many aspects of your life, but where it is possible to make choices you should.

Sally and Bob, for all of the obstacles thrown up by fate, maintained a sense of direction and positioned themselves to make sound choices for themselves. This should be your objective as well.

4
Overview of Career Planning

A story about the late Supreme Court Justice Oliver Wendell Holmes may have some relevance for law students embarking on the job search. One day during his 88th year, Holmes was traveling by train. When the conductor asked for his ticket, the embarrassed justice could not find it. As Holmes was checking the contents of his pockets, the conductor, who recognized him, assured him there was no problem. "The railroad will trust you to mail your ticket back when you find it," he said. With great irritation, Holmes replied, "My dear man, that is not the problem at all! The problem is not where my ticket is. The problem is, where am I going?"

Law students, too, are traveling. Many of them do not know where they are going, and will take whatever the world gives them. Others will take matters into their own hands, and take steps to order the choices they make about their future. This process is called career planning.

The term should not suggest that you can look into a crystal ball and somehow divine where your career is going and how to get there. On the contrary, career planning is hard work, and the answers are seldom clear. It is also a never ending process, something you do throughout your adult life.

There are two distinct parts to any job search: The career choice process and the job search process. A fundamental rule is that the first must precede the second.

In other words, you have to know what you are looking for if you expect to find it. This sequence may seem obvious, but many people skip the first step, fail to find a satisfying job, and then do not understand why.

Throughout this book you will see the terms, *career planning* and *career choice process, placement and job search process*. The career choice process is the means by which career planning is undertaken, and the job search process leads to placement.

The theme of placement through career planning will be repeated throughout this book. From the time you first decide to attend law school until you finally choose a job, you are evaluating, either consciously or unconsciously, the opportunities.

That there are so many opportunities is fortunate; yet it is unfortunate that many people either do not investigate or are not aware of the full range of possibilities. The following overview of the career choice and job search process briefly describes each step. The steps are covered in greater detail in the chapters indicated. You should focus your efforts on the particular steps that apply to you.

The Career Choice Process

This book talks about career planning in terms of a specific model, the career choice process, because the term planning may infer that there is some magic formula that will allow a person to map out his or her future with a degree of certainty. For most of us, this is simply not possible. Too much of our fate lies beyond our control. Factors such as economic conditions, luck and personal handicaps will affect our goals.

Career choice, on the other hand, is a process based on effective decision-making. It attempts to allow the individual to make the best possible choices when the decision is made, and to increase the alternatives available in making the decision.

If you are not sure about which direction your professional life should take, you should take the time to organize your thoughts. It is undoubtedly better to go through the trauma of uncertainty while you are in law school than to go to work in a position you later discover you do not like, where you have not foreseen what was foreseeable.

The career choice process begins with **analyzing your skills** (Chapter 5), which you should think of as interesting and challenging rather than painful. Only by beginning with a perfectly honest appraisal of yourself can you make this a valid evaluation.

You need not look up a psychiatrist— this is a subjective analysis. What are your likes and dislikes? What are your skills, abilities, interests, needs, values, goals? Anyone who says, "I don't have any," is giving up too soon.

This might well be the most difficult step in the career choice process, as well as one of the most intrinsic to success. Seeing yourself as you really are, not as you were, or could be, or should be, or will be, is not easy.

If you *do not* like the image you see, by all means take steps to remedy the situation. Do not rest your later decisions, however, on projected self-images which are not accurate. There are methods in your self-analysis which can help you to focus your skills and other factors. Many law students never will have done this kind of thing before, but an honest self-appraisal is the essential first step.

After you have undertaken self-analysis, which is essentially subjective, you should begin **evaluating the market** (Chapter 6), which is more objective. This step, no less than self-evaluation, requires scrupulous honesty. Here, however, you are required to look outward, to view your environment, to see things the way they are. You must be able to confront the facts honestly and determine the relative importance of them.

Once again, for this analysis to be most effective and helpful, you must consider the positive as well as negative—balance the weaknesses against the strong points for an entirely accurate picture. You may find yourself both expanding and narrowing alternatives by obtaining more options while limiting the areas from which you will eventually make your choice.

Obviously, your market analysis is going to involve not only research on the facts, but the interpretation of those facts, which is the next step: **ranking priorities** (Chapter 7). Your goal here is to develop a list of options, ranging from the most desirable situation you could imagine to the bottom line; i.e., what you would find acceptable if worse came to worst. Never expend all your options; there should always be an alternative. At this point, we are talking about broad categories as opposed to specific positions.

By synthesizing the self-analysis and the market analysis you should be able to generate some options. If this does not work, you have either not done your research homework or you are not being realistic.

If you have a hard time making up your mind about the appropriate direction for your career, you might need to work on developing decision-making skills. Uncertainty is the element of any decision that makes it so difficult. Even though you can control the decision, you are probably aware that the element of chance influencing the outcome of your decision makes it impossible for you to have ultimate control. There will always be a certain amount of risk or chance, but you should try to minimize the degree to which chance affects the outcome.

You should chart a middle course between leaving everything to chance, which could be disastrous, and expecting to eliminate it, which is impossible. In other words, you should know what you want, be well informed of the facts, and be alert for opportunities.

The Job Search Process

After the career choice process has given you some direction, the job search begins. There are five steps to the job search: packaging yourself, researching potential employers, building a network, selling yourself, and making a decision.

Job hunting requires a set of skills which can be *learned* and which will always stay with you. Job hunting skills are covered in greater detail later in this book.

Packaging yourself (Chapter 11) includes preparing a resume, developing good interviewing techniques, and securing other support for your search such as references and writing samples. How many students would take a final exam cold, with no preparation? Very few. But many students fail to give adequate attention to details prior to beginning the job search, and this is often costly in the long run.

Researching employers (Chapter 12) is hard work for which there is no shortcut. To make a decision you must take affirmative steps to gather relevant information about employers. When your inaction or indecision results in the closing of an alternative, for example, by letting an application deadline pass, you have forfeited to some extent your control of your destiny. Research should be easy for law students, but many forget that the same skills they have developed to research a legal problem can be transferred to research on legal employers.

The process of **networking** (Chapter 13) is aimed at expanding your opportunities by increasing your contacts with individuals who may know about career opportunities that would interest you, help you to open doors, and provide support for you. These contacts are your eyes and ears in the world of work. They are your allies in the war against unemployment.

Many students aver that they do not have "contacts" in the legal profession. Networking involves developing new contacts, as well as tapping old ones. It requires work to build a network and effort to maintain it. Yet, informal channels of information represent a major source of legal jobs that you should not ignore.

Using your plan to seek specific positions in the priorities you have established, you can begin **selling yourself** (Chapter 14). As you start to apply for specific jobs, begin with priority #1. The possibilities are that you get a job or you do not. If not, you turn to the next possibility and so forth throughout the list. When you exhaust the employers in your highest priority group, you go to the second, and so on.

The final step in the process is **making a decision** (Chapter 15). If you have only one choice the decision is easy—yes or no. If you have several choices, then you must sort out the factors in order to reach a final decision that is best for you. This is easily said, but not so easily accomplished.

Reassessment

Bear in mind that even the best plans may not yield the results you expected. You might discover in mid-stream that new skills are required for the position you want. Can you realistically obtain them, or would it be wiser to consider another field? Do the latest statistics show that competition in your chosen area is so fierce as to render it an unrealistic choice for you? What happens when the student (or graduate) goes through the whole job search with no results?

Careful analysis and thorough preparation at lower levels of the process should help you avoid this situation. However, if it does happen, it is probably best to go back to the beginning and start anew. At this point, you will probably need the help available through the law school placement office. It can be very helpful to talk about your situation with someone who has a broader view of law careers and the current job market.

This career planning model may help you to visualize the processes we have discussed. The entire model is basically a continued narrowing of alternatives until a final decision is reached,

Chart 1
Munneke's Pyramid – Overview of the Process

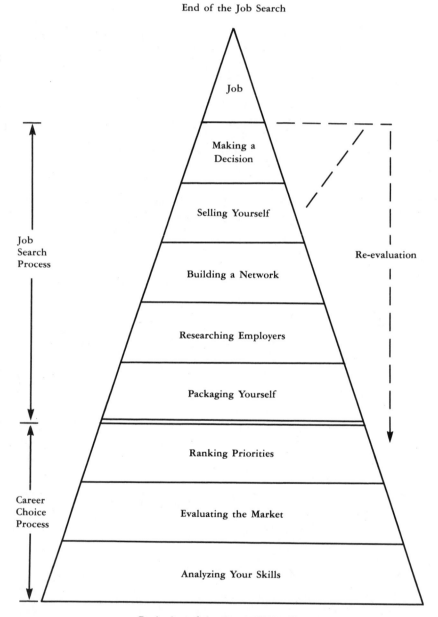

End of the Job Search

Job

Making a
Decision

Selling Yourself

Job
Search
Process

Building a Network

Re-evaluation

Researching Employers

Packaging Yourself

Ranking Priorities

Career
Choice
Process

Evaluating the Market

Analyzing Your Skills

Beginning of the Career Choice Process

from a starting point where the individual has no idea of what the final decision will be.

The time frame is flexible. One person may have reached the third level by the beginning of the second year in law school. Another may not begin the first until after graduation. You should allow whatever time is necessary to work through the possibilities, although ideally the career choice process should begin during the first year of law school and the job search process no later than the beginning of your senior year.

In the end, you can look forward to a job that is personally and professionally rewarding. But that is seldom the end of the story. Your career is a process, rather than a product, and is likely to grow and change with time. The average lawyer will make at least three (and many lawyers more) job changes in a legal career.

If you understand this model, the skills and self-awareness you have developed for the job search will help you to make career decisions throughout life, to provide for continued professional development, and to be prepared for those unpredictable turns of fate that the future may hold for you.

5
Analyzing Career Skills

Once a law student has accepted the notion that law is not a career, but rather that there are many different careers in law, it is a short step to the conclusion that choices must be made during law school regarding options available to graduates. One cannot simply wait for the right thing to come along, or postpone until after graduation critical career decisions.

The need to make career choices implies a correlative need to assess one's skills. Many law students are surprised—even dismayed—to learn that they must undertake this skills assessment. Did they not, after all, go through the very same thing when they decided to go to law school? Is it not now the most important job to find a job? Does a busy law student have time to worry about playing silly psychological games? Can one actually plan a career?

There is a natural impulse to shortcut the process of making career choices, not only because it is uncomfortable to ask hard questions about life choices, but also because most law students do not understand how to manage effectively the process by which such choices are made. Just because one made a career choice in deciding to come to law school does not mean that one will not make other choices during law school, or after graduation for that matter.

Another problem many law students face in making career choices is the role that subjectivity, non-rationality, and personal feelings play in the process. The law school teaches students that the rule of reason is paramount, that every decision can and should be made rationally.

The law student who deigns to bring personal feelings and subjective judgments to analyses of hypothetical cases is inevitably portrayed as weak-minded by professors. Eventually, most law students learn to sound as if they can analyze questions in a coldly rational way, untainted by emotion. Some even believe this. Unfortunately, it is impossible to divorce personal feelings from career choices, and it is unwise to try because feelings are an important dimension in the process of making career decisions.

While the analytical skills developed during law school clearly should be viewed as assets in choosing a career, the individual must maintain a clear perspective on the role of the rule of reason. When hard facts seem to fly in the face of gut feelings, it is sometimes best to follow one's feelings. An offer that looks good on paper may be less attractive where subjective feelings point to deep-seated doubts about one's long-term satisfaction while working in the environment being considered.

This chapter will provide techniques to allow law students to sort out feelings and attitudes, and to get a handle on such abstract concepts as abilities, talents, and skills. It will suggest to the reader ways to apply the steel-trap logic that law school has inculcated to what could otherwise become a guessing game or a high-stakes crap shoot.

Career Theory

An understanding of some of the underpinnings of career theory may be useful to the uninitiated reader. Although there are many books on career planning, some of which are discussed in this chapter, the basic theory is probably best set forth by John Holland in *Making Vocational Choices.*

Holland argues that individuals tend to like activities in which they succeed, and that they will succeed in the future in activities utilizing the same skills or activities that have helped them to succeed in the past. It follows, according to Holland, that job dissatisfaction, or "dissonance" as he calls it, is related to the lack of skills necessary to perform work successfully. When we are frustrated in this way, there are three possible responses: we change ourselves (the skills we possess), we change the environment (the skills we utilize), or we leave the frustrating environment.

It is therefore essential that each individual assess his or her skills, not just in terms of specific jobs, but also in transferable terms that can be understood in a wide variety of endeavors. For example, a preacher, a politician, a trial lawyer, and an actress may all possess the oral skills of speaking and persuading.

An analogy may be helpful in applying these principles to law careers. Students sometimes believe, or are led to believe, that job opportunities are like a ladder, with practice in a large firm as the top rung, based on some vague notion of prestige, and employment in a nonlegal job as the bottom rung, only slightly more desirable than standing in a breadline or begging on a street corner.

In fact, Holland and most career theorists suggest that the ladder should be turned on its side so that various jobs are perceived as options. Instead of reaching for the top rung and then falling down the ladder until it is possible to grab a rung and hold on, one should view the entire ladder of possibilities and find the right place among them.

The important idea in the latter approach is this: What is right for one person is not necessarily right for someone else. "What is right" is partially determined by correlating the skills which a job requires and the skills an individual possesses. The closer the match between these two, the greater is the likelihood of finding satisfaction, as well as long-term success, in one's career.

Job dissatisfaction may be partly a natural product of the transition from school to the working world, and endemic to contemporary civilization. The frustrations of living and working in the last decade of the 20th century would be similar in many other career fields.

Some of the dissatisfaction, however, may be a product of certain aspects of the practice of law. Furthermore, different kinds of practice have different sources of dissatisfaction as well as different levels of overall satisfaction. The goal of the career choice process is to identify potential frustrations and problems and to avoid them by making sound choices based on the alternatives available.

Making good career choices can affect long-term career satisfaction, but there are some pragmatic considerations as well. One's resume, interviewing style, and cover letters will be more powerful if they are based upon and reflect skills that have been identified through the career choice process. One's ability to recognize the right job when it comes along is enhanced also by an understanding of these skills.

Adele Scheele in her book *Skills for Success* contends that the frequently cited reason given by successful people for their success—

being in the right place at the right time—is not so much a product of good fortune as it is a specific ability to identify the right opportunity. This ability is based upon a number of skills, including the skill of knowing what transferable career skills the person can bring to a given job.

To use another analogy, it is somewhat like entering the New York City subway system without knowledge as to which train to catch. Someone could stand on the platform or ride for hours without reaching the intended destination.

Too many people approach career decisions as victims. They take the first train that comes along and go wherever it leads them. If they would only realize that they are in control of their destinies, they could find the right train the first time, and avoid much frustration.

Taking the time now to ask and answer questions about job skills and career goals can prevent hours of frustration during the job search, and perhaps years of unhappiness later in life. Too often, busy law students want to skip this part of the process, and get on to serious job hunting. But you are unlikely to bag the job you want if you cannot recognize an opportunity when it comes along.

The exercises presented in this chapter are designed particularly for law students, and are modifications of similar exercises that may be found in many contemporary career planning manuals. They are intentionally simple in recognition of the time limitations many law students face.

Those who wish to pursue this self-evaluation in greater depth may obtain one of other commercial books available. Perhaps the most popular of these is Richard Bolles's *What Color Is Your Parachute?* which guides its readers through a series of exercises aimed at finding the ideal job.

Its drawback is that in his exuberance, Bolles seems to suggest that if one simply follows the formula, the right job can be found. The failure to achieve that goal may be seen as the fault of the individual for not carrying out Bolles's plan as a true believer would. Also, since the manual is aimed at a general audience, law students will find some parts less helpful than others. Bolles's smaller book, *The Quick Job-Hunting Map,* may be a more useful guide to the skills analysis exercises, but it lacks any explanation of the underlying theory.

Another manual, *The Complete Job Search Handbook,* by Howard Figler, was written in response to the "true believer" approach of

Parachute. Figler's book contains 20 chapters on 20 different job search skills with exercises for each. Although it also was not aimed specifically at law students, many have found it to be useful.

Other career planning manuals deal in great depth with the related but distinct issue of values clarification, another factor ultimately reflected in career choices. Values clarification is not treated in depth in this chapter. Those, however, who are plagued by questions such as, "How do I feel about prosecuting people and sending them to jail?" or "Could I represent a client with whom I am personally in disagreement politically?" may find values exploration useful.

Put Your Degree to Work, by Marcia Fox, is a hard-nosed pragmatic, although not widely recognized, tome on career and job Research techniques for professional level individuals. Finally, *Lawyers in Transition* by Mark Byers, Don Samuelson, and Gordon Williamson represents a serious effort to apply sound career skills analysis to the legal environment. Although written for practicing lawyers, law students will find the chapters dealing with career planning to be particularly helpful.

Another recent development has been the use of personal inventories (e.g.—Myers-Briggs Type Indicator) to test how well an employee will fit into a given work environment. These tests have the advantage of a scientific method of development and validation, and they can provide valuable insights about the individuals tested. An increasing number of career counselors and legal employers are using personality tests such as the MBTI in the career planning and placement process.

A danger exists that such instruments will be misused by poorly trained administrators or by interpretations that suggest, "If your type is X, you must become a Y." The flaw in the logic is that not only X's may become Y's, and certainly not all X's must become Y's. The tests merely show a correlation between X's and those who have in the past become Y's.

For example, we often picture litigators as erudite, aggressive, and self confident. Although many litigators fit this mold, many trial attorneys do not. It would be unfortunate if they had chosen to avoid the courtroom because they did not fit the profile on some test.

Like any other analysis, the results of these tests can help you to find areas of practice that you may enjoy, but they cannot make your decisions for you. There may be other reasons leading you to different choices.

Exercises in Skills Analysis

The information you distill from the following exercises can be equally helpful to you analyzing your career skills. To complete the exercises, you need only have plenty of paper, a pencil (to erase), and a block of several uninterrupted hours in a place that permits thinking. Before getting into the exercises, however, there are several caveats:

1. *Tell the truth.* No one else needs to see this, so there is no reason to lie. Absolute, total, brutal honesty is the only way to do the exercises. Anything else will taint the results.

2. *Spend the time to do it right.* A block of several hours is necessary to work through the exercises. The exact time will vary from individual to individual, but there is a limit below which the results will have diminishing usefulness.

3. *The career choice process is ongoing.* This activity is not something to be done once and put aside forever. The career choice process continues throughout life. It may not be necessary to reconsider the results as the job search progresses. But it may be advantageous to rethink the questions asked here from time to time during your career, particularly at points of choice, transition, or frustration that inevitably will occur.

4. *Pre-law career planning is not enough.* The law school classroom experience, clerking, and other extracurricular activities, and learning to "think like a lawyer" make it necessary to continue career planning already done, using both the insights gained earlier in the process and those later discovered. By the same token, it is impossible in one sense to know if a job is satisfying until it has been tried. It is not uncommon for a law student to believe that a certain choice, such as litigation, may be ideal, only to find that as a lawyer he or she hates the work. There are inevitably elements of any work that must be experienced to be understood. This means that career planning cannot end with finding a job or graduation from law school. It is a lifelong activity.

5. *The career choice process is not the same as career planning.* The term planning seems to suggest that there is a formula that will get you from here to goal X by following steps 1, 2, and 3. Things seldom happen according to plan, and many well-intentioned career planners become frustrated with the unplanned, and lose confidence in the career choice process. It is more like following a path through the forest, making choices at various forks using the

best information available at the time with only a compass as a general guide for direction, as opposed to following a map driving the Interstate from New York to Chicago.

6. *Do not procrastinate.* Because making career choices means facing personal limitations, fears, and skeletons in the closet (both real and imagined), it is a frightening and anxiety-producing process. Too many law students cope with this anxiety by ignoring the problem. This procrastination has the unfortunate result of foreclosing many opportunities as time passes. The individual who starts the process during the first or second year of law school has a greater range of choices than one who begins after completion of the bar exam.

7. *Finally, more questions may be raised than answered.* Do not be discouraged if the result of completing these exercises is a sense of confusion. The issues are seldom black and white. This tension is healthy, and is indicative of awareness. Someone who is absolutely sure of his or her career choices may be someone who has not given them much thought. Anyone recalling the first year of law school knows that when you are sure you know all the answers, you really do not understand; only when you feel confused are you beginning to get close to the answers.

The skills analysis exercises that follow are intended to make you think, dream, and dredge up forgotten experiences. They can be an adventure or a chore. They can be as enlightening as you allow them to be.

Most of us have little experience at identifying skills. Because we seldom identify skills, we cannot articulate them when we need to in the job search process, much less in these exercises. This stumbling block is the single biggest impediment most law students have to effective job hunting.

It can now be revealed: Skills are things one can do; they are actions. Doing is expressed in the English language through transitive or action verbs, such as analyze, propose, organize, direct. Thus, articulating skills requires no more than being able to describe actions using the full richness of the English language.

For example, someone who has participated in a moot court competition may have developed the following skills: speaking, persuading, organizing, researching, responding, listening. By analyzing an activity in detail it is possible to break it down into component skills.

Frequently, it is difficult for law students to make the shift from describing job-specific skills to describing more general job-transferable skills. In other words, when completing these exercises you will want to take skill descriptions from specific activities and describe them in terms that could be applied to other activities. Furthermore, when applying for a specific job you will want to take these general terms and describe them in the language of the job.

In the previous example, a moot court participant may be able to identify an array of oral skills. As stated before, however, those same skills may be useful not only in work as a litigator, but also as a minister, politician, salesperson, or actor. In searching for a job, you may not have experience as an associate in a law firm but you may be able to demonstrate that you have done the things that associates do: speaking, persuading, organizing, researching, responding, and listening.

It may be useful to use a thesaurus to facilitate word choice as an aid during the exercises as well as throughout the job search. You may also want to refer to the list of law-related action verbs in the appendix.

Exercise 1
The Party

This exercise is taken from Richard Bolles's *Quick Job Hunting Map* and is intended to provide a rough sense of skills orientation by broad skill groups.

1) On the next page (see Chart 2) is an aerial view (from the floor above) of a room in which a party is taking place. At this party, people with the same or similar interests have all gathered in the same corner of the room.

2) Which corner of the room would you instinctively be drawn to so that you would join the group of people you would most enjoy being with for the longest time? (Leave aside any question of shyness, or whether you would have to talk with them.) Write the letter for that corner in this space: _____

3) After fifteen minutes, everyone in the corner you have chosen leaves for another party crosstown except you. Of the groups that still remain, now which corner or group would you be drawn to the most so that you would join the people you would most enjoy

Chart 2
The Party

A

People who have athletic or mechanical ability, who prefer to work with objects, machines, tools, plants, or animals, or to be outdoors

F

People who like to observe, learn, investigate, evaluate, or solve problems

B

People who like to work with data, who have clerical and/or numerical ability, carry things out in detail or follow through on other's instructions

E

People who have artistic, innovating, or intuitional abilities, and like to work in unstructured situations, using their imagination or creativity

C

People who like to work with people—influencing, persuading, or performing or managing for organizational goals or for economic gain

D

People who like to work with people—to inform, enlighten, help, develop, or cure them, or who are skilled with words

From the 1992 edition of *What Color Is Your Parachute? A Practical manual for Job-Hunters and Career Changers,* by Richard Nelson Bolles, copyright 1992. Used by permission. Available from Ten Speed Press, P.O. Box 7123, Berkeley, CA 94707, $12.95 paper, $17.95 cloth.

being with for the longest time? Write the letter for that corner in this space: _____

4) After fifteen minutes, this group too leaves for another party. Of the groups which remain now, which one would you most enjoy being with for the longest time? Write the letter for that corner in this space: _____

After you have completed these four questions, save your responses and move on to Exercise 2.

Exercise 2
Accomplishments

Mentally review your life history from your earliest memories to the present. Then on 10 sheets of paper write your 10 greatest successes or achievements. It is not necessary to limit these activities to school, or jobs, or any other specific endeavor.

After listing the 10, fill out your listings by describing what you did and why you were successful. Then for each entry make a list of verbs describing the skills you used or developed. When you have a preliminary list of verbs, attempt to break those described into finer terms by asking what other skills were required to perform the listed skills. Save your lists.

Exercise 3
Law School Classes

On three sheets of paper, list your three favorite law school classes or those where you did your best work. (First year students can go back to undergraduate and graduate school.) As before, describe what you did in those classes and why you did well.

Then make a list of skills you used or developed in these classes. Break down the skills into subskills if you can. Again, save the list.

Exercise 4
Law Work

Think back to your law-related work experiences. Note the use of the word *experiences,* which is not limited to jobs or to work during law school. List three different experiences on separate sheets of paper. If there are more than three, choose those in which you felt most successful. Then describe what you did.

In the case of a job or activity that involved regular hours, you may find it productive to summarize your activities for a certain period, say one week, to get a handle on what you did. Next, repeat the steps followed in Exercises 2 and 3 to produce a list of skills.

Exercise 5
Fantasy

Close your eyes and imagine what work you would be doing in five years if all your dreams came true, good fortune was always with you, and you had unlimited options. After having this fantasy, describe it on paper. Remember: You will probably only be able to record a fraction of what goes through your mind, so be selective.

Instead of looking back, look forward, and describe what you will need to do to be successful in this fantasy. Then make a list of skills you will need to use or develop in this work.

When you have completed this exercise, repeat it for 10 and then 20 years. Keep in mind that this is a fantasy, not a career goal, so do not get hung up on details.

Exercise 6
Strengths

In addition to skills that communicate what you can do, you have a number of strengths that describe what you are. If skills can be characterized as action verbs (i.e., *I can* _____), strengths can be communicated as adjectives (i.e., *I am* _____). Just as you need to be able to tell employers about your skills, you need to be able to explain what your strengths are.

Some of us may remember the words of our mothers, "Don't toot your own horn." When it comes to jobs, you should forget what your mother said. This is the time to talk about your skills and your strengths.

Professor Peter Kutulakis of Dickinson Law School has developed an Inventory of Strengths for Law Students which we refer to as the Dickinson Model (See Chart 3). Using the Dickinson Inventory, you can assess your strengths quickly and easily. Take a few minutes to complete the inventory now. Keep these results separate from the results of the skills exercises above.

Chart 3
Dickinson Inventory of Personal Strengths

Below you will find a list of strengths. Some of these strengths very much describe you and others will not be like you at all. By completing this exercise, you will hopefully obtain a clearer image of what type of person you are and what types of strengths you have to offer. With this information, you can better evaluate yourself and how that self can relate to the world of work.

Step 1   Read through the list and underline each word that describes you. Use the phrase, "I am a(n) _____ person."

Step 2   Read through the words that you underlined and circle those that you feel are very descriptive of you. Use the phrase, "I am a(n) _____ person."

Step 3   Read through the words that you circled and rank order them according to how closely they describe you. Use the space to the left of each word that you circled to write a choice number, (i.e., 1, 2, 3, etc.)

Step 4   Write below each of the circled words in the order that they were ranked (i.e., 1, 2, 3, etc.)

Step 5   Give blank copies of this list to people whose opinions you trust and have them check your perceptions.

_____ academic	_____ democratic	_____ ingenious	_____ reserved
_____ active	_____ dependable	_____ innovative	_____ resourceful
_____ accurate	_____ determined	_____ intellectual	_____ responsible
_____ adaptable	_____ dignified	_____ intelligent	_____ responsive
_____ adventurous	_____ diplomatic	_____ inventive	_____ self-confident
_____ aggressive	_____ discreet	_____ kind	_____ self-controlled
_____ alert	_____ dominant	_____ lighthearted	_____ sensible
_____ ambitious	_____ dynamic	_____ likable	_____ serious
_____ artistic	_____ eager	_____ logical	_____ sincere
_____ assertive	_____ easygoing	_____ loyal	_____ sociable
_____ attractive	_____ efficient	_____ methodical	_____ sophisticated
_____ aware	_____ emotional	_____ meticulous	_____ spontaneous
_____ bold	_____ empathetic	_____ modest	_____ spunky
_____ broad-minded	_____ energetic	_____ natural	_____ stable
_____ businesslike	_____ enterprising	_____ objective	_____ strong
_____ calm	_____ enthusiastic	_____ obliging	_____ strong-willed
_____ capable	_____ excitable	_____ open-minded	_____ sympathetic
_____ careful	_____ fair-minded	_____ optimistic	_____ tactful
_____ caring	_____ flexible	_____ organized	_____ teachable
_____ cautious	_____ forceful	_____ outgoing	_____ tenacious
_____ challenging	_____ formal	_____ patient	_____ thinking
_____ charming	_____ frank	_____ peaceable	_____ thorough
_____ cheerful	_____ friendly	_____ penetrating	_____ thoughtful
_____ clear-thinking	_____ generous	_____ perceptive	_____ tolerant
_____ clever	_____ gentle	_____ pleasant	_____ tough
_____ competent	_____ good-natured	_____ poised	_____ trusting
_____ competitive	_____ healthy	_____ polite	_____ trustworthy
_____ concerned	_____ helpful	_____ practical	_____ understanding
_____ confident	_____ honest	_____ precise	_____ unexcitable
_____ conscientious	_____ humanizing	_____ progressive	_____ uninhibited
_____ conservative	_____ humorous	_____ quiet	_____ verbal
_____ considerate	_____ idealistic	_____ rational	_____ versatile
_____ cooperative	_____ imaginative	_____ realistic	_____ vigorous
_____ courageous	_____ independent	_____ reasonable	_____ warm
_____ creative	_____ individualistic	_____ reflective	_____ wise
_____ curious	_____ industrious	_____ relaxed	_____ witty
_____ daring	_____ informal	_____ reliable	_____ zany
_____ deliberate			

Exercise 7
Work Values

Another area that all career planners should explore is work values. These are subjective attitudes you hold concerning work generally that will affect your perceptions of any job you take. They reflect how you feel about yourself, your colleagues, and your work environment.

Sometimes people who are good at what they do hate their work. If we looked at skills alone, this would not make sense, because we predict that someone who has the skills to do the job will be successful at the job, and if she is successful she will be satisfied. But if the work does not satisfy her work values, then she will not be happy even though she is competent to handle the work.

Because work values go directly to how you feel about your job, you should try to identify them. The following exercise, also developed by Professor Kutulakis for the Dickinson Model, is designed to help you recognize these important work values (See Chart 4).

If you can identify values that are important to you, you should be able to look for a work environment that will support those values. Remember: no job is perfect, and sometimes it takes time to establish a supportive atmosphere in a work setting. Many elements of the environment will remain hidden from you until after you go to work because they are difficult to assess during the interview process. Yet if you have an idea about what values are important to you, and look for clues as you interview, you can maximize your chances of making a sound choice in the end.

Pulling It All Together

At this point you should have the results of the Party Exercise and 17 to 19 sheets of paper with a great many skills listed. To sort this out, list all the skills you have identified on all the other sheets on one sheet of paper (See Chart 5). It is very likely that some skills will appear several times on the list, having come up in more than one exercise.

Next, rework your list by ranking the skills on the basis of the number of times each appears (See Chart 6). Then place your ranked skills in one of the six major skill groups described in Exercise 1 (Chart 7). This winnowing process is designed to help you

Chart 4
Dickinson Work Values Rating Sheet

Step 1   Look at the definitions of these values and rate the degree of importance you would assign to each, using the scale below.

Not Important				Reasonably Important				Very Important	
1	2	3	4	5	6	7	8	9	10

Step 2   Rank the top ten.

1. _____   2. _____

3. _____   4. _____   5. _____

6. _____   7. _____   8. _____

9. _____   10. _____

Step 3   Choose the three you would take if you could have no others.

1. _____   2. _____   3. _____

_____ **Help Society:**   Do something to contribute to the betterment of the world I live in.

_____ **Help Others:**   Be involved in helping other people in a direct way, either individually or in small groups.

_____ **Public Contact:**   Have a lot of day-to-day contact with people.

_____ **Work with Others:**   Have a close working relationship with a group; work as a team toward common goals.

_____ **Affiliation:**   Be recognized as a member of a particular organization.

_____ **Friendships:**   Develop close personal relationships with people as a result of my work activities.

_____ **Competition:**   Engage in activities which pit my abilities against others where there are clear win-and-lose outcomes.

_____ **Make Decisions:**   Have power to decide courses of action, policies, etc.

_____ **Work Under Pressure:**   Work in situations where time pressure is prevalent and/or the quality of my work is judged critically by supervisors, customers, or others.

_____ **Power and Authority:**   Control the work activities or (partially) the destinies of other people.

_____ **Influence People:**   Be in a position to change attitudes or opinions of other people.

_____ **Work Alone:**   Do projects by myself, without any significant amount of contact with others.

_____ **Knowledge:**   Engage myself in the pursuit of knowledge, truth, and understanding.

_____ **Intellectual Status:**   Be regarded as a person of high intellectual prowess or as one who is an acknowledged "expert" in a given field.

_____ **Artistic Creativity:**   Engage in creative work in any of several art forms.

_____ Creativity: (General)	Create new ideas, programs, organizational structures or anything else not following a format previously developed by others.
_____ Aesthetics:	Be involved in studying or appreciating the beauty of things, ideas, etc.
_____ Supervision:	Have a job in which I am directly responsible for the work done by others.
_____ Change and Variety:	Have work responsibilities which frequently change in their content and setting.
_____ Precision Work:	Work in situations where there is little tolerance for error.
_____ Stability:	Have a work routine and job duties that are largely predictable and not likely to change over a long time.
_____ Security:	Be assured of keeping my job and a reasonable financial reward.
_____ Fast Pace:	Work in circumstances where there is a high pace of activity; work must be done rapidly.
_____ Recognition:	Be recognized for the quality of my work in some visible or public way.
_____ Excitement:	Experience a high degree of (or frequent) excitement in the course of my work.
_____ Adventure:	Have work duties which involve frequent risk-taking.
_____ Profit, Gain:	Have a strong likelihood of accumulating large amounts of money or other material gain.
_____ Independence:	Be able to determine the nature of my work without significant direction from others; not have to do what others tell me to.
_____ Moral Fulfillment:	Feel that my work is contributing significantly to a set of moral standards which I feel are very important.
_____ Location:	Live in a town or geographical area conducive to my lifestyle and which allows me to do the things I enjoy most.
_____ Physical Challenge:	Have a job that makes physical demands which I would find rewarding.
_____ Time Freedom:	Have responsibilities which I can work at according to my own time schedule; no specific working hours required.

focus on the specific skills and skill groups you have developed in your life. This information will be invaluable to you at every stage of the career planning and job search process.

Finally, in order to summarize the results of these activities, you may want to record your findings. (See Chart 8.) This handy sheet will give you a thumbnail sketch of what assets you will bring to your work, and what assets you have to sell.

Now look back at the six skill groups described in Bolles's Party scenario and your results from that exercise. Are the emphases in your skills similar to the preliminary preferences? If not, why not?

Are you surprised or not at the results? Do your skills correlate with your preconceived notions of your strengths and abilities? If not, what accounts for the differences? Are there skills that you feel need to be developed to a greater degree in the future? Which ones? Will your resume look different as a result of this experience? Will your career plans or job search take a turn?

Chart 5
Listing Your Skills

For exercises 2-5, list the skills you identified in the appropriate column.

2	3	4	5

Chart 6
Ranking Your Skills

Using the skills you identified in Chart 5, use this two step process to rank the most important ones.

A. Weighted (Record each skill once, indicate the number of times each skill appears)	B. Ranked (List the skills in descending order of the number lines each mentioned)
	1.
	2.
	3.
	4.
	5.
	6.
	7.
	8.
	9.
	10.
	11.
	12.
	13.
	14.
	15.
	16.
	17.
	18.
	19.
	20.

Chart 7
Grouping Your Skills

Using the skills identified in Chart 6, group your ranked skills according to these six major categories. You may list a skill in more than one group.

A Athletic	B Numerical	C Influencing	D Helping	E Creative	F Investigating

Chart 8
Pulling It All Together

Exercise 1
Skill Groups   Interests

  1. _____   1. _____

  2. _____   2. _____

  3. _____   3. _____

Exercise 2
Ten Successes

  1. _____

  2. _____

  3. _____

  4. _____

  5. _____

  6. _____

  7. _____

  8. _____

  9. _____

10. _____

Exercise 3
Three Favorite Classes

  1. _____

  2. _____

  3. _____

Exercise 4
Three Work Experiences

  1. _____

  2. _____

  3. _____

Exercise 5
Fantasy

_____

_____

_____

_____

_____

_____

Exercise 6
Top Ten Values

1. _____
2. _____
3. _____
4. _____
5. _____
6. _____
7. _____
8. _____
9. _____
10. _____

Exercise 7
Top Ten Strengths

1. _____
2. _____
3. _____
4. _____
5. _____
6. _____
7. _____
8. _____
9. _____
10. _____

Charts 5-7
Top Ten Skills

1. _____
2. _____
3. _____
4. _____
5. _____
6. _____
7. _____
8. _____
9. _____
10. _____

Most law students find that their perspective on who they are and where they are going shifts—for some slightly, for others radically—as a result of skills analysis. There are many so-called experts—psychologists and career counselors—who can give and interpret career and vocational interest or aptitude tests. They may be able to help, but they can cost money. Many students can gain sufficient insights for their purposes through this process of regimented self-discovery just described. Friends, family, and co-workers will all be ready to tell you what you can and ought to do with your talents. Their impressions, while worth noting, do not compare to your own assessment of what you can do.

For many law students, the most difficult part of the entire process is identifying their skills. While people in general have little experience in skills analysis, law students probably have less. If their pre-legal education did not lead them away from subjective inner directed methods of solving problems, law school undoubtedly did.

Despite the fact that skills analysis may make some students uncomfortable, it is not a mystical process which can only be understood by an elect few. Remember these concepts integral to an individual understanding of his or her skills:

• Law students possess both the innate intelligence and the training to think rationally about employment.

• You alone have total responsibility for your life and its direction.

• You have to make choices. When the road forks, you have to take one path or the other. Whenever you make a choice, you open up some options and foreclose others; you gain something and you lose something. Know how you make decisions.

• Act at a time when you have the greatest control over the outcome of your decisions.

• Not only should you act to minimize the risk, but you should know what kinds of risks you are willing to take in the job search.

• You possess an array of skills which are transferable from one job or career to another. Too often, we think of skills in the vocabulary of one field and fail to see that the same skill might be transferred to a different area.

As you proceed through this book, the conclusions you reach in this chapter will have several uses. Throughout the process of considering broad career fields as well as specific jobs, it will be important to compare the skills required by the job with the skills you possess. At this point—having gone through these self-assessment exercises—defining the skills required by the job may still present a formidable problem while defining the skills you have should not.

6
Evaluating the Market

One of the most important steps in the career planning process involves evaluating the market to see what is available. Some students may need to spend less time on this step because they already have a clear idea of what and where they want to practice. On the other hand, realities of the job market may require subsequent modification of initial objectives.

For many law students, taking a broad look at the job market can be a useful or even necessary stop in the selection of alternatives. Surprisingly, a substantial number of law students do not have a good feel for what opportunities exist for lawyers.

There is a great deal of misinformation floating around. Some of it is perpetuated by the news media and legal press. Some of it is passed from student to student at school. Some of it is perpetuated by pre-law advisors, practicing lawyers, and other supposedly informed individuals. As a smart consumer, you will undoubtedly listen to what everyone has to say, but believe only what you can verify yourself.

Another reason to conduct this market analysis is that the market itself is always changing. Before this book is published, some of the information it contains will be out of date. Whatever you read or hear should be subject to review to determine whether the information is still valid.

There are five areas which you will want to investigate in your market analysis:

1) What substantive areas of law or fields where law training is useful are possible alternatives?

2) What organizations will be employing law graduates at the time you want to go to work?

3) What credentials will employers require of prospective employees?

4) Where are these employers located?

5) What economic conditions will come into play in the hiring decision? (Not only what is the state of the economy generally, but what are the financial rewards and prospects with individual employers?)

Market analysis is a component of the career planning process and should precede the job search itself. To establish priorities upon which a job search will be based without looking at the parameters of job availability would be an exercise in futility. You are much more likely to conduct a successful job search campaign if you take a look at the job market opportunities earlier in the process rather than later.

Part III of this book contains overviews for a number of common types of career choices. You should view these comments as jumping off points for your own research rather than the research itself. The remainder of this chapter addresses some basic questions about where you will work and live which you should ask as you look at the job market. Each of these factors should play an important role in your analysis of the environment.

Places to Work

Substantial differences exist in the way you are likely to spend your time on the job in different areas of law practice. This may be relevant to the type of organization where you work.

Larger organizations, whether law firms, corporations, or agencies are likely to be more hierarchical, structured, and institutional than smaller organizations. Organizations may vary widely as to how entrepreneurial they are, as well as how entrepreneurial they expect their employees to be.

Different organizations may have different ideas about acceptable deviation from group norms of behavior, dress, attitude, and philosophy. Different organizations espouse different views about training and nurturing new employees. And different firms will hold widely varying institutional goals and objectives that inevitably have an impact upon the careers of the people who work for them.

It is not always easy to get a feel for the "personality" of legal employers from the literature or statement of official representatives. It is even more difficult to make generalizations about classes of employers.

You should investigate different sources to gain a clear picture of the various job market settings. A conscientious investigation should lead you to some conclusions about the various categories of employment that interest you. In one sense, you are comparing your career skills to the requirements of the market in order to ascertain where you are most likely to be successful and consequently happy.

Places to Live

Where you live can be as important to your happiness as where you work. You should look carefully at different localities not only in terms of the jobs that are available, but also the lifestyles that are likely to be supported in that setting.

As for the job market, how many lawyers practice in the area? What do they do? Practice in law firms? Corporations? Government agencies? What substantive fields of law are supported by the state and local economy? What are the prospects for growth in population? In the business community? In the legal field? What opportunities for professional development are you likely to find in these various geographic settings?

Places vary widely, as to the types of lifestyle they support as well as those they tolerate. Urban, suburban, and rural areas offer unique advantages and present discrete disadvantages. The considerations that go into this analysis are limitless. They can include everything from whether there is a church or community supporting your religious faith to whether you can get to the opera often enough to satisfy your cultural pang.

Increasingly, cities, states, and regions are becoming less unique. You can get tacos in Boston and lobster in New Mexico. Shopping malls all seem to have the same stores. Some factors such as climate, ethnic mix, and history may distinguish geographic areas but on the whole there are more similarities than differences from place to place today than ever before.

This does not mean that you should not look at a geographic setting, it only means that your investigation may not be an easy one. It may also be the case that some of your preconceptions about places prove to be inaccurate or dated. It is likely also that you will be able to find opportunities in similarly situated cities in different parts of the country. Those who are not tied to a particular geographic location by family, working spouse, or other roots, may find greater flexibility than previously imagined.

Narrowing the Options

Before leaving this subject, it may be useful for you to put some flesh on the bare bones that have been presented. Before you start, try to make a list of all the settings you might consider. "Anything" is not a sufficiently narrow response.

Combining the factors, type of organization, type of practice, and type of community, list all the combinations you would be willing to consider.

Based on this list, spend some time investigating the job market in these settings. Look carefully at your own needs and requirements. Use information interviews and other oral techniques as well as reading to collect your information. This research process can take days to months depending on the number of options investigated, the depth of research, and the amount of time available. You will find, however, that this provides a much clearer picture of the prospects than simply listening to one or two people or reading a single publication. After completing your research, you are ready to establish some priorities and develop a timetable for your job search.

7

Establishing Priorities and Developing a Timetable

The final steps in the career planning process involve establishing priorities and developing a timetable for the job search. Many law students omit these steps because it seems self evident to them that after they have looked at their own skills and reviewed the market they can proceed directly to the job hunt.

The importance of ranking priorities is that it gives you focus. It forces you to organize your job search in a manageable and rational way. Similarly, establishing a timetable for the job search early in your law school career relieves the panicky feeling that you must find something—anything—in the last month.

Developing a Ranked List

It makes sense to begin your job search with the highest priority and to proceed down the list. Many law students have problems identifying specific employers during the job search process because they have not taken the time to set priorities during the career planning process.

It is not necessary to rigidly follow this list of priorities. If a job opportunity comes up that falls under another listed priority while you are still working on the first, you can pursue the job if you want to. The idea is to make the process work for you, not you for it. The paradigm merely calls for you to devote the greater part of your energies to the categories at the top of your list, and pursue other avenues only if your first ones do not pan out.

Chart 9
Ranked Options

	Type of Position	Type of Employer	Location	Substantive Area
1.				
2.				
3.				
4.				
5.				
6.				
7.				
8.				
9.				
10.				
11.				
12.				
13.				
14.				
15.				

So, how do you rank priorities? At this point, you should have selected quite a bit of information from your self analysis (Chapter 5) and your evaluation of the job market (Chapter 6). All you have to do is to convert your original list of market choices into an ordered list based upon what you have learned about yourself and the market. Your investigation may have uncovered one or two new alternatives. You will also probably want to drop some of the alternatives you had initially considered based upon what you have learned.

At this time, rank-order your possibilities on a sheet of paper (See Chart 9). List no fewer than five or more than ten. The reason for these limitations is to impose a degree of manageability to the list. If the list is too short, you may find yourself unemployed and out of options, an unfortunate combination. If you have too many options, your job search will not seem to have any clear definition. You may find that you have not forced yourself to make choices, but rather merely rearranged a big, unmanageable list.

Maintaining Options

As you go into the job search, your task will be to identify specific employers who meet the criteria defined by your ranked list. Begin with option one and proceed down the list.

As you near the end of the list, but before the list is exhausted, you should add additional options to the list. Hopefully, you will not reach this point. It is better to be prepared for the worst case scenario, however, than to find yourself out of ideas as well as options.

Developing a Timetable

You began the career planning process before you came to law school, but it does not stop when you matriculate. Many students spend a significant amount of time during the first year of law school going through the steps explained in the last three chapters. They begin the job search during the second year of school and complete it sometime during the third year. If this is the rule, then the rule is the exception.

In reality, the process is much more complicated for most law students. For one reason or another, many law students do not begin the process of career exploration until later in their law school careers, some not until graduation. The closer in time that you are to the date you start work, the more compressed the entire process will be, and the greater the temptation to shortcut the career planning process.

Many law students discover that experiences during law school itself alter their original visions of what they want to do. Career planning choices made during the first year of law school may not hold up during the third year. For this reason, it is almost always necessary to review your analysis at least annually. In fact, this is something that you should do on a regular basis throughout your legal career. We all change, and our plans should keep step with our identities.

For many law students, the planning process can be interrupted by diversions into the job search process from early in law school: part-time jobs during the school year, summer jobs, or even full-time jobs taken temporarily so that you can earn enough to complete law school.

In short, it is not always possible to proceed on a straight line through the career planning process. It may be necessary to jump forward and deal with elements of the job search (e.g., to look for a job, you have to have a resume.)

In one sense, jobs you obtain during law school represent another facet of the career planning process. You could call this a testing process. As you engage in the career planning process and form opinions, these may be viewed as hypotheses subject to testing in the crucible of the marketplace.

The fact that you may pursue jobs during law school does not alter the fact that career planning is the first step in the process of obtaining employment after graduation. Chart 10 describes a time line that illustrates alternative timetables for the career planning process. You will note the different schedule for day and evening students.

This chart reflects the fact that the longer you wait to begin the career planning process, the more compressed will be the time frame, and the less flexible will be the options. The chart also illustrates the point that there is no one "right" schedule for the process for all students. It will be useful to understand the cycle of this process in order to maximize the effectiveness of your efforts. See also Chart 23, Timetable for the Job Search, to see how the career choice and job search process are related.

Chart 10
Career Planning Timetable

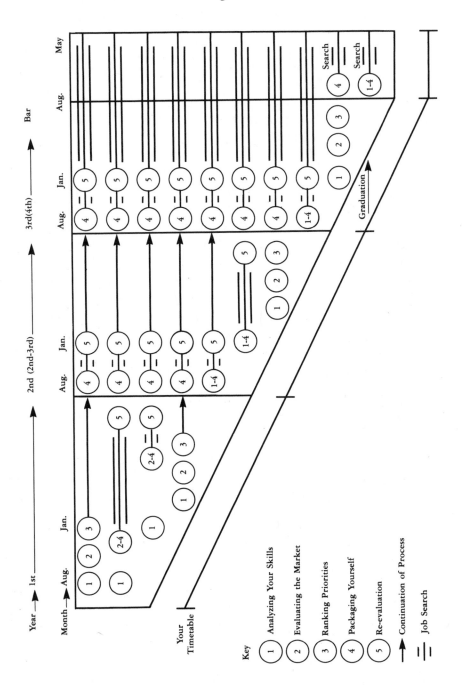

It may be helpful at this point for you to insert your own timetable in the space provided in the exhibit. This will give you an easy point of reference as you proceed through the career planning process.

One way to develop a personal timetable is to start at the end of the process. For instance, if you know when you plan to start working at a permanent job, you can work backwards to the point in time where you are now.

This simple technique can help you to avoid considerable stress as you proceed through law school. Aside from the demands of study and your personal life, the question of what to do after graduation looms ever-present in the background throughout your legal education. For some, the pressures associated with making career choices can produce acute anxiety.

The best way to negate such stress is to plan for it. Anticipate your most stressful periods. Spread out your activities. Get control of your career before it gets control of you.

Part II

The Job Search

Two roads diverged in a wood, and I –
I took the one less traveled by,
And that has made all the difference.

Robert Frost

8
Psychology of the Job Search

A job search can be lonely if for no other reason than that you are putting yourself on the line. The situation is made lonelier still when you are seeking your first legal position and are surrounded by peers with whom you compete for jobs. There are allies out there; you must take the trouble to develop them.

Much of this book addresses practical considerations and pragmatic problems about planning a career and finding a job. Implicit in much of this advice is a fundamental psychology that if you can identify what you want, you possess the tools to attain it.

Perhaps a more reflective look at this "psychology" for success will help to place the career planning process in perspective. Too many self-help books ring untrue. They seem to suggest that you can talk yourself into success. Or they imply that there is a secret formula that when imparted to the uninitiated will allow them to achieve happiness and success.

Too often, these works read like the high school cheerleading squad exhorting the football team to win. Self-help writers feed on the American dream that if you want something enough you can have it. The converse, of course, is that if you fail to achieve your goal, the reason is because you did not want it enough.

There is no doubt that a positive mental attitude is absolutely critical to success in any job search. Employers are not impressed by the "hat in hand approach" of a candidate who says in effect, "I know nothing, but if you teach me, I might be a good lawyer some day." Of course, you do not know everything there is to know about practicing law when you graduate law school. Employers understand that. You do not need to remind them how little you know.

What you must do instead is tell them what you have to offer. This simple, fundamental necessity in many cases is the biggest hurdle separating the job seeker from the job. Why? Because many people do not learn the skills of identifying and presenting their qualifications to others. Self knowledge and personal marketing skills are important. Returning to our football team analogy, these skills are the running, tackling, and blocking that we need to have to reach our goal.

Chapter 5 of this book discussed the need to identify the skills you bring to the job. These skills are defined in your past achievements. Your future accomplishments will utilize old skills as well as new ones you develop as you grow. It is important to take the time to develop a professional identity. With that knowledge, you can recognize and place yourself in situations where your particular talents can most effectively be utilized.

This book provides a formula to help you figure out who you want to be and how to get there. There is nothing mystical about this formula. The book does not say that if you fail to proceed step by step, you will not find a job or happiness.

What it does offer is a logical approach to a fundamental problem that everyone faces: deciding what to do with their lives.

The psychology of winning as presented here is more than desire. It is a positive presentation of your skills based upon careful analysis. The confidence you take to the job search should be based upon preparation, and not hype. The line between winning and losing an oral argument is often preparation, and preparation also provides a psychological edge when you stand up to speak. Good BS without preparation is just BS. Anyone who has been through eight weeks of law school knows this. Why should it be any different when you look for a job?

Another underlying concept throughout much of this book is self-determination. Too many people are willing to give up their self-respect by handing over the power to make decisions about their lives to others. We come into this world and go out alone. When we make fundamental career decisions no one else can be inside our heads. A host of individuals and forces can influence and contribute to these decisions, but no one else can make them.

This book makes the assumption that you are willing to take responsibility for your life and make decisions that serve your personal best interests. Many of the "don'ts" described throughout this book relate to various devises used by job seekers to abdicate this basic responsibility. Only when you can be your own woman or man can you exercise this existential right. For many it is simply a matter of making the decision. For others the task may be complicated by emotional baggage from outside the legal environment. For those people, personal counseling may be a necessary part of this process.

Mindset for Success

It may seem trite to say that you must maintain a positive attitude if you are to be successful in the job search. Books have been written about the importance of positive thinking in attaining personal goals. Although it would be simplistic and unrealistic to suggest that one could attain success simply by willing it, the history of humankind is replete with stories of people who achieve seemingly impossible objectives through the strength of their personal will.

What separates the achievers from the always dreamers? Surely the beggar on the street once had dreams just as the successful person. But is it enough to say that one was a quitter and one was not? Is it enough to say that one got the breaks when one did not? Or to say that in the final analysis one had talent and one did not? The intellectual traps of social Darwinism, metaphysical predestination, and existential nihilism all suggest that events shape our destinies, and that personal decisions are meaningless in the course of our lives.

If you accept the notion that you are not in control of your life, then you will probably not be in control of your life. If you want to say that blind luck, God, or society hold the strings in your life, then you minimize the importance of personal decisions.

You must take control. You must decide that your decisions make a difference in what happens to you. You must accept the significance of your responsibility for your own career. Saying this does not mean that luck does not have a role in what happens to you, nor does it preclude a relationship with God, whatever your conception of a Supreme Being may be. It certainly does not suggest that your family, cultural inheritance, societal norms, or personal talents and limitations have no bearing upon what happens to you.

Events and forces outside your control do affect your life. Much of what happens, however, lies within your own control. Too many people give away too much in this sphere. They abdicate choices which are theirs to make.

It is no mean feat to assert control over decisions that are not intrinsically dictated by external forces. It is easy to go with the flow and difficult to take charge. Frequently we run up against brick walls and get knocked down in our efforts to scale them. There is a distinction between an insurmountable barrier and a challenge that can be overcome.

The fact that you are in law school attests to your ability to overcome obstacles in your life. Law school will give new meaning to the word challenge. From the law school you attend, to your class rank, to your extra-curricular activities, to your work experience, everything and everyone will seem to conspire to stand between you and the job you want. You must adopt a mind set for success.

In order to devolve this discussion from the esoteric to the practical let us look at some ways that you can achieve a positive attitude:

1. *Pick your friends wisely.* Surround yourself with people who are realistic but supportive. Why spend time with pessimists, doomsayers, and negative thinkers? You can choose your friends, so pick ones who are upbeat and positive.

2. *Eat right and exercise.* There is a definite correlation between a positive self-image and a healthy lifestyle. Law school tends to push you away from physical activity, good dietary habits and reasonable patterns of sleep. Trust me on this one: you will feel better about yourself if you get plenty of sleep, eat something besides fast food, and work out regularly.

3. *Reward yourself.* Since much of the career planning and job search process involves setting and achieving goals, you can enhance your performance by imposing some simple conditioning on yourself. Set up a base schedule of rewards for accomplishing objectives. Give yourself small rewards for small accomplishments and big rewards for major ones. Let yourself be happy when you succeed. Pavlov would be proud of you.

4. *Meditate.* Many law students blanch at the idea of meditating, but meditation is simply a period each day when you clear your mind of the thoughts and pressures that normally clutter it. It is important to find a peaceful setting uninterrupted by telephone calls, noise, and other people. For many law students, such as those who are also working mothers, finding time alone is almost

impossible, but if you can take just fifteen minutes each day to clear out the cobwebs, your attitude will improve markedly.

5. *Take the time to plan ahead.* This book is a blueprint for planning. By following the logical steps presented here, you can provide yourself a methodology with a track record of success. If you know that you are doing all you can to maximize your opportunities and further your career, you can approach this process with confidence and vigor.

Alternatives

The importance of using options as a technique for maintaining a good mental attitude in the job search cannot be overemphasized. The concept is simple: always give yourself an alternative.

Desperation is an insidious thing. It starts with those little seeds of fear we all have that no one will ever hire us. It sprouts into panic when our initial plans fail to materialize. It can blossom into full blown depression when we perceive that there are no viable options open to us.

When that happens we are likely to say, "I'll accept any job." And when we do, it often turns out to be a mistake.

Maintaining a list of options can preclude the sense of helplessness brought on by having no options. Even though you will naturally spend more time focusing on options at the top of your list, periodically review what you would like to do if you do not get your first or even second choice. You can avoid much grief later on by following this advice.

9
Where to Look for Help

The placement office at the law school is not the only place to get assistance in your job search. Personal contacts and other sources may be just as helpful. The placement office is for many students, however, the focal point of a career search.

Your Placement Office

Two caveats are in order. First, every law school is different, and it follows that every placement office should be different in order to meet the needs of its particular student body, administrative requirements, and employment pattern for graduates. It is difficult therefore, to make any absolute statements.

Second, the ultimate responsibility for getting hired must fall on the student, not the placement office. The office is a resource and service center that can and should support your efforts, but when you get to the interview room there is only you and the interviewer.

In 1978 the American Bar Association added to its Standards for the Approval of Law Schools the provision that "the law school should provide adequate staff space and resources in view of the size and program of the school to maintain an active placement service to assist its graduates to make sound career choices."

• The law school should have specific personnel whose responsibility it is to administer the school's placement program. Administrative responsibility for placement should be in the hands of a person trained in law or in a profession related to placement. If a faculty member assumes the placement responsibilities, that person should be granted a reduced teaching load.

• The law school should have specific space set aside for placement activities, including a career library and interviewing and advising areas which assure privacy. In addition, the privacy of student records should be protected.

• Interviews conducted under the auspices of the law school should adhere to the National Association for Law Placement Principles and Standards for Law Placement Activities (See Appendix.)

• The school should conduct programs on legal career options, resume preparation, interviewing, and other job hunting skills as needed. Career education should be taught as an integral part of the educational process.

• The placement office should assist students seeking part-time (no more than 20 hours per week) and summer positions as well as permanent employment.

• The law school probably participates in the annual employment survey of the National Association for Law Placement. Thus, information on employment patterns of its graduates should be readily accessible to students.

• The law school should provide career advising or counseling. Ideally there should be at least one full-time equivalent counselor or advisor for every 750 students enrolled. In cases where a trained counselor is not on staff at the placement office itself, career advice may be provided by faculty members, student services of the parent institution, or in cooperation with bar or alumni associations.

• The law school should provide placement services to alumni of the school as well. Services extended to students should be granted to recent graduates until they have obtained permanent employment after graduation.

What function does placement play in the scheme of things at the law school? The answer is not too difficult. There are more law graduates than ever, and the job market is tight.

In a purely academic environment, there would be no need to rank students. It is the fact that legal employers rely heavily upon the collective assessment of the law faculty as to the performance of individuals being considered for employment that prompts the law school to assign grades and class rank. It is the fact that law school grades are relied upon heavily by legal employers that motivates many students to excel in their studies. More than a few students see their grade point average plummet as soon as they have attained employment.

Teaching law students about the variety of legal careers and employment prospects in these careers is integral to the academic program of the law school. Certain job hunting skills can and should be taught in the law schools.

Finally, the educational process is influenced by the employment during law school of students who are working in summer and part-time jobs, thereby supplementing the students' formal education. In a sense, summer and part-time work provides the residency or practical education that the law school does not or cannot offer. A high percentage of law students participate in these opportunities, since almost no law school offers a comparable program that would provide all students a practical internship.

Students who embark on a legal education generally have a reasonable expectation that they will be able to find employment in the field for which their education has prepared them. Law schools have a responsibility to law students and to the public to consider the employability of their graduates. Educators cannot divorce the real world filled with students' expectations from purely academic concerns.

Because the placement office can be where the academic and real worlds meet, you should find out what services it offers. At most schools, the placement office contains a wealth of information about legal and law-related careers. It will answer such questions as: What types of positions do most of your school's graduates accept? What are the current salary levels being offered to graduates of your school? Are there new materials available on careers? Are alumni lists available to those who seek positions outside the usual placement pattern of the school? Where can you find the materials about careers in law?

Of course, the placement office also receives information about specific job opportunities. Some, but certainly not all, will be in connection with on-campus interviewing.

Get acquainted with your placement director. Do not pick the busiest time of the year, such as the fall recruiting season. Set up an appointment to sit down and discuss your professional goals.

Give the director an opportunity to share with you his or her experiences gleaned from aiding in the career plans of many, many others. In turn, you will have the advantage of becoming something more than a number on an application form to the director. That can be of tremendous help as you begin to narrow your search.

By cooperating with your placement office, you can increase the network of its storehouse of expertise. Keep in touch with your law school placement office after graduation. Many openings do not develop until you have been admitted to the bar. If you have already been placed, your information on the position you have accepted and the compensation you are receiving will be helpful to graduates coming after you.

Personal Contacts

Many students who enter law school do not personally know any lawyers. If you are in this situation, you will want to develop a network of professional mentors. Your objective is not to develop specific job opportunities, though that frequently occurs, but to develop a better understanding and knowledge of what it actually means to practice law.

If you do not know any lawyers, perhaps you have friends in the business community who regularly use lawyers' services. They might be willing to ask lawyers they use to talk to you about the profession.

Go to court. Observe not only the procedures but also the interaction of members of the bar involved in trial work. Try to define what it means to be a professional person earning a living by practicing law, as opposed to a student learning about the law.

Often overlooked as sources of contacts are bar associations. The American Bar Association offers student memberships, as do many state and local associations. In addition, many offer the opportunity for enrollment in a section devoted to a substantive area of practice.

Take advantage of meetings which allow you to mingle informally. If a chance is offered for student participation, take it. It will mean extra responsibility, but it will also increase your chances of knowing lawyers with whom you may be professionally associated later.

If bar association activity is for any reason not open to you, consider subscribing to bar periodicals. Note the names of the bar leaders and their views on the legal issues of the day. Keep a scrapbook of articles and news notes that are tied to specific lawyers. This resource will be invaluable to you when you begin your actual job search.

Professors are often overlooked as personal contacts. Not only are they in a position to know your work as a student, but they also have a professional and even a personal acquaintance with many members of the bar. Their opportunity for comparative analysis of employers and opportunities can make them invaluable guides for you.

In all of these contacts, seek to develop an understanding of the practicing bar. Such contacts also give you a chance to ask each lawyer one important question: "Knowing what you know now, what career course would you recommend to a lawyer just entering the profession?"

Someday you will have ten years of experience behind you. You will know and understand things that can be perceived only through such experience. But by meeting and talking with lawyers now, you have the chance to develop your own plans based upon the experience of those who have gone before you. The better you understand the profession you are about to enter, the better your chances for a successful job search. For more information on how to develop a network, see Chapter 13.

Other Resources

There are other resources available to you outside the ordinary circles of the legal profession. Many students particularly those considering alternative careers, overlook these contacts.

What follows is not a comprehensive description of all possible resources, but rather some possibilities for the student who is imaginative enough to develop his or her own ideas. Do not hesitate to be creative in coming up with ideas for job hunting. Things like group or team research efforts have been successfully employed by some students. You may be successful because you are able to come up with an angle that no one else has considered before.

Libraries—Do not limit yourself to the law library, but use public and university libraries as well. Many universities have offices which conduct research into business and population trends; many private research organizations conduct such research also. Information available through these organizations can save you hours of digging.

Placement Offices—Remember that the undergraduate placement offices at many universities can help you with general information.

Many law schools provide reciprocity of services with offices at other schools.

Newsletters and Newspapers—Placement newsletters abound in certain areas of practice and geographical locations. While they may require a subscription fee or membership in an affiliated organization, the job information is often worth the investment. The want ads of most bar journals and legal newspapers list openings for positions also.

Agencies—Many state and local governments, in addition to the federal government, provide employment services. While the effectiveness of these agencies may vary from place to place, the careful student will want to cover all bases. Also, if you are unemployed, find out whether you are entitled to unemployment benefits.

10
Investing in Yourself

Your investment in a legal education represents a substantial amount of time, money, and effort. But even though classes and exams may have far more immediacy, they are in fact only a preparation for your future.

While you have many allies, the future of your career rests squarely and inescapably in your own hands. To reach your career goals requires a major commitment of time, effort, and in a limited way, money, if you are to succeed. You have put a great deal into your legal education; be ready for the additional investment necessary to utilize it to your full advantage.

Identifying Marketable Skills

The sooner you have some idea of the course you would like your career to take, the sooner you can point your education and/or work experience in that direction. Some fields of law put greater emphasis on research and work experience; others stress high academic achievement.

In all cases, planning ahead is important. Be sure you have completed the exercises in Chapter 5 so that you know well the product you are selling - yourself. It may mean the difference between successfully working toward a goal or settling for what's left over.

Academics

Law school grades are a factor taken into consideration by most legal employers. Emphasis on grades may vary from slight to heavy depending on the employer. Remember that grades are not the only factor an employer considers. Each year many students sell themselves to employers who would not have hired them on the basis of their grades. Likewise, some students with outstanding grades have difficulty finding jobs for reasons which totally escape them.

The trap is to blame everything on grades. While one should not be blind to the importance of academic performance in law school, one should not use grades as an excuse any more than a student with high grades should use them as a crutch.

The best advice to students is probably to be frank in discussing grades, no matter what they are, and to avoid sounding defensive when talking to potential employers. You do not need to say, "I would have done a lot better if that S.O.B Professor X hadn't been out to get me." If you sound like you think your grades reflect some sort of innate inferiority, you will turn off even the employers who do not place total reliance on law school grades in their hiring decision.

If you can manage to be positive, and show that you have skills which the employer can use, your chances will be substantially improved. If an employer is not persuaded by what you say about yourself, you have to be able to believe that it is his loss and not yours.

While grades can represent an ability to work hard and write well, innate intelligence or analytical skill, and successful competition in a highly charged environment, your own experiences outside the classroom may demonstrate the same qualities. If your grades are not spectacular, seek to gain other experiences and let employers know that you have other positive work habits: you get along with others; you are a self-starter; you have integrity.

You will undoubtedly want to look at employers' past hiring patterns. Since none of us likes to get shot down, we all play the odds in deciding whether to "go for it." It is important to know what kind of a risk-taker you are. Or, put another way, how stringent would an employer's requirements have to be, before you simply would not apply for a job?

Students might want to think of themselves as arguing a case (their own), and having to meet a certain burden of proof (some may have more of a burden than others). What kind of argument will be persuasive? How well do you build the evidence? How can you convince someone that you are more than a number? Other factors are likely to be important in the employer's consideration:

your personality, your interest in the job, your hometown or state, your interests, your maturity, or a variety of other variables.

It is, of course, easier to tell someone how to do this than to face the prospect personally. But what is the alternative? Too often, fear of rejection or failure, or anxiety caused by uncertainty about the future causes law students to procrastinate in order to avoid facing the situation. Many people wait to deal with these issues until all of their options have been foreclosed.

Summer Jobs

Many students work during the summer months to earn money for school, to gain valuable experience in law-related work, or simply to get away from school. It is becoming more common, too, for students to take a semester off and work full-time during either the fall or spring semester. The opportunities with legal employers are generally greater for students who have completed two years of law school than those who have finished only one.

Most medium-to-large-sized law firms, and many agencies and corporations conduct formal summer clerkship programs. These are usually well organized, high paying. They afford the opportunity of a permanent job. The bulk of the recruiting for these clerkships is done in the fall through on-campus interviews and job listings.

Many small firms or agencies will hire law clerks for the summer also, even though there is no organized clerkship program. The pay is often lower, and the employer is probably more interested in work than in recruiting permanent employees, although permanent associations do result from such clerkships.

Many of these clerkships are listed on the placement bulletin board of law schools or through outside organizations like the local bar association. Students often locate the employers themselves, however, and even convince some employers who have not hired law clerks previously of the need to do so.

Some students will work at nonlegal jobs to earn money. These often pay better than many legal jobs although the experiential value is diminished. The nonlegal placement offices on your campus often have information on jobs in their fields. However, many jobs can be located through want ads and personal contacts.

Summer school is an alternative for many students who hope to finish law school early or to lighten a course load. Others in order to get a different viewpoint or to be near home, take courses at other law schools. Summer school abroad is one possibility more students should consider. It allows a student to travel as well as receive course credit for law work.

Students need to consider their summer plans early in the academic year. By the end of March, many summer jobs are filled—and there are *not* enough to go around. Some jobs always come through the placement office after finals in spring, but waiting until then will leave you hanging until the last minute.

Part-time Jobs

Placement offices usually post part-time job listings for law clerk positions as well as nonlegal work. Many students do not wait for job notices but write or call local attorneys personally, or talk to friends who are currently working as clerks. Many jobs are passed on from clerk to clerk informally. It is common for many firms near a law school to select permanent associates exclusively from the ranks of their law clerks.

A word of caution: experience has shown that outside work will have a detrimental effect on academic performance. The value of the outside work must be weighed against the sacrifice in terms of education.

Full-time first-year students particularly are strongly advised not to attempt to work during the first year of law school. The ABA requires that outside work for full time law students must be limited to 20 hours per week, and urges first year students not to work at all. If you avoid working during the first year, you will have made a sound decision. If you must work, talk to an academic advisor or counselor to get suggestions on how to manage your load.

Education/Experience

Many students who did not pause after undergraduate school before starting their legal education find themselves with little or no work experience to complement their schooling. Conversely, students who have been out of school for some time complain that their years away from academia leave them out of sync with legal education and legal employers.

Even during school, students must frequently balance the costs and benefits of pursuing purely educational objectives (i.e., grades) against developing experiential skills through extracurricular activities (e.g., moot court) or work (e.g., clerking for a law firm part-time).

There are no easy answers to this question, partly because the solution may vary according to the various career paths law graduates pursue, and partly because it answer may vary from individual to individual. It is probably overly simplistic to say that one should attain the most experience possible without sacrificing academic objectives. In essence, however, it is necessary to weigh the advantages and disadvantages of choices made during law school, as much as it is to engage in career planning concerning post-graduate job choices. Although you may not be able to do anything about some parts of this equation, like how much and what kind of experience you acquired prior to law school, you do have control over decisions you make during law school.

Choices about how to balance your education and work experience inevitably must be made in light of the career planning process. In other words, what you should do now depends on where you want to go later. With the exception of some highly focused individuals, law students generally do not integrate long term goals into short term plans.

The earlier in your law school career you begin to engage in career planning, the greater opportunity you will have to apply your insights in that process to academic planning during school. Additionally, your assessment of your skills and marketability may lead you to pursue different avenues during school than you would have otherwise.

Writing and Law Review

A final topic that deals with your credentials involves writing experience and law review. Undoubtedly, law review experience can add panache to an otherwise ordinary resume.

Many schools now have two or more journals and there may be an unwritten pecking order of prestige usually related to comparative selectivity. Since law review experience tends to enhance your marketability, you should pursue law review if you have the opportunity. Aside from the boost to your credentials, the experiences of research, writing, editing (and being edited), working as a part of a team, and managing such a publication inculcate a variety of useful skills for the practice of law.

For those who do not have the opportunity to write for a law review, it is nevertheless important to develop your skills as a writer. Unfortunately, at some law schools it is possible to graduate with no legal writing experience after the first year.

Considering the important role that legal research and writing play in virtually every type of lawyering, it is unfortunate that the educational system does not require more. And considering the number of prospective employers who want to see writing samples of students they interview, it is tragic that many candidates can produce nothing but a first year moot court brief.

You can do something about this problem. Opportunities for writing are varied: "paper" seminars and courses, essay contests, advanced moot court competitions, research assistance for a professor, and part-time or summer jobs.

Push yourself to compose the best possible work product. Subject your writing to editorial review by others. Spend some time every week doing research and writing in school or in a summer job, and you will have plenty of samples to show prospective employers. When you plan to use written work from a job or judicial clerkship as a writing sample, however, be sure you obtain permission from your judge or supervising attorney before you release the document.

Debt Load

One material factor in the job search equation for many law students today is debt load. If your parents were not wealthy, if you did not get a full scholarship, if you were not supported by a working spouse, if you did not work night and day to pay tuition, then you probably have student loans to pay off.

The cost of legal education on top of college (and sometimes graduate school) can be staggering. It is not unusual for law school graduates to owe thirty, forty or fifty thousand dollars to lenders when they graduate. Such students begin practice with a cash flow problem.

Unfortunately, loan repayment must begin when school is over. Since defaulting on these student loans is not likely to make a strong impression on the bar admissions authorities, the prospect of carrying a built-in financial obligation with you into the real world can be an unwanted burden.

In practical terms, a heavy debt load often can limit the career choices available to students. Graduates looking at student loan payments may be forced to forego certain lower paying alternatives (e.g., public interest law) in favor of higher paying positions because of these obligations. The reality is that choices you make during and even before law school may have consequences for the options available to you after graduation. It may be necessary to grab the money and run by taking the highest paying job available.

If you face this problem, it will be necessary to incorporate your financial obligations into the analysis of your career plans. You should discuss the possibilities not only with your financial aid officer, but your placement director as well. Initiate a plan that keeps borrowing to a minimum. It may make sense to go to law school part time while working during the day, eschew law related jobs during law school for higher paying nonlegal positions, actively seek scholarship or fellowship money, and investigate work-study possibilities through your school.

To deal with economic problems, it is essential that you be honest with yourself concerning your needs. Determine whether there is any degree of flexibility you might be able to show to obtain a particularly desired position. Once again, your placement office can supply valuable information about the range of compensation currently being offered to graduates of your school, and it should be those figures upon which you base your financial analysis of potential income as related to your need.

Dual-Career Families

A new limitation has arisen in recent years for married lawyers. For those with professional spouses, the question is whether there will be equal career opportunities for your spouse in a particular community. Dealing with that issue has brought many interesting and varied answers.

For law graduates with lawyer spouses, there is an additional dimension to the general problem. For many years law firms have had an unwritten, but very real, rule that they will not employ lawyers married to each other. The only answer that many couples have had was to go into practice together if they wanted to work in the same office.

There has been a gradual relaxation of the rule, but in many smaller communities you will still find that if a law firm hires one-half of a lawyer couple, the other must seek employment in a corporation or government office. No other law firm in the community will consider this spouse for employment because of the potential conflict of interest. Employers themselves may understand that this danger can be avoided (as pointed out in the Model Rules of Professional Conduct, Rule 1.8j) but they are fearful of the reaction of their clients. These attitudes are changing, to be sure, but very slowly.

Other Limiting Factors

Oddly, the very breadth of choices offered by the legal profession can be a limitation because it is a physical impossibility for you to explore fully all the potential career options. But you can examine the vast array of possibilities, picking and choosing those that appear most likely to provide career satisfaction as a basis for further examination. The range of options open to you does provide room for personal choice.

One area of limitation is your own law school. This is far from an absolute limitation, merely a relative one. It arises from the employment market served by an individual school. That market is defined both by geography and by the type of office the school's graduates most frequently enter.

For example, it is not surprising that graduates of law schools in the Washington, D.C., area tend to be heavily concentrated in the federal government. Or that graduates of the Indiana University School of Law often find work with the firms in that state. If you are in doubt as to the type of market your law school serves, ask your placement office for its reports on the first positions held by graduates of your school during the last five years.

The limitation of the marketplace is not purely arbitrary. Consider the role of the employer in determining that market. The preference of alumni for hiring graduates of their own law school has long been noted. There are some very sound reasons for this preference. First, having attended a particular law school, a prospective employer is fully aware of the standards that the school maintains, the caliber of its academic program, and the suitability of that training for the client market to be served.

Second, the employer may personally know many of the professors of the law school and will therefore feel comfortable in calling and talking to them concerning an applicant's educational qualifications. The employer may even ask for a gut reaction regarding the applicant's ability to fit comfortably into the employing organization. Favorable comments from professors can be of immeasurable help in a job search, particularly if the graduate is not one of the top-ranking students but has demonstrated qualities of personality and character that may not be highlighted in a formal resume. Additionally, the employer may have had an opportunity to get to know you personally, having met you through law school alumni activities and functions.

On the other hand, what if your career goals lie outside the particular area served most frequently by your school? Here your imagination and aggressiveness in developing position resources will be your best ally. Arm yourself with literature that will demonstrate the quality of your school, and be ready to provide references to professors with whom the prospective employer may talk freely. Lists of alumni now located outside the school's market may also be obtained through the placement office or the alumni office as an aid to direct contact.

Still another way in which your law school will exercise a certain restriction is the matter of grades. It may be a painful subject, but it is one on which you and your law school stand united. Both of you recognize that there are factors other than grades that will determine your success in the practice of law.

Employers recognize that situation as well. Their difficulty lies in trying to establish some standards of measurement that will permit them to make value judgments concerning one candidate in relationship to another. Employers rely heavily on grades as basis for what they hope is a reasonably rational judgment about your potential. Equal opportunity employment laws have underscored the importance of this issue by making it necessary to make objective, rather than subjective, evaluations regarding individuals being considered for employment. When all is said and done, however, importance of the grades is minimized as you acquire a work record that can be evaluated.

Another possible limitation will be your undergraduate or nonlegal experience. For instance, in the field of patent law if you do not have undergraduate training in a scientific or technological field, you will find it extremely difficult to find a job.

In most situations, however, undergraduate training and nonlegal experience serve more as an advantage in the job search. Undergraduate work or an advanced degree in accounting, or experience in tax work will definitely receive priority consideration by prospective employers in the field. It behooves anyone with special training or experience to analyze the job market for potential employers who may fully utilize these skills in addition to your legal training.

11
Packaging Yourself

Successful job hunting requires a set of skills which, once learned, can be used repeatedly throughout your career. Writing a resume is an exercise in self-assessment and organization necessary for success at any level. Composing a persuasive and impressive cover letter is a good practice for all those times in the future when you will be required to present yourself or an idea in a letter. And the job interview is, of course, only the beginning of many such encounters. The current job seeker may become the future employer, the attorney interviewing (or being interviewed by) a prospective client, or once again a job seeker hoping to move on to a better position.

Preparing a Resume

A recent cartoon shows a portly gentleman seated in the office of a lawyer search consultant. The caption reads, "My resume, sir, is what you see sitting before you!"

Since most of us are unlikely to be hired simply on the basis of our compelling presence, it is generally useful to have a resume. The employer who will be evaluating your qualifications needs to have a resume. The resume tells the employer who is a likely candidate for the position and who is not.

In this respect the resume is a baited hook. It provides the prospective interviewer enough about the candidate to pique the interviewer's interest, leading the interviewer to think, "I would really like to meet this person."

The resume also provides a framework for the interview. A great deal of time can be wasted in a twenty minute interview if the employer knows nothing about the applicant beforehand and the applicant has to answer many tedious questions about grades, experience, and other basic qualifications. Under these circumstances, the applicant might become confused about names of employers, dates, or other details, and lose valuable time in which he or she could be asking questions about the firm or corporation. With a good resume, the employer can review the applicant's qualifications in advance and use the interview time to clear up important details and get some sense of what the applicant is like as a person.

What follows is a step-by-step description of how to create an effective resume that will make employers want to meet you. Do not short change yourself by plugging your data into someone's boilerplate form.

Do Your Career Planning Homework

Your resume should help focus on your goals and objectives. While compiling your resume, you will be forced to evaluate your goals, your skills and abilities, and your limitations. You will also have to consider the job market: given your career and geographical preferences, what is available?

Do not make the mistake of thinking that all this self-analysis can wait until later. Your resume will have to be aimed at the kinds of employers you hope to work for if it is to be effective. Compiling a general resume and firing it off to hundreds of employers in hopes that one of them will respond is reminiscent of the famous line, "I shot an arrow into the air; it fell to earth I know not where!"

You do not shoot an arrow into the air if you want to hit a target—you *aim* it. If you want to aim several different resumes at several different career targets, that is perfectly acceptable.

As you prepare your resume, ask yourself the following objective questions: Who will you be interviewing? Who does the interviewer represent? What information will the employer want to know about you? What personal characteristics and aptitudes do you possess that would be most attractive to an employer? What accomplishments should you stress in applying for this kind of employment?

The answers to these questions, as you perceive them, will determine in a large part the structure of your resume.

The second consideration is your subjective assessment of what you want. At this point, a certain amount of self-knowledge and a good deal of thought are needed, but the investment of time and energy will be well worth while if the result is an effective resume.

List Your Qualifications

When you have identified your employment objective(s), you are ready to take out a pencil and paper and start working on the resume itself. First, jot down a brief statement or statements of your objectives. Then record in outline form everything you think might be relevant to these objectives, including your educational background, work experience, and other relevant factors.

Start with the present (law school) and move backwards to college. Include all honors, activities, and publications, as well as your GPA.

Do not include high school experience unless your high school record contains something especially relevant. One student, for example, had attended the same prestigious private high school as a partner in the firm to which he was applying. While his other qualifications were excellent, you can be sure that mentioning his high school in his resume did not harm his chances.

Another student might have had some special achievement or honor in high school that would have direct bearing on the type of job she was seeking. But except in very unusual cases, it is not necessary to go back to the year one to give the employer relevant information.

Next, summarize in outline form your entire work history, including names of employers, dates, and general statements of the most important duties for each job. Make a note of significant skills developed on each job. Again, list everything you can remember.

Edit or Expand Your List

Having listed the information usually included in resumes, you should now edit ruthlessly. If you are a second or third year student, or a graduate with some work experience, your task may be to cut irrelevant material from your list. Leave out undergraduate activities if they have little bearing on what you want to do. If you have had summer or part-time clerking experience, do not bother including the construction job you had in your junior year of college, or the summer you waited tables in a resort.

If you are a first year law student hoping for a summer or part-time clerkship, your problem may lie in not having enough on your resume to make much of an impression. In this case, expand your list.

Include college activities and important papers and projects. Include titles of law school courses taken or in progress to show that you have some familiarity with the work you will be doing. Describe work experiences that show you to be hard working and dependable. Add any references that would mean something to the employer.

Shape and Arrange Your Qualifications

Once you have a rough list of items to be included in your resume, it is time to shape and arrange those items in the pattern that will be most effective. In some ways it is very difficult to give general advice about writing a resume because each person's resume should be a unique representation of a unique individual.

In order to present yourself as such a unique individual to prospective employers, your resume—your proxy—must stand out. Employers tend to view students as generic or fungible. You, on the other hand, must establish yourself as a gem, or at least diamond in the rough.

Academic honors provide immediate identifiers. There are, however, others. Look at your list again. What have you done or accomplished that distinguishes you from most of your classmates? Work those accomplishments into your resume in the appropriate sections.

The standard approach is to begin the resume with your **name, address and telephone number(s).** These should be prominently presented at the beginning of the resume to make it easy for employers to contact you.

If your current address is temporary, provide a permanent mailing address, such as that of a family member. If necessary rent a post office box. But use a good, easily accessible address. If at all possible, supply a telephone number where you can be reached easily so an employer can make an appointment for an interview quickly and conveniently. If there is someone who is willing and able to accept appointments for you, you are in luck. If you have access to a fax number, list it also.

If no other avenue is open, a telephone answering machine or even a professional answering service for a period of time may be the answer to your needs. An employer who is moved to action by your resume, should be able to pick up a phone and arrange an appointment immediately. An employee who cannot reach you at a time when interest is high may be less inclined to call back on another occasion.

Education is usually the first major category in your resume since it is often the area of greatest interest to employers. For experienced attorneys, work experience may be more important.

There are several ways of presenting your academic performance. You can include your grade point average (most employers expect to see it), or list the courses in which you did particularly well. Group courses according to area of concentration to show expertise, or chronologically to show improvement. Some students prefer to make grade and class standing information available only in the interview, but many employers assume that if your grades are not on your resume they are not very good. Check with your placement office to find out your law school's policy on grade representation. Activities and honors usually should be listed as well, but they can be included in a separate category to showcase them.

List your college or university, the date and type of degree you received, and all pertinent honors and activities. Again, the way you arrange the material will influence the message you communicate about yourself. Try to be more selective about prelegal than law school entries.

If you attended graduate schools or special programs, you will want to list those as well. Some older students who have attained several academic degrees may need to leave out or summarize some of their educational experiences in order to conserve space.

The way you classify your academic record and activities will depend on how you can best highlight your strong points. Chart 11 depicts a matrix with which you can group entries by educational level (legal/prelegal) or by content (academics/activities).

Experience is usually the next category. Note the use of the term experience rather than employment. Concentrate on legal work by listing these experiences first and in greater detail, with the present or most recent job listed first.

For relevant jobs you can include the name of your employer, dates of employment, and a brief description (using action verbs)

Chart 11
Education Matrix

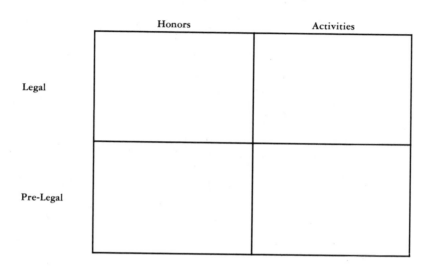

Chart 12
Experience Matrix

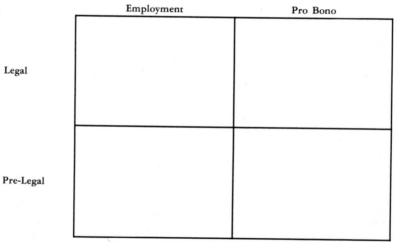

of your most important responsibilities. If you were chairperson of a committee, helped with a political campaign, lobbied, or volunteered in some other capacity, you acquired valuable skills, and this information should be included, especially if your other work experience is limited. As for nonlegal work experiences, try to focus on those aspects of the job that built skills that could be useful in your work as a lawyer. Chart 12 illustrates a matrix based upon experience.

Publications, if you have them, can appear in the context in which they were written (under education or experience) or, if there are several, can be listed in a category by themselves.

Personal information if included at all, is usually best listed at the end of the resume. As the name implies, this information tells briefly who you are and what you are like.

It is unlikely that a single list could serve to describe all the possibilities to incorporate in this section. What you include here will depend on what sort of image of yourself you want to present.

Employers cannot legally ask you date of birth, marital status, whether you have children, or other similar personal information that might be used to discriminate against women or minorities. Whether you elect to make personal information known to employers is up to you. In some cases you may make an employer uncomfortable by raising such issues (e.g., marital status).

If you include personal information, you may want to list things like place of birth, nationality (if non-U.S.), special skills or languages, geographical preferences, hobbies or travel (if pertinent or especially interesting), and when you will be available for the job. Information about your health, height, and weight might be relevant if you were going to work on a construction project or entering a beauty contest, but not for most law-related jobs. Also irrelevant (and often negative in impact) are the name and/or occupation of your spouse, the names and ages of your children, your religious beliefs, political persuasion, and self-laudatory statements (e.g., "highly motivated").

Remember, anything that is likely to create a negative impact is best left out altogether. Say "single" instead of "divorced" if you feel you must reveal your marital status. You need not mention the ages (or even existence) of children, particularly if they are very young and you are a single parent. If you have a noticeable health problem or handicap, do not mention it in your resume, but be prepared to explain in your interview that your problem would in no way affect your work performance.

References may be included if you need to fill up the page or the names will be recognized by employers. Legal employers are not likely to ask for references if you do not list them, so the commonly used "References available upon request" may let employers know that you have references but fail to motivate evaluators to contact the references.

In lieu of using valuable space on your resume, prepare a separate reference sheet listing names and telephone numbers (as employers are much more likely to call references than to write to them). Three to five references, not relatives or counselors (such as ministers), is usually enough. Try to use at least one law professor and make sure your references know that you will be listing them.

Although the common practice is to the contrary, some students include **professional preferences,** areas in which they have particular interest and/or experience. Here is a good place to bring in special qualifications even if they are nonlegal in nature. Beware of listing preferences if you have not decided to specialize in the areas you list, because doing so will probably typecast you. The same advice applies to inclusion of an "Objective" statement which is popular in many business resumes.

Lay It Out, Type It, Review It

Today almost all law students have access to PC's with powerful word processing programs. Some have access to graphically-oriented desktop publishing software. If you don't have a computer yourself, ask you can someone with a word processor to type the resume for you. Such technology not only permits easy editing, ready retrieval, and visual help in drafting, it also allows you to prepare different versions of your basic resume.

Single page resumes are definitely preferred by legal employers looking at law students. Remember that you can fit more on a page by using a smaller type size or scalable fonts, but do not select type so small that it is hard to read. Use an 8 1/2" × 11" format, not legal size. An oversized resume is unwieldy and gets dog-eared in the employer's briefcase and files.

Evaluate both the content and appearance of your first draft. It should be clearly organized and neat. Your name and heading

should stand out and the text should be placed in pleasing propor-
tions on the page. Make sure that you have clearly emphasized
your strong points. Ask yourself, "Does this resume present the
image of myself that I want to communicate potential employers?"

As you draft your resume, try to incorporate the skills you identified in Chapter 5. (*See* Chart 8.) As you describe your activities and
experiences, utilize action verbs to convey a sense of accomplish-
ment. Sometimes law students have difficulty communicating their
skills in a resume format, and articulating their nonlegal skills in a
way that looks credible in a legal context. The appendix contains a
list of law-related action verbs that may help you with this step of
the process if you are struggling.

Revise and improve your draft. Make effective use of white
space, type sizes, and boldface or italics. Cut out unnecessary facts
and direct the information specifically to the employers you want to
reach. Have someone else objectively evaluate your resume: your
placement officer, a fellow student, a professor, or an attorney.
Remember that everyone has a different opinion about what will
make the best resume. In truth, there is no perfect model. In the
end, you must decide what pleases you.

Some Resume Examples

Charts 13 and 14 contain sample resumes that illustrate different
interpretations of the conventional approach. Because the resume is
somewhat brief, the first student has used a large type face to create the illusion of more information.

The second resume demonstrates a slightly different arrangement. This resume emphasizes and places near the top of the
resume two qualifications that will interest employers: an editorial
position on a law review and excellent grade point average.

These examples illustrate two of the more conventional ways to
arrange an effective resume. They have been "aimed" at the
desired audience. Information has been carefully selected and
grouped for effective presentation. The next two resumes show
how much of a difference careful planning and arrangement can
make in a resume.

Chart 15 represents the resume of a third year law student, who
was going to use for fall interviews before a member of her placement staff encouraged her to revise it. At first glance, it looks some-

Chart 13
Sample Resume

JUAN VALDES
4000 Red River
Austin, Texas 78705
(512) 555-3660

EDUCATION

University of Texas School of Law; Juris Doctor Degree expected May 1992

> Associate Editor, *Texas Law Review*
> GPA: 83 (82.5 = approximately top 10%)

University of Pennsylvania; B.A. in Business Administration, 1985

EMPLOYMENT EXPERIENCE

Law Clerk - Wilson & Trump, Washington, D.C., Summer 1991

> Prepared comments for several national trade associations for submission to federal regulatory agencies; conducted research and drafted memoranda for litigation on behalf of American Indian clients.   Worked with the FCC, the Federal Reserve Board and other agencies.

Law Clerk - Hunter & Lansing, Austin, Texas, January 1990-May 1988

> Researched legal issues in both civil and criminal practice; wrote legal memoranda; prepared and drafted legal documents, motions, interrogatories, jury instructions and appellate briefs; and assisted in trial preparation.

Law Library Assistant - Clark & Koe, Philadelphia, PA, April 1985-June 1987

> Processed legal periodicals and treatises; assisted attorneys in locating research material; prepared catalogue cards; and prepared invoices and checks for payment of library bills.

PERSONAL

Birth: May 23, 1964, Philadelphia, Pennsylvania
Interests: Latin American Law and History
Languages: Spanish and French. Have traveled extensively in Latin America and throughout the United States.

REFERENCES AVAILABLE ON REQUEST

Chart 14

Sample Resume

U. Charles Cullen, III
1300 North South Road
Harrisburg, Pennsylvania 17999
(717) 111-1111

Legal Education

Widener University School of Law   J.D. expected May, 1993
Harrisburg, Pennsylvania

Honors:	Moot Court Honor Society
Activities:	Class Representative, Student Bar Association
Memberships:	American Bar Association, Law Student Division
	Pennsylvania Bar Association, Student Division

Legal Experience

Judicial Clerk Intern   Summer 1991
Dauphin County Court of Common Pleas

   Assisted Judge's law clerk in reviewing briefs, petitions, and orders; researched legal and procedural
   issues; assisted in trial preparation and trial conferences; drafted opinions.

Pre-Legal Education

Gettysburg College   B.A. awarded June, 1989
Gettysburg, Pennsylvania

Major:	Finance
Honor:	Dean's List

Other Experience

Dormitory Resident Assistant   September 1988 - May 1989
Gettysburg College

   Served as counselor for 75 coed students in university residential hall. Coordinated dormitory activities;
   acted as student liaison in dealing with university administration; and performed various counseling
   functions.

Department Manager   Summers 1987, 1988, 1989
The Department Store

   Ordered all merchandise for several departments; maintained the stockroom inventory for these
   departments; assisted customers in locating and choosing merchandise.

what carelessly done. Indentations wander all over the page and all the spacing is the same with nothing set off to emphasize its importance. The first impression is that this is a foreign national who is divorced, has two small children, and no telephone where she can be reached. Her degree in comparative literature and the prominence given to hobbies unrelated to a legal career complete the picture that this person may not make a very dedicated attorney. Because the average employer spends only thirty seconds scanning each resume, most would not even get to the part where she mentions having written for the *Urban Law Review*. If they do, they will be turned off by the list of four jobs, only one of which is related to law, and references who have nothing to do with the legal profession. A couple of typographical errors become exclamation points for incompetence.

Now look at the revised resume in Chart 16. The arrangement of type and headings on the page is pleasing and balanced. Margins and indentations are consistent throughout the page, and major headings are clearly set off by the double lines. The use of varied line spacing (single line within a classification, double between them) also contributes to a harmonious and easy to read page.

The content of her resume has been similarly revised. She includes the essential telephone number, making it easy for employers to reach her for offers of office visits or jobs. The employer can immediately see that although her grades are not spectacular, she has several honor grades in areas that pertain to her legal interests and she has a scholarship. She also has published articles related to city planning (her main area of professional interest), and is active in law school organizations. Instead of listing unrelated jobs, she has grouped her "experience" to include important volunteer positions which demonstrate an interest and expertise in her chosen field. The descriptions of each job use action verbs, which convey the impression of an energetic and purposeful employee. Prelegal education and personal items are included briefly at the bottom of the page and the unnecessary references to marital status and potential family complications are deleted. Instead, she appears to be a competent and experienced professional.

Have It Printed

You are now ready to prepare a final draft of the resume for printing. Unless you are having your resume typeset, it will be

Chart 15
Resume of Ann Applicant

ANN APPLICANT

PEROSNAL

Born: April 18, 1956, Heidelberg, Germany

Marital Status: Divorced

Children: Two (Tommy, 4 and Carol, 2)

Health: Excellent

Address: 2610 Cherrywood

Austin, Texas 78722

PRELEGAL EDUCATION

Kent State University, Kent, Ohio

University of Texas, Austin, Texas: B.A. in Comparative

Literature, June 1987

HOBBIES: Tennis, dog training, photography

Languages (French and German)

Member U.T. German Club

ACTIVITIES

Academic Scholarship (Kent State University)

Volunteer, Austin Tomorrow Program

Volunteer, Student Attorney's Office, Kent State University

Dean's List, University of Texas 1986-87

LEGAL EDUCATION

The University of Texas School of Law, J.D. expected May 1990

Activities: URBAN LAW REVIEW

Assault & Flattery

Women's Law Caucaus

EMPLOYMENT EXPERIENCE

Clerk, Murphy's Five and Dime, Austin, Texas, July-August 1984

Library Assistant, Kent State University, Summer 1985

Teaching Assistant, Univeristy of Texas German Department, 1987-88

Law Clerk, Dewey, Cheatham, and Howe, Austin, Texas, 1988-present

REFERENCES

Mrs. Georgia Grumbly, 1616 Sixteenth St., Austin, TX 78716

Mr. George George, 1801 South St., Houston, Tx

Rev. John Jones, 99 Ninth St., Kent, OH

Chart 16
Revised Resume of Ann Applicant

ANN APPLICANT
2610 Cherrywood
Austin, Texas 78722
(512) 555-4004

Candidate for Doctor of Jurisprudence Degree - May 1990
The University of Texas School of Law

LEGAL EDUCATION

The University of Texas School of Law

Academics: GPA 78.6
                Am Jur in Contracts
                Honor grades in Torts, Property, Civil Procedures

Honors: Jane Doe Scholar, 1989

Publications: "The New Integrated Neighborhoods: A Review of Recent Trends in Major Texas Cities," *Urban Law Review*, June 1988, pp. 36-51. "Urban Renewal and Historic Landmarks: Legal Questions When Public Interest and Heritage Clash," *Austin Citizen*, August 6, 1989, p. 10.

Activities: Women's Law Caucus: Chairperson, Community Relations Committee, 1989; Student Bar Association: Fund Raising Committee,1989; Assault and Flattery: Wrote and directed skit, May 1989.

LAW-RELATED EXPERIENCE

Law Clerk: Dewey, Cheatham and Howe, Austin, Texas, June 1988 to present.
    Briefed, researched, interviewed clients, prepared materials and accompanied clients to rezoning hearings before City Council.

Volunteer Neighborhood Coordinator: Austin Tomorrow Program, Austin, Texas, 1987.
    Worked with neighborhood group to propose and plan for future development of integrated Austin neighborhood. Plan involved rerouting public transportation, increasing use of schools and parks for recreation and community practical skills courses, and adding bicycle lanes to proposed new highway through the area.

Intern: New York City Planning Commission, Summer 1987.
    Worked as team member on Inner City Development Project, prepared statistical data, supervised three other student interns.

Volunteer: Student Attorney's Office, Kent State University, 1986.
    Answered telephones, received initial inquiries, referred clients to outside help when necessary.

PRELEGAL EDUCATION

The University of Texas at Austin: B.A. June, 1987
        Dean's List 1986-87
Kent State University, Kent, Ohio
        Academic Scholarship 1985

PERSONAL

Hobbies: Tennis, training dogs, photographing animals.

REFERENCES AVAILABLE UPON REQUEST

Compiled 7/30/89

reproduced from the version you produce. Whether you type it yourself, or have it typed by some else, be sure to use a laser quality printer so that the letters are crisp and dark and will reproduce well. Variety on the page is desirable; some items can be in **bold** or *italic,* for instance; but be sure that the main body is typed in an easily readable script. Desktop publishing programs increase the options available for layout and design of a resume. This software combined with a laser printer can give the appearance of typesetting at a fraction of the cost.

Even if you do not have a desktop publishing system available, you can use transfer lettering (available at most campus bookstores) to get larger letters for headings in lieu of typed headings. Painstaking care must be taken to transfer type neatly, but the result is attractive and cheaper than typesetting. For the ultimate in a professional looking resume, you can have your resume typeset. Most people feel that the improvement in appearance with typesetting however, is not worth the high cost.

After the page is typed, proofread it very carefully for errors. Use the spell-checking feature of the word processor to make sure all words are spelled correctly. Your original must look exactly the way you want your resume to look. A good quality copy can only be reproduced from a good quality original.

The next step is to decide how to print your resume. You can run off quality originals with a laser printer which is the best and cheapest option; you can print one original and photocopy more on bond paper if you have a good copier; you can have your resumes printed at a "quick print" shop; or you can have the resume produced by a professional printing service.

Regardless of which method you use to have your resume reproduced, be sure to choose a good quality paper. There are usually a variety of textures and colors to choose from, but do not get carried away and choose a bright or intense color. White, cream, pale beige, or something similarly conservative, generally works best with legal resumes.

Distribute It

A resume is not only a blueprint for the interview, it is a marketing piece. Often, the employer will decide whether to grant you an interview on the basis of your resume. Therefore, getting your resume into the hands of the person who can decide to interview or hire you is just as important as producing a good resume. Chapter 14 deals with cover letters. Remember, however, that frequently the resume is hand delivered or passed on to a lawyer who does not have the benefit of a cover letter. For this reason the resume should be able to stand on its own. At the very least, your resume should cause the employer to want to meet you in person.

Elsewhere in this book, the tactics of the job search process are covered in detail. Regardless of how your particular job search proceeds, keep in mind the most effective means of distributing your resume. Do not blanket the world. On the other hand, make sure that references, friends, business contacts and past employers who may be contacted get a copy.

Be considerate of other people's time. Coordinate mail, telephone, fax, and personal visits when appropriate to get your message across.

Revise It

Resumes do not stay current forever. In fact, any resume older than three months is probably out-of-date. As a job seeker, you should regularly update your resume as your credentials evolve. You also may want to modify your resume to reflect changes in tactics or direction. If your resume has been prepared with a word processor and stored, making changes should not be difficult.

Remember to circulate the new version to everyone who has the old resume, including references, current employer, and potential employers who have it on file. This not only updates their information, but gently reminds them that you exist.

In addition to a personal resume many job applicants will need to produce a number of other documents as a part of the application process: transcripts, writing samples, application forms, and letters of reference. Not all employers will expect you to produce all of these documents, but you should be prepared to do so if necessary.

Transcripts

All law schools will distribute official transcripts when requested to do so by students. Federal law prohibits the institution from releasing such information without your permission. Thus, employers cannot obtain a transcript without your written authorization.

Many corporations and government agencies routinely ask for transcripts, although few law firms do. As cases of resume fraud increase, however, this may change. Handing an unofficial copy to the interviewer is insufficient. Instead, you will be asked to sign a release before, during, or after the interview.

Writing Samples

Some employers ask applicants for a sample of their writing. A substantial number of firms and most judges want to evaluate your research and writing skills directly, rather than indirectly through professors or references. Accordingly, you should always carry with you a copy of a writing sample to hand over if requested. Don't routinely send out a writing sample with every cover letter and resume.

Students sometimes ask: "What should I use for a writing sample?" Generally, the answer is to use your best work. If you are not sure, have someone else read the possibilities.

For most third and fourth year students their best work probably came after the first year of law school. For second year students this may not be the case. As suggested in Chapter 10, you should do everything you can to produce written work during law school, not only because of the importance of writing skills in law practice but also because of the relevance of writing samples to the evaluation process.

Application Forms

Take special note of the requirements for individual application forms, which in a sense are a variation of the resume. If you are planning to apply for a federal government positions, obtain Form 171 from your local post office because virtually every federal office requires this form to be filed to be eligible for consideration. Make one original and copy it for each separate application, but sign each form separately.

Many state and local governments also require a form. If you are seeking a state or local government position, inquire about this possibility before an interview or, if possible, even before submitting your resume.

Letters of References

As a rule, legal employers are not impressed with reproduced letters of reference. Somehow, they know that you would not give them a letter that said, "I would *never* recommend Ms. Smith for a job!"

Even unsolicited letters sent directly by your references to employers may be viewed as annoyances. Your best strategy is to make the names, addresses, and phone numbers of your references available when asked, so that those employers who are interested can contact your references directly.

A Final Note

Remember who you are interviewing. Who does the interviewer represent? What will employers want to know about you?

Your resume should facilitate the interview process, introducing personal characteristics and skills most attractive to an employer. It should highlight the accomplishments to be stressed in applying for a job. A certain amount of self-knowledge and a good deal of thought are needed to present the best possible picture, but if you manage to succeed in this effort it will be well worth your time.

12
Researching the Employer

As you may have gathered by now, finding a job involves a lot more effort than merely showing up for an interview on time. There is considerable behind-the-scenes homework involved. Taking shortcuts will only leave you with less control of the situation and fewer good possibilities to pursue. Researching the employer is one area where students may be tempted to take shortcuts. Resist this temptation. A key to successful job hunting is learning enough about prospective employers to be able to demonstrate why *they* need *you*. To accomplish this objective you must do your homework.

Much employer research is tedious, but your three years at law school deserve a planned and thorough effort to find the best employer and working situation possible. Applying to employers at random or going into an interview cold is as sensible as buying an expensive pair of shoes without trying them on. Your job will be a major part of your life for the next several years, perhaps as many as 40. It may make the difference in the level of happiness you attain in life.

When researching an employer, find out as much about the organization as possible. Remember these two questions:

1) What type of person and skills do they need?

2) How do your skills meet this need?

Some of the specific information you need to discover about each employer includes:

• What is the employer's philosophy of law practice management?

• What is the work environment like?

• What are the backgrounds, ages, accomplishments, and interests of members of the firm or organization?

- Who are the clients? What services do they perform?
- How do they obtain clients?
- What is the size of the organization in terms of employees and volume of work?

The following program requires work. If you break down your efforts into small, manageable segments, however, it can be handled with much greater ease. For example, writing a hundred personalized letters at one sitting is a Herculean task, but writing five letters a week can be managed.

Many information resources are too expensive and bulky for you to purchase and keep for ready reference, although you will find them in your placement office or law school library. Materials not in the law school might be found in a university or public library. Some law schools also offer computer databases for their students' use. Those living in a small town or attending a smaller law school may be able to use sources in law offices, banks, and similar institutions.

A file box of 3 by 5 inch index cards or laptop computer can be transported easily to the libraries and other places where resources are maintained. Information can be recorded and carried away with you for later retrieval.

The index card is a convenient form for notations about job applications as well as information about employers. If you use a computer, you can record this information in a database or spreadsheet program. (See Chart 17 for an example of how such a spreadsheet can be organized.)

What information should you record? First, you will want the name, address, and telephone number of each prospective employer you wish to contact. Since legal directories do not give the name of the person responsible for hiring within a particular firm, you may need to select the senior partner, a partner whose bar affiliations indicate a strong practice interest in the area of specialization to which you are drawn, an alumnus of your law school, or another person you believe should receive employment inquiries.

In a corporation, government law department, or similar organization, the general counsel usually assumes the same role as senior partner in a law firm, and frequently has direct hiring responsibility. If there are other individuals listed to whom your inquiry more logically might be directed, however, note the name and the reason for selection. For almost any employer, a phone call can provide

Chart 17
Model Spreadsheet or Database

Name of Employer: _____

Address: _____

City: _____

State: _____

Zip: _____

Phone: _____ – _____ – _____

Hiring Partner: _____

Recruitment Administrator: _____

Contact: _____

Type of Employer:* _____

Application: _____/_____/_____

Interview 1: _____/_____/_____

Interview 2: _____/_____/_____

Offer: _____/_____/_____

Reject: _____/_____/_____

Salary: _____

Notes:

*LF Large Firm	GF Government Federal	PR Prosecution
MF Medium Firm	GS Government State	PI Public Interest
SF Small Firm	GL Government Local	LS Legal Services
CL Corporation Legal	JG Military (JAGC)	ED Education
CT Corporation Tax	JC Judicial Clerkship	MI Miscellaneous
CO Corporation Other		

the appropriate name to which your letter should be addressed.

Since your job search should not be restricted to advertised openings alone you should seek to find potential openings using other sources. You can utilize legal directories and telephone books from cities across the country. You can contact various placement organizations that provide legal job search assistance. Finally, if you want to know which firms and corporations have shown an interest in graduates of your law school, thumb through the resumes of employers who interview at your school.

Many unconventional and exciting ideas for researching and approaching employers can be gleamed from Richard Bolles's *What Color is Your Parachute?* The book has step-by-step instructions for job seekers, covering a variety of topics including the art of conducting information interviews and gathering facts. This manual may be especially helpful for students who feel overwhelmed by the job search and need some extra encouragement and motivation.

Deciphering Employer Resumes

The employer resume—can anyone discern meaning among the platitudes? The resumes sent by employers to your school soliciting applications can be slick professional productions or simply two- to four-page summaries on company, agency, or firm letterhead. Regardless of form, these marketing pieces may tend to obscure rather than to clarify the picture of employers for you.

It is possible, however, to find meaningful information if you know where to look and how to systematize your findings. Keep a sheet or 3 × 5 cards on each employer with a list of questions for which you would like answers. As you read the resume, fill in the answers to your questions.

The unanswered questions may give you ammunition for the interview. In addition, when you review the answers, you may discover other questions to ask. The whole interview process should be aimed at collecting and utilizing information make sound decisions.

Some of the information commonly incorporated in resumes includes the following:

- History and background of the firm, agency, or corporation;
- Organization, structure, and practice of the office;
- Clients and major areas of practice;

- Hiring standards or requirements;
- Hiring needs for the upcoming year;
- Description of summer clerkship program, if any;
- Starting salary, benefits, and salary potential;
- Special advantages which would attract candidates, such as provision for pro bono or public service activities;
- Training and opportunities for professional development;
- Advantages of living in the city or community where the employer is located;
- Other factors which make this employer different from others you may be considering; and
- Biographical information about lawyers working for the employer (if not included in *Martindale-Hubbell*).

A good resume will reflect the employer's philosophy of practicing law and hiring and help answer many of your questions. A bad resume can make your job much more difficult.

Many legal employers who participate in full on campus interviews complete a standardized NALP form. (See Appendix.) Not only is it much easier to compare one organization to another using the NALP form than a firm resume, it is easier to track changes in an organization from year to year.

The NALP forms contain a wealth of information from areas of practice, to hiring patterns, to salary structure. Recently the NALP forms traditionally published in a *Directory of Legal Employers* have become available on Westlaw under the name *NALPline*.

If you are interested in small firms or other organizations that do not recruit on a regular basis, there may not be either NALP forms or firm resumes to guide you. Even for entities that have resumes and NALP forms, many of your questions may still remain unanswered. Where can you find out about working conditions, reputation, and attitudes toward new lawyers? For the answers to these questions you may have to ask other students and contacts or read between the lines.

Directories

Classes have started, and you are busy! Nevertheless, you have to spend hours in your placement office and the library researching potential employers with whom you may or may not have an opportunity to interview. Is there an easier way to get through fall interviews? Perhaps. If you learn how to use the *Martindale-Hubbell Law Directory,* the state legal directories, *Standard and Poor's Register of Corporations,* the *U.S.Government Manual,* and other resources available in the placement office or library, you can find out what you really need to know about legal employers and what they want you to know.

Martindale-Hubbell

The 22-volume *Martindale-Hubbell Legal Directory* is arranged in alphabetical order by state. In each of the first seventeen volumes there are three main sections. The first lists all licensed attorneys in the states included in that volume. The information here is abbreviated and coded according to a key found on the inside cover of each volume.

In this section you can discover when an attorney was born, his or her date of bar admittance, firm and status within the firm, undergraduate and law degree, and the firm's competence and ethics rating (e.g., av). No telephone numbers are listed, but the addresses of solo practitioners are included.

The second part of each volume is the largest and most familiar. Here you will find most firms with over five lawyers, but remember that only those who have paid for space are listed. This section includes full addresses and telephone numbers of firms, biographies of members, areas of specialization, and representative clients. Look for graduates of your law school among members, and check members' professional affiliations to see what their interests are. This is one way to find out before the interview whether the firm will really be interested in you, and you in them.

You should also pay attention to the firm's listed areas of specialization, but do not be misled by generalizations. Terms like "general civil practice," "real estate," "probate," and "trials and appeals" could apply to most firms, and so do not tell you much about a particular firm. On the other hand, the terms "insurance" and "defense" seldom appear in the same listing with "negligence" and "worker's compensation," and terms like "criminal," "tax," and "public housing" give you a very good idea of the kind of work you might do if you worked for that firm. The list of representative clients is also a good source of information, but bear in mind that probably only businesses, corporations, and banking institutions will be listed. A small town lawyer or one who represents only individuals would probably not list representative clients.

The third part of these volumes includes information on legal support services and suppliers of products for lawyers. Ostensibly a service to the bar, this section appears to be more of a means of raising advertising revenue than anything else.

The last four volumes of *Martindale-Hubbell* can also be very helpful. Volume 15 includes a directory of corporate law departments. The last five volumes contain a directory of Canadian and international lawyers, and digests of Canadian, international and American laws by state, the District of Columbia, Puerto Rico, and the Virgin Islands. A good idea for anyone interviewing with out-of-state firms would be to read through the relevant jurisdictions in case legal questions arise during an interview.

Since *Martindale* has become available both on *Lexis* and CD-ROM (Compact disk read only memory), the potential for accessing information is greatly expanded. It is now possible to construct complex searches covering a number of different variables to identify lawyers or firms that meet your profile. Chart 18 includes a summary of ways you can use *Lexis* to support your job search.

Not to be outdone, *Westlaw* has established an online *West Legal Directory* that replicates much of the information in *Martindale*. West also produces a booklet available through most placement offices covering online placement research.

When used in conjunction with *NALPline* (containing the *Directory of Legal Employers* mentioned previously), *Westlaw* becomes a powerful research tool which rivals *Lexis/Martindale*. Your choice may depend on which system you are more comfortable with, your specific search needs, and availability, but whatever you do, remember that electronic research can enhance the depth and quality of your job search just as it can traditional legal research. Since both *Lexis* and *Westlaw* are available free to law students, there is real incentive to use these systems prior to graduation.

State Legal Directories

If you do not find all you want to know in *Martindale-Hubbell,* try the appropriate state legal directory. Many of these directories are blue paperbound or hard cover volumes published by the Legal Directories Publishing Company, Inc.

Chart 18

Preparing for an Interview on Lexis

- *Use LEXIS/NEXIS to locate information to help you with your job search.*

- *Use specific libraries and files to target information on:*
  - *Law Firms*   - *Government Agencies*
  - *Corporations*   - *Trends in the Legal Profession*

LAW FIRMS

− *To locate a profile on a particular law firm*

Lib:	COMPNY
File:	TRINET *(Company and Establishment Database)*
Search:	name (williams w/2 connolly)

- *To locate a list of clients that a law firm represents*

Lib:	COMPNY
File:	SPCORP *(Standard & Poor's Register of Corporations)*
Search:	law-firm (fried frank)

- *To locate information about a recruiting partner*

Lib:	NEXIS
File:	CURRNT *(Stories dated 1988 or later from full-text NEXIS files)*
Search:	kevin pre/3 baine

- *To review recent general information about a law firm*

Lib:	NEXIS
File:	LGLNEW *(A collection of legal publications that primarily cover legal news)*
Search:	skadden arps and date is 1990

- *To review recent cases where a particular firm represented one of the parties*

Lib:	GENFED
File:	CURRNT *(Combination file of federal court files from January 1988 to present)*
Search:	counsel (akin gump)

CORPORATIONS

- *To review an annual report for a particular corporation*

Lib:	COMPNY
File:	AR *(Annual Reports)*
Search:	name (nabisco)

– *To find information on a particular corporation's executives*

    Lib: COMPNY

    File: SPBIO *(Standard & Poor's Register of Directors and Executives)*

    Search: name (nabisco)

- *To review general business information about a company*

    Lib: NEXIS

    File: BUS *(A collection of publications and wire services that primarily cover business news)*

    Search: rjr nabisco w/50 nabisco and date is 1990

GOVERNMENT AGENCIES

- *To gather information on a specific division of a government agency*

    Lib: NEXIS

    File: CURRNT (Stories dated 1988 or later from all full-text NEXIS files)

    Search: department w/2 justice w/20 civil rights division and date is 1990

- *To find general information on programs that an agency is working on*

    Lib: NEXIS

    File: DREXEC *(Daily Report for Executives)*

    Search: environmental protection agency or epa w/20 policy or program and date is 1990

GENERAL TRENDS/INFORMATION

- *To locate the most recent annual survey of the nation's largest 250 law firms by <u>The National Law Journal</u>:*

    Lib: NEXIS

    File: NTLAWJ *(The National Law Journal)*

    Search: date is 1989 and section (NLJ 250)

- *If you are interested in restricting your search to a particular law firm, modify the search by transmitting:* m; and (the firm name)

- *To research emerging areas of law*

    Lib: NEXIS

    File: LGLNEW *(Legal publications)*

    Search: grow! or trend or emerg! w/10 practice law firm

- *To locate salary and benefit information for attorneys*

    Lib: NEXIS

    File: LGLTME, NTLAWJ, AMLAWR *(Legal Times, The National Law Journal, American Lawyer)*

    Search: lawyer or attorney or associate or partner w/15 salary or compensat! and date is 1990

For additional information or search assistance call our CUSTOMER SERVICE Department, 1-800-543-6862 (24 hours a day).

Each directory contains a biographical section on blue paper which is roughly comparable to the second part of *Martindale-Hubbell*. Here again, the listings are for paid subscribers only. The yellow section of advertisers which follows many also provide useful information.

The first two parts of the directory (on yellow and white paper) are perhaps most useful for job seekers. Here you will find listed the staffs of various federal, state, and local government departments and agencies, the courts, and both U.S. and state legislators. If there is a judiciary section, it contains biographies of judges within the state.

To find a particular attorney in a state legal directory, you would first look up his or her name in the alphabetical list. The listing will tell you the city and county in which he or she practices and the telephone number.

For an address and the name of the firm, turn to the roster section. This section is organized in alphabetical order by counties, and within each county by cities. There you will find the attorney's name, abbreviated name of firm, complete address, and telephone number. For more information about the firm and its members, consult the blue biographical section.

Corporation Directories

If corporate law is your main interest, your most valuable tool may be the three-volume *Standard and Poor's Register of Corporations*. Volume One is an alphabetical list of corporations by name, showing their address and telephone numbers, officers, accountants, banks, and law firms used, revenue for the past year, number of employees, products, and other information. (See the front of each volume for directions.)

Check to see if the company has a corporate counsel in-house, or if it engages a particular outside firm for its legal affairs. Volume Two lists directors and executives of corporations, with biographical information and home addresses. Volume Three indexes the information in the first two volumes according to industrial classifications and geographical location, and also lists the names of individuals listed in Volume Two. In addition to *S & P*, you may find useful *Dun & Bradstreet*, the *Law & Business Directory of Corporate Counsel*, Volume 15 of *Martindale*, as well as the annual reports of various companies.

Government Directories

For similar information on federal government agencies, try the *U.S. Government Manual,* which will tell you the names of officials and agency staff members. *Now Hiring: Government Jobs for Lawyers,* published by the American Bar Association Law Student Division, is another valuable guide to federal jobs. The emphasis in this book is on information pertaining to jobs for lawyers. Thus you can find out how many male and female lawyers are employed by the agency, how many openings are anticipated this year, the locations of the positions, the entry level qualifications, the nature of the legal work in that department, and many other items of interest to job seekers.

Another fine source of information about employers in Washington, D.C. is the Congressional Quarterly's *Washington Information Directory.* The *Directory* claims over thousands information sources in government and private associations on the following topics: economy, energy, health, consumer protection, education, employment, housing, justice, transportation, minorities, communications, defense, science, international affairs, environment, and women.

Work the Directories

Work the directories you are using for every possible bit of information that may be useful. What kind of clients does the firm have? What is the principal business of the corporation? The amount of information that these directories convey is tremendous. Make use of the codes and symbols that are used to identify the organizations.

If a job with state government appeals to you, check the library reference department to see if a guide to state agencies has been published in your state or in the state in which you hope to live. Some guides of this nature contain information on the structure and functions of every state agency, but may not tell you anything about the staffs of the agencies. For names of individuals to contact, you will go back to the state legal directory (yellow section in front).

If none of the above resources covers the employers you are considering, ask for help in your placement office or the reference department of your school or public library.

Computer Databases

In addition to the Lexis, Westlaw, and Martindale-Hubbell databases described earlier, there are literally hundreds of specialized databases and directories available online through such commercial networks as ABA/Net, Prodigy, The Source, CompuServe, or on CD-ROM (compact disk-read only memory). CD-ROM systems are increasingly available in libraries and many private businesses.

Although it is difficult to predict specific developments, it is virtually certain that the 1990s will usher in even more information systems that will benefit law students astute enough to utilize them. Thus, it may be worthwhile to acquaint yourself with electronic communications if you are not knowledgeable now.

Summary

Preparing for fall interviews or the independent job search can be a laborious and time-consuming process, especially if you are not quite sure how to go about it. If you know where to go for information and how to interpret what you discover, you should be able to save time and trouble, and avoid scheduling interviews with legal employers in whom you are not really very interested.

13
Building a Network

The term networking is sometimes overused and often misunderstood. Some people think that networking merely means using contacts to find jobs. Others dismiss it as psychobable, a campy way to mystify something that is very simple.

Both these perceptions contain grains of truth, but miss the big picture. Certainly, networking means using personal contacts in the job search process. And the basic idea is quite simple: Everyone has a network. Some people are born with family connections, but all of us develop personal and professional ties along the way.

Not everyone understands how to utilize their contacts. There are steps involved in creating, maintaining, and utilizing a network. It should not be something that you do just when you need a job, but rather as an ongoing activity.

Creating Your Network

Everyone has contacts. While some folks may start out with more than others or do a better job of making contacts, anyone can build a network. Begin by making a list of all the people you know well enough to call on the phone and not have to explain who you are.

This list can include relatives, friends, college and law school acquaintances, lawyers, business associates, social and political contacts, and other people you have gotten to know along the path of life. They do not have to be people you see every day, nor do they have to be lawyers. It is a common mistake to assume that only lawyers have information about legal jobs.

Keep a record of as much information as possible on all these people: addresses, phone numbers, employers, birthdays, etc. You can use file cards or a spreadsheet as described in Chapter 14. The point is that you need to organize this information so that it is easy to retrieve when you need it.

The second step in building a network involves expanding it. As time passes, you will encounter more individuals who will become a part of your network. This process of accretion occurs naturally, but your biggest difficulty will be following up on initial contacts to establish them as part of the network. Social custom seems to dictate that a one time meeting is just that. It takes follow-up to create an ongoing relationship. If you are willing to take the initiative, you will be surprised how quickly your network grows.

Additionally, you should not wait for chance meetings. Go out and find people who can help you professionally, with whom you share some common intellectual, philosophical, or professional ground. Pursue contacts you have developed through informational interviewing. Go to CLE programs, bar association meetings, and community activities. Do volunteer work and become active in professional and social organizations.

Let people know who you are, what you are doing, and what your interests are. If you are looking for a job, you will find that more opportunities are developed from resumes mailed to your network than to unsolicited employer lists. When you are looking for a job, try to meet personally with as many people in your network as possible. Let them know your plans and expectations.

Maintaining Your Network

While you are always building your network, you must take time to maintain it. This means not only updating information about people (something that is easy to procrastinate until you forget the information), but also communicating with people on a regular basis.

Even if you are not looking for a job, keep in touch with your contacts so that they do not think you only call when you want something. In fact, you can develop your network by giving something to your contacts: information. Send them clippings, articles, and comments about issues that you know will interest them.

If you fine tune the network, you will discover that contacts with some individuals will be more regular than with others. You should try to communicate at least annually with everyone on your list.

You can use holiday greeting cards for this purpose, although most of us do not usually think of holiday information sharing as a time to massage our broader network. Some lawyers have extended the concept of the holiday letter to a permanent, regular, professional newsletter.

In order to do a good job of maintaining your network, you need to spend some time contacting your network virtually every day. You can use the phones, mail, computer bulletin boards, FAX, and personal meetings (e.g., lunches). This may seem to be a formidable task at first, especially given the crunch of day-to-day activities. If you get in the habit of taking a little bit of time each day when you answer mail and make phone calls to contact a couple of people from your network, the process will become second nature to you if you think about how people you know could use information that comes across your desk.

Utilizing Your Network

If you have built and maintained a good network, then utilizing it in the job search will be easy. It is important to articulate what you are looking for, so do not be afraid to tell people what you want.

If your current employer is not aware of your interest in leaving, you will obviously have to be more discreet and ask those you talk to to maintain confidence. There is a tradeoff here. The more people you talk to, the more your job hunting plans become common knowledge. In a small legal community, this does not take long! On the other hand, the more people who know about your plans, the more likely you are to come up with solid opportunities.

Visit as many people as you can in person, call others, and send everyone a resume. This does not have to be done all at once. If you assume that a job search will take six months and that you will work on it every day, you can gather a tremendous amount of information during the course of your search.

Do not be disappointed when some people let you down. Inevitably, some of your contacts will promise to get you an interview with Ms. X at XY & Z or to give you names of firms with openings, but fail to deliver. Do not hold it against them; this is just the nature of the process. It is just as likely that someone from whom you expected no help at all will come through for you. So, in the end, things balance out.

Do not forget to follow up. Keep records of your contacts with people and get back to them periodically as your job search continues. If they do not hear from you, they may assume that you have found something and that you are no longer in need of their help.

When you do land a job, let these contacts know so that they do not continue to work in your behalf when it is not necessary to do so. Everyone's time is valuable, so it will benefit you to respect the time of your network contacts.

As a final note, the heart of your network may well come from law school contacts: your graduating class, professors, and graduates who preceded you. You belong to a very small club. You can help each other. Talk to each other; support each other. The placement office, the dean's office, and the alumni office at your school are all committed to increasing the level of communication among graduates of the institution. You can further this aim simply by building, maintaining, and utilizing your own network.

Revise your list: Indicate people you can contact directly, and contact them. Try to track down as many of the missing links as possible. Chart 19 will help you to develop your list of contacts. Do you know where these people are? Do they know where you are? What legal skills would these contacts be most interested in knowing? What legal employers are these contacts likely to know?

Remember that networking is an activity that you must pursue tirelessly. You must make a point of keeping in touch with people, and not merely calling when you need something. On the other hand, you should expect to help out your contacts when they call, as they will when they know the lines of communication are open.

In this light, utilizing your network means considerably more than keeping a list of contacts for job search purposes. These are the people you may turn to throughout your professional career for advice on everything from a specific case to discussing more personal thoughts and concerns. College and law school afford you opportunities to build both close friendships and casual ones. Once you enter the working world, however, such opportunities diminish considerably.

Chart 19
Networking Checklist

A. Five friends from childhood through high school:

1. _____
2. _____
3. _____
4. _____
5. _____

B. Five friends from college through law school:

1. _____
2. _____
3. _____
4. _____
5. _____

C. Five teachers or professors:

1. _____
2. _____
3. _____
4. _____
5. _____

D. Five work supervisors or business associates:

1. _____
2. _____
3. _____
4. _____
5. _____

E. Five lawyers or professional contacts:

1. _____
2. _____
3. _____
4. _____
5. _____

14
Selling Yourself

The statement, "You are unique," may not strike you as particularly profound. Of course you are unique; you have been told so since childhood. Your many accomplishments set you apart from the crowd.

Unfortunately, many law students lose their confidence in their own uniqueness as soon as they begin to look for a job. They act like they are fungible. They talk like they have no special skills. Part of the reason lies in the law school experience itself while another part relates to the job search process. These two elements can combine to undermine your ability to sell yourself to employers.

Law school is a little bit like marine boot camp. The course of study strips away your old identity and replaces it with a new one as a lawyer. For better or worse, you will never be a "nonlawyer" again. During your first year, you learn that you are almost never right. By your senior year, you discover that despite years of studying legal theory and black letter law, you know little about practicing law. Unlike previous school experiences, you can put everything you have into a course and still not get the highest grade.

The job search process is tough on the ego, also. Whether or not this is your first experience looking for a real job, it doesn't take long to discover the debilitating effects of job hunting. You may find it extremely difficult to feel unique in the face of this adversity. Many law students have encountered little adversity in their careers, so the job search can bring a rude awakening.

What can you do to maintain a strong sense of individuality? First, the better you understand your own skills, interests, and values, the easier it will be to articulate to employers that you are not just another grain of sand on the beach. Focus on your skills in relation to the job you seek rather than to the skills of your class-mates.

Second, keep in mind that this is not a new battle. Throughout your life you have confronted pressure to be ordinary, and the fact that you are where you are suggests that you have resisted. Resist again.

Third, always identify a nexus between what you have to offer and what you believe an employer wants. Finally, keep in mind that you only have to score once in this game to win. The wildcatter only has to strike one gusher to make up for all the dry wells, and you only need one job despite the fact you may apply for many more. Maintain that "wildcatter" mentality.

In order to market yourself, you must know the product you are selling. You need to know its strengths as well as weaknesses, its appeal to potential consumers, and its value in the marketplace. Whether you perceive this product to be one of a kind or one of 35,000 identical items produced in the current model year can have a significant impact on your ability to sell the product in the marketplace.

Identifying Your Target

Just as you are unique, each employer is unique. Sometimes that truth is lost in the mass of employer lists and placement information. Your goal as an applicant is to identify an employer who needs someone like you.

This does not mean that you cannot apply for more than one position at a time. It does mean that you should learn enough about each employer to whom you apply to be able to articulate why that employer needs to hire *you*. This becomes almost impossible to do with a mass mailing campaign.

Your school's fall on-campus interview program represents the largest single group of employers you can hope to manage at one time. The more carefully you dissect employer information the more readily you will be able to make informed choices about interview selection. This pre-selection or self-screening process on your part, whether you are interviewing on campus or going out on your own, will enhance your chances of being selected for an interview, being hired, and being happy after you go to work.

Earlier chapters of this book dealt with techniques for researching employers. If you have followed the advice there, you should have a significant compendium about employers at your disposal. As you narrow your leads from classes of employers to specific organizations, you should seek increasingly detailed information about potential employers prior to the interview.

Some of the information will be in written form, prepared by the employer or compiled by some other source. Much can be learned by talking with your network sources beforehand. A great deal of information can be obtained orally and then confirmed or amplified during the interview process. You will be eliciting oral information from the interviewer. When you can anticipate the interviewer's answers about the organization, your level of sophistication will be perceived as interest in the job, while lack of knowledge is often perceived as disinterest by interviewers.

Talk to professors, students who have clerked for the employer, judges, other lawyers, and even clients before the interview. Not all of these people will be helpful, but some will, and they will give you the information you need. When you talk to contacts, know exactly what you want to find out and get right to the point. Try not to telegraph the answers you want to hear when you ask questions (e.g., "Isn't X, Y and Z a good firm?"). Unless it is obvious or necessary, do not specify that you will be applying for a job with the organization. Just say that you are curious or conducting research.

At this point, legal employers may be horrified at the prospect of thousands of law students calling everyone under the sun for background checks on them, but in reality few law students will take this advice. They will not have the time, consider it too intrusive, or simply believe that the return will not justify their efforts. Those of you who do dig beneath the surface will gain a decided advantage in the job search. You will be better prepared for interviews and can also use your research to eliminate many prospective employers or at least lower them on your priority list.

You do not need reams of information on each prospective employer, however. If you can articulate in a paragraph or less what makes this employer unique, you will generally have all the information you need to know. The best way to gather answers to your questions about an employer is through an information interview. This can be a formal appointment, a chance meeting, or a phone conversation during the pre-employment process to gather information.

In his book *What Color is Your Parachute,* Richard Bolles talks about information interviewing at an early stage in the career planning process. He suggests that you go to the person in the organization who ultimately will have the power to hire you for the purpose of gathering information even before you apply. Then, when you come back to apply for a job, you will already have the information you need to sell yourself and know your interviewer.

Even if you do not conduct, as Bolles suggests, a surreptitious pre-interview, many information interviews can lead to real interviews and jobs. Whether you are going directly to the organization or meeting with someone else, keep in mind the rules for any interview. Look good. Be prompt. Establish rapport. Question effectively. Listen actively.

Keep in mind what you want to learn and pursue that information assertively. If the interviewee does not have or know the information you require, ask for additional leads. Leave a business card or resumeä, since sometimes people will have an idea after the interview and want to contact you.

Take notes during the interview, or as soon as you leave, because this information will fade quickly. Send a follow-up note or thank you letter if appropriate.

Finally, many of the individuals you meet can become part of your own network of contacts. By logging them into your database, you can build upon these contacts for future reference far beyond the employment process.

Contacting Your Target

Once you have written your resume and researched potential employers, you are ready to contact your target. You may be sending it to employers you interview through your placement office or in response to specific job notices posted at the placement office or in legal publications. You may also want to use your resume to solicit interviews with employers whose type of practice interests you and who are located in an area in which you would like to live.

In many cases, a cover letter is a necessity. If your letter specifically targets the organization's needs, it can greatly enhance your chances of being hired.

Mass mailings to law firms, on the other hand, can be a costly and time-consuming task with little result. As direct mail advertisers know, a response rate of one for every 100 letters is unusually good. The approach you take and the language with which you state your interest can determine whether your letter comes to rest on the hiring partner's desk or in the trash can. You must use the letter to convey your interest in the type of practice a firm, corporation, or agency engages in, and your desire to become part of such a practice.

Your letter should describe how your skills and interest complement the firm's goals. It should reflect a little of your personality while getting its message across clearly and succinctly. Neatness, punctuation, and spelling are important. An error can eliminate your chances to be hired, especially if your letter is the only impression an employer has of you.

Several approaches can keep communications open. You may ask for an interview; you may even suggest a time. You might tell the employer that you plan to visit the office "unless it is inconvenient." It all depends on how assertive you want to be.

Do not neglect, however, to say something about a future meeting as you are unlikely to get a job on the strength of your resume alone. Highlight one particularly strong point from your resume in your letter, but do not restate the resume in prose. In one sense, your cover letter should persuade the interviewer to turn the page to read your resume. Together, the cover letter and resume should pique the reader's interest enough to get you in the door.

A follow-up letter or phone call may be useful to assure that you are not forgotten. You walk a thin line between assertiveness and pushiness, so use your discretion.

On the following page are a general purpose letter of application and other letters likely to be useful in the job search. Remember, these are merely suggestions.

You must write letters in your own words if you want them to truly represent you and your interests. Word processing allows you to personalize letters quickly and easily, although most students simply use a word processing program to merge addresses with a boilerplate body. The problem with computer-generated letters is that they look and sound impersonal. Not surprisingly, many law firms react to such applications the way you do to junk mail. The more personalized your letter sounds, the better the odds.

If you have maintained a card file or database of potential employers, you are now ready to begin your letter-writing cam-

Sample Letter of Application

```
                                        Your address
                                        City and state
                                        Date of writing

(Inside address)

Dear _____:

First paragraph: Tell why you are writing, name the position for
which you are applying and tell how you heard of the opening.

Second paragraph: State why you are interested in working for this
employer, and specify your interests in this type of work.  If you have
had experience, be sure to point out what particular achievements you
have accomplished in this field or type of work.

Third paragraph: Refer to the attached personal data sheet or resume
which gives a summary of your qualifications as well as a photograph,
or to whatever media you are using to illustrate your training,
interests, and experience.

Fourth paragraph: Have an appropriate closing to pave the way for the
interview by enclosing a return envelope, by asking for an application
blank, by giving your phone number, or by offering some similar
suggestion for an immediate and favorable reply.

                                        Yours very truly,
```

Sample Letter of Application
When On-Campus Interviews Are Oversubscribed

```
                                        Your name (typewritten)

Enclosure

Dear Mr. or Ms. _____:

    I had hoped to meet you in _____.  I understand, however,
that your time is limited and you will not be able to see everyone.  I am
planning to be in your vicinity Thanksgiving weekend and hope very much
to see you then.  If possible, I will telephone you in advance to arrange
for an appointment.  My resume is enclosed.

    I am looking forward with pleasure to meeting you.

                                        Sincerely,
```

paign. If not, you will have to do some research (See page 115.) The length of each letter is not nearly as important as its content, but as a rule, keep the letter short and direct.

The first paragraph of your letter should indicate why you are contacting a particular firm or organization. Your primary reason will usually be the nature of its work as evidenced by its clients, professional affiliations, and the like. But perhaps a speech or a position taken by a member of the firm struck a responsive chord in your own view of the profession and its goals. Or you may have been referred by someone to the organization or established your own contacts in the firm. Regardless of what your reasons are, be sure the first paragraph of your letter describes them.

This first paragraph is important because you are asking a busy lawyer to take the time to review your application. It should indicate that you have taken the trouble to become acquainted with the firm and that you know enough about the organization to believe it might be interested in you. The fact that you have done this kind of research indicates that you are serious about seeking a position, and is also subtly flattering to the organization.

If you send your resume to an alumnus(a) of your own school, you should still indicate why you chose that particular firm or organization, and ask that your letter be passed along to the individual responsible for hiring decisions.

The second paragraph of the letter should expand on your reason for contacting the firm by pointing out some part of your background or experience that you feel might be relevant to the firm's needs. Generally, you will refer to your resume at this point in the letter (e.g., "As my enclosed resume indicates....")

There may be other background information not shown on your resume that would be important to employers. For example, if you contact a firm with a large number of Spanish-speaking clients, you could mention that you have studied Spanish for eight years or speak Spanish at home.

The third paragraph should indicate how to contact you and arrange for an interview. Be as specific as possible. If you will be in the law firm's community during a certain period of time, state when, and, if possible, give a local address and telephone number to reach you during that period. Repeat addresses and telephone numbers from your resume to encourage action.

Employers understand that you cannot sit by the phone 24 hours a day. The following statements are entirely appropriate:

- "I will be in class most of the time, but I have arranged for an answering service to accept appointments for me."
- "I will call your office to confirm the time you find most convenient."
- "The person answering the phone has a complete scheduleof my time commitments and will be glad to arrange aconvenient time for you to meet with me."

If you have been farsighted enough to arrange an interview schedule to meet the employer's convenience, that thoughtfulness will not go unnoticed.

The appearance of your cover letter is just as important as the content. With desktop publishing software, you can create your own letterhead at a fraction of the cost of printing. Keep the appearance neat and conservative, using quality stationery in white or cream. Proofread everything. A single typographical error can be the kiss of death for your application.

As you send out your letters and resumes, note the dates on file cards (see sample on page 141) or on a computer database. As replies are received, note the dates and the nature of the responses as well. If you do not hear from an employer within a reasonable time, use follow-up letter or phone call. If you are not sure what is reasonable, consult your placement director or some other knowledgeable person. If your application will be under consideration for several months or longer, periodic communications from you may help keep your application fresh, but try not to become a pest.

Keep working on your file cards, increasing the number of cards and the amount of information on them. In addition to providing further contacts for your letter-writing campaign, the cards will be essential at the next step—the interview.

Interviewing Your Target

Is there a magic formula that guarantees a successful job interview? An elixir to cure knocking knees, sweaty palms, and a blank mind? Unfortunately, no. Interviews involve a complex interaction between the people involved, reflecting the various values, needs, and personality traits of each. By arming yourself with knowledge

Sample of File Card

Front:

```
┌─────────────────────────────────────────────────┐
│                                                   │
│                                                   │
│   Organization: _____  │
│                                                   │
│   Contact: _____   │
│                                                   │
│   Address: _____   │
│                                                   │
│   City, State, Zip: _____   │
│                                                   │
│   Phone No.: _____   │
│                                                   │
│   Practice: _____   │
│                                                   │
│                                                   │
└─────────────────────────────────────────────────┘
```

Back:

```
┌─────────────────────────────────────────────────┐
│                                                   │
│   Letter:                 Response:               │
│                                                   │
│   Interview:                                      │
│                                                   │
│   Thank You:              Response:               │
│                                                   │
│   Follow-Up Interview:                            │
│                                                   │
│   Offer:                                          │
│                                                   │
│   Comments: _____   │
│                                                   │
│   _____   │
│                                                   │
└─────────────────────────────────────────────────┘
```

of the employer's needs and preferences, as well as your own strengths and weaknesses, you will have a better idea how to conduct the interview and what questions to ask.

A successful interview is not necessarily one that results in a job offer. It is, instead, one that allows both the employer and the potential employee to discover what the other wants, what goals are important, what working conditions are most desirable—in short, to gain an honest impression of whether or not a working situation would be mutually satisfactory.

This is not easy to discover in the limited time available in the interview situation, and to avoid any misconceptions, both parties should be entirely honest. An important rule is to be yourself. Otherwise, you might find yourself in an uncomfortable employment situation.

The primary goal of any interviewee should be to become more aware of the dynamics of the interview situation, and thereby to to control it. An interview can be any face-to-face meeting between an employer and potential employee to discuss the employment possibilities of the former with the latter. The dynamics of the interview are the interactions, both verbal and non-verbal, between the interview participants. They will constitute each party's basis for evaluating the interview.

In order to control the interview, you must recognize which aspects of your background to emphasize and establish specific objectives to accomplish during the interview. Because of time limitations inherent in the interview situation, it is important to select and control the information you give the interviewer.

The primary area under your direct control is the attitude with which you approach the interview—your mindset. Imagine yourself as an investor approaching a prospective banker. You have funds to invest, and the banker has services to offer. In such a setting, the banker will naturally have questions regarding the amount you wish to deposit, the percentage of return that you expect, and the length of time the bank would have use of your funds.

You, in turn, would want to know the advantages and disadvantages of the various forms of investment the bank has to offer, the degree of safety of your funds, and the types of services you would receive. What should result is a businesslike exchange of information aimed at reaching a mutually satisfactory arrangement. If that could not be achieved, you would then proceed to consult with other bankers along the same line. The typical interview lasts 20–30 minutes and consists of a greeting, a discussion, and a closing. There are generally one to three interviewers. But remember: an interview may not be a formal one in the office or at school; it may occur during a chance meeting at some other place.

One thing that should be avoided at all costs is tardiness. You should be on time or a few minutes early whether the interview is at the law school or at the employer's place of business.

A conservative, neat appearance is generally advisable. In both dress and demeanor you can come on too strong just as easily as not strong enough. It might be necessary to purchase a new interviewing wardrobe to project a professional image. The expense may be considerable, but you should think of it as an investment.

Once your attire has been selected, you can then concentrate on the most important aspect of preparing for an interview—knowing the employer. Review your file card or database on the particular prospective employer.

You may also want to see other sources of information, like a corporation's annual report. Your placement office may have a complete description of a law firm on file for you to consult. A government agency may publish a brochure that describes in detail the work of the agency including the work of its legal department. Too much information is better than not enough.

As you review the information you have collected, formulate the questions you would like to ask regarding the organization and its opportunities for you. Jot them down. Include the names of people to whom you may be speaking. Oral introductions can be hard to recall, but once you see a name in writing, remembering it is much easier.

While the interviewer is sizing you up during the greeting phase of the interview, you should be aware of your reaction to the interviewer as well. Researchers have found that people develop strong and often lasting impressions about the appearance, attitudes, values, and abilities of other people within the first few minutes after meeting them. If you feel an initial dislike or uneasiness about someone, move more slowly into the interview and attempt to ascertain why you feel that way with direct or indirect questions. If a first impression is favorable, adopt a more informal stance, or approach the interview itself more aggressively.

While good eye contact, a firm handshake, a memory for names, and a big smile are helpful, too many people get so wrapped up in carrying out these functional activities that they lose all spontaneity, as well as the ability to think quickly. They may come across as shallow and rigid. It is more important to be relaxed and natural at the start of the interview than to perform some kind of ritual.

The types of questions asked in an interview situation often address what kind of law practice interests you, what substantive knowledge you possess, and other goal-related questions. Not only will the employer want to gain an accurate impression of your goals at this point, but you will have an excellent opportunity to discover whether the employer is doing the kind of work you would find challenging and enjoyable.

Honesty is vital at this stage of the interview, or you are likely to create an image of yourself which you would not be comfortable living with should you eventually go to work for the employer. For example, if you indicate that you are interested in doing research, this is probably what you will be doing if you are offered a job.

The potential employer may evidence some interest in your past employment experience, academic qualifications, and interests. You are, for the most part, in control of the direction the questioning takes at this point, since you have drafted your resume, and it reflects those points you want to discuss. It is important, both in the resume and in the interview itself, always to stress those facts about yourself that you consider outstanding — those that in some way separate you from the other interviewees. If you are honest and straightforward, you are much more likely to discover an employment situation in which you have the freedom to be yourself and do the things that you enjoy.

Interviewing Styles

An interviewee who is alert enough to ascertain the interviewer's approach to the process can "key" on the interviewer in phrasing answers to questions. Differences in personality account for some differences in interviewing style. Although the following synopsis is an oversimplification, it may be useful to think about interviewers in terms of a number of distinct interviewer types.

The Collector—Some interviewers may be interested only in collecting information such as where you went to school, activities, and areas of principal interest.

The Shrink—Others might take a more psychological approach, questioning you about areas such as attitude toward school, goals, and aspirations, conceptions of various issues, and so forth.

The Conversationalist—Some seem more interested in merely talking or in gaining an overall impression of you through less direct questions. With this type of interviewer, it is often important to keep the discussion from straying too far from information about the job itself or your particular qualifications.

The Professor—Still other interviewers ask rapid fire questions about legal issues. It is important to avoid yes or no answers, and do not be intimidated. Remember that this is no worse than law school.

There are a few somewhat atypical interviewers who deserve mentioning also:

The Dud—In a bad interview, the student and employer are just unable to communicate. The Dud, also known as the Ego Deflator, prematurely rejects you without asking any questions or telling you anything.

The "Ego Deflator"
A Premature Rejection

The Interrogator—This interviewer will press you quite hard on difficult questions, sometimes of a personal nature, or does something to test your reactions; (e.g., drawing an "X" through your resume before you sit down.) This technique, known as the stress interview, is common in the business school setting. If something like this happens to you, do not lose your cool or you lose all control of the situation.

The Violator—This interviewer shows definite signs of unethical or discriminatory conduct. Do not hesitate to terminate the interview and take appropriate action. For more information on how to handle discriminatory interview tactics, see the NALP guidelines in the Appendix and consult with your placement officer.

Normally an interview is concluded by the interviewer, but take the initiative if the interview appears to be running overtime. It is possible that the interviewer is hoping that you will stop talking, but is reluctant to cut you off. A timely exit can be as important as any part of the interview. Do not leave without determining how, when, and where you can expect further communications concerning your potential employment.

Once you have left the interview, immediately make notes for your file cards or database, including the names of the individuals who interviewed you and the date. That will prevent the embarrassment of forgetting someone's name should you meet again, professionally or personally.

As soon as possible after your interview, write an acknowledgment letter. Such a letter is not only a thank you for the time and courtesy of the individuals with whom you have spoken, but, more importantly it is also an opportunity to repeat your special qualifications and to note any areas in which there appeared to be a true meeting of minds. If there were any decisions reached regarding future contact, restate these as well.

The acknowledgment letter is also a way to notify the office that you have a continuing interest in the position. Unfortunately, this courtesy is not extended frequently enough. The exception to this rule involves fall on-campus interviews, where employers interview hundreds of candidates in a short period of time. In that situation, acknowledgment letters may be viewed as superfluous, so use your discretion.

Employers consistently mention two common negative factors among law students they interview. These are the students' apparent lack of interest in the job and their apprehensiveness about the interview. The former problem can usually be avoided by scheduling to see only employers in whom you are genuinely interested. Demonstrate your interest by being well-informed.

The second problem may be more difficult. It is perhaps little consolation to say that everyone has butterflies before an interview. Dress comfortably, sit down somewhere if you have to wait, and relax your mind. Talking to someone else may also be helpful in easing the tension. Take two or three deep breaths just before going into the interview room to lower your blood pressure and calm your nerves.

The Office Visit

The office visit is always important, whether it is a follow-up to an on-campus interview or a first meeting. Because the office visit is usually longer than a screening interview, you often get an opportunity to see a law office in action. It is often much more difficult, however, to keep up a front for both you and the interviewer(s), so make a conscious effort to stay calm. Before you leave, try to get some commitment regarding your possibilities for employment and if it is clear that you will not receive a letter, seek new leads from those you interviewed. It is possible that they were impressed with you but just can't make you an offer.

If you manage to get one or more invitations for office visits, here are a few things to keep in mind:

• Be observant. What is the general tone of the office? What are the individual personalities? What do the relationships between individuals appear to be? If you are sensitive only to the impression you are seeking to make, you miss valuable opportunities to assess the office in ways that no amount of research can provide.

• Get your facts straight. When and for how long do they want to see you? How do they handle reimbursement of expenses? Are spouses or "significant others" invited? Who arranges travel and hotel rooms? Many students find themselves in a bind because they do not ask about these things and the firm does not say anything either. Generally speaking, big firms reimburse; small firms do not. If you are visiting more than one employer in an area, you should suggest that they split expenses (and *never* ask for multiple reimbursement). Also, if an employer invites you to visit an out-of-town office, it is customary that your expenses are paid. If you suggest the meeting, this is not the case.

- Get directions and a good map. Do not get lost and miss an hour of your interview. If you plan to interview with more than one employer, plan your movement from one to the next to avoid being late.
- If you have gotten this far you have probably already done your homework, but do more. Reread the firm or agency resume. Find out if there are other students being invited for office visits, and what the firm's hiring patterns have been in the past. Check carefully the composition of the firm for age, schools attended, etc. Look to *Martindale-Hubbell* to find out such things as the composition of the firm, the ages of the partners and associates, the law schools that they have attended, where they are originally from, and the type of clients they handle. Ask other students or professors who may know the firm to share their thoughts with you.
- Read the local newspapers and regional magazines to get an idea of what the community is like and what current issues concern its citizens. Married students will need to assess whether the area will appeal to their family. If your spouse accompanies you, he or she may need to spend the time looking for a job, checking out the housing market, or visiting schools.
- If you interview an employer from out-of-state, do some additional background research. Read the pertinent digests in the last three volumes of *Martindale-Hubbell*. This will help you to discuss local legal issues with the interviewer.
- You may also get some substantive legal questions, so be prepared. Since you are more likely to get questions about an area you know than something totally off-the-wall, re-read your law review note or other research mentioned in the resume.
- Office visits vary considerably from employer to employer. Not all office visits last a full day, but almost all are grueling. A recruitment administrator may take you from attorney to attorney; you may be led to the next interview by your last interviewer; or you may be sent from office to office on your own. You can expect to see as few as three lawyers in a half-day interview, or as many as fifteen in a full day, individually or in groups. At some point during the day, frequently at the beginning or end, you will be given a tour of the facilities. Be observant and ask questions during this guided tour.
- Ask about office operations, such as time-keeping and billing systems, secretarial and paralegal assistance ratios, structure of the office and assignment of new attorneys, word processing and other office equipment systems, library size and check out system, filing

system, and office space allocation and configuration. Do not be timid about asking challenging questions.

• Do not write off the younger lawyers you visit: many employers rely heavily on them for input into hiring decisions.

• Each appointment should be considered a separate interview so give each one your best. Your campus interview was just the first hurdle. You must pass muster in each of these subsequent interviews to get an offer. Ask similar questions of everyone you meet in order to better get a "flavor" for the firm. Study individual personalities when meeting with attorneys on a one-to-one basis. It may be helpful to ask interviewers what they do each day.

• Entertainment, very often with associates or younger lawyers, is intended to put you at ease, so enjoy yourself—just do not spill the vichyssoise in your lap. Evening entertainment is less frequent and ranges from stuffy to sporty. It is more likely to include partners or senior attorneys and spouses.

• No matter how many people you see, treat each interview as if it is your first and most important one. During on-campus interviews, the recruiter may be tired while the candidate is fresh. This dynamic is reversed in the office interview, so make sure that you remain alert. For example, do not stay out late the night before your interview. And during the office interview, ask for time to freshen up, if it is not offered.

• Remember the same principles of effective interviewing that got you to the office visit: be yourself, emphasize what you can offer, and control the situation. Add to this a little stamina, and you are on your way.

Another area of particular interest to students is how a firm goes about making a hiring decision. Again, this often depends upon the size of the firm. In a large firm, a committee may be responsible for hiring decisions, even though other attorneys have input into the process. In a smaller firm everyone is involved. You generally must receive a unanimous confirmation. As a result, there may be two or three office visits to find out early whether or not everyone feels they can work with you. Large firms are more likely to screen out candidates at an earlier stage of the process than small firms where hiring decisions involve all or most of the lawyers. Large firms also tend to play a numbers game with offers. Small firms on the other hand often make only one offer at a time. These differences are reflected in different approaches to the interview process generally.

Tough Questions

Certain lines of questioning may prove very uncomfortable for many candidates. Two critical topics, salary and benefits, must be addressed at some point. If the interviewer brings up the topic it may indicate that the firm plans on tendering you an offer, since, as a general rule, they will not discuss salary with those students who do not interest them. You should not raise the issue during the initial interview. Wait until you are sure the employer is interested in you.

Although many interviewers will have little power to negotiate, they should be able to give some indication of whether or not your expectations are reasonable. Be sure you know both the range of starting salaries in your geographical area and the salary range for the type of job you are seeking. Your placement office should have current statistics.

You should consider a number of other factors in reviewing a salary offer: What kind of insurance program (life, disability, health) does the employer offer? Is there a starting bonus or an annual bonus? Pension or retirement plan? Vacation? Leave (illness, parental, sabbatical)? What are the possibilities for advancement on becoming a partner? Does the employer provide a profit sharing or other incentive program for the newer lawyer? What about "perks" such as club memberships, travel expenses, professional dues and journals, continuing legal education, and parking? Will you have staff support including paralegals and secretaries? What is the cost of living in the community? Will there be employment for a working spouse? When considered together, these many factors may give a very different picture of the compensation than the original salary quoted.

In some instances, salary is not negotiable. For example, in government positions where the salary level is beyond the employer's immediate jurisdiction. Otherwise, you may have a minimum figure in mind that you believe is necessary to cover your expenses and financial obligations. If you have obtained information regarding ranges, you will know whether the offer falls in the acceptable pattern. Negotiation in such cases is acceptable. See Chapter 15 for more information on negotiating your job offer.

Here is where the problem may arise: If you give the interviewer an outrageous requirement, she is likely to think that you are unrealistic, or simply pricing yourself out of the market. On the other hand, if you quote an unusually low figure, she may perceive you as underselling yourself and your abilities, and she may take that as a sign of little or no self-confidence. (Of course, she may also hire you on the spot because you are so cheap.)

The key to surviving this minefield successfully is to identify the employer's salary range, which is probably competitive within the geographic area and type of position for which you are interviewing. Large firms will offer the higher salaries and small firms will offer figures in the lower part of the competitive spectrum. Salaries for 1990 law school graduates fell between $15,000 to over $85,000 according to the National Association for Law Placement, so employers' offers may be anywhere in this range.

In recent years fringe benefits have become a major concern of law graduates, but often their importance is overrated. Most benefits are tied to long-range employment prospects, but today, increasing numbers of lawyers are moving laterally from position to position. The traditional pattern in which an entry position becomes a lifetime professional commitment is no longer necessarily the case.

Early in the game, therefore, your best evaluation of the fringe benefits probably will contemplate their immediate value to you. By the time their long-range value becomes important, you may have moved several times. One time that benefit packages may be a factor is when you are evaluating similar offers. The opportunity for professional growth should be your primary concern, but if that criterion appears to be equally met, consideration of fringe benefits in your comparative analysis may be helpful.

In addition to finding out about salary and benefits, ask how the firm is organized and whether cases are handled by teams, whether associates work with one partner only, how specialized the firm is, and how new clients are obtained.

There are certain areas where open discussion may not only be unnecessary, but may harm your chances of being hired. For example, many students are very interested in knowing the turnover a firm has, or how many people come and go within a year. Rather than inquire directly and antagonize the interviewer, check *Martindale-Hubbell* and the law school placement office figures back on campus.

When you interview with a bank, public accounting firm, or other organization, you might be asked about the possibility of your leaving to enter private practice. It is not uncommon for the

Chart 20
Five Least Desired Questions

Question	Proposed Answer
1.	
2.	
3.	
4.	
5.	

interviewer to raise such a question, and more often than not, she will be quite sensitive about this subject. The key to avoiding problems in this area is to appear enthusiastic about the work without really making a lifelong commitment.

Another rather sticky question involves the amount of time you will be expected to work. A direct line of interrogation about working hours is likely to create an impression of laziness and lack of ambition in the interviewer's mind. Instead, find out the answer indirectly by calling the office after hours or on Saturday. As a general rule everyone works hard and a 60- or 70-hour week is not unusual.

Another risky question is the potential for future earnings. While it is perfectly natural to wonder about your future, the question seems to disturb quite a few interviewers. It may be better to glean the answer to this question from several sources. Ask other young attorneys in the firm or check *Martindale-Hubbell* for a high turnover rate which may indicate low growth potential.

You could also ask other related questions in the hope that the interviewer may mention growth potential as one of the firm's benefits. Try to get the interviewer to make a comparison among firms or between the firm and a corporation's legal department. Never ask something like, "How much will I be making in 10 years?" or "How much do you make?" You not only come off sounding mercenary; you will antagonize the interviewer.

Similarly, avoid asking questions about the length of time until you reach partnership or how many associates make partner. Consult *Martindale-Hubbell* or use other indirect channels instead. Forget about asking questions about salary differences between new and senior partners. Ultimately, the answer is that, as a partner, you are getting a "piece of the pie," and your income is much more tied to your output.

There are, however, different ways of making partner. In some firms you spend the entire time you are an associate saving up to buy in or to purchase a share of the firm. In others, that is not a major consideration. It varies from firm to firm.

If you can get someone to talk about the organization, you can figure these things out very easily. Questions dealing with money or partnership should be raised with the person you believe to be the one with the most power in the hiring process—a managing partner, senior partner, or the chair of the hiring committee.

The last area in the line of delicate questions is the skeleton in your closet. It might be your grades. It might be where you went to school. It might be something in your background. Everybody has some questions they would like to avoid, but it is best to be prepared for the worst. Here are some specific pieces of advice: first, do not apologize; second, do not be evasive, and, third, prepare a response. Instead of praying that you will not be asked, make a list of the five questions you would least like to be asked in an interview and develop answers before the interview (See Chart 20).

In conclusion, do not hesitate to ask questions. Observe everything going on around you in the office. In this respect, the office interview is much easier than the on-campus session because new topics for discussion and conversation are constantly being raised. Prepare beforehand by researching the firm or organization and record your impressions and new information learned as soon as you leave.

15
Making a Decision

How will you receive an offer? Will the offer be made through a phone call or letter? How much time will you be given to make a decision? It is an old maxim that offers are communicated by telephone and rejections by mail.

After completing the interview process, firms may not give you any direct indication of your status. While you may have some idea of how well you did, you may possess little or no indication of whether or not an offer is forthcoming. The official notification will be received several weeks later. Occasionally, offers are made during the interview process, but more commonly, you will have to wait.

Receiving an Offer

If you do receive an offer and are not prepared at that time to make a decision, it is vitally important to show a continuing interest in the employer. Explain that presently you are interested but are talking to other employers and you feel it would be unfair to accept this offer without reviewing all your options. You might stress also the importance of the decision by saying that you simply need time to think. Emphasize that you enjoyed your interviews and that you were very impressed with what you saw of the firm.

There is no need to succumb to pressure. Certainly the firm will want to know as soon as possible whether or not you plan to accept, but usually it will allow you a reasonable amount of time to make a decision. Firms interviewing on campus during the fall generally follow NALP guidelines requiring offers to be held open until December 15 (See Appendix.) Check your own placement office for details.

Sample Letter Responding To an Offer,
But Delaying Final Decision Whether or Not to Accept It

```
Dear Mr. or Ms. _____:

    I appreciate your interest in me for the position we discussed
in our earlier meeting.  I am still very interested in the possibility
that we can reach some mutually satisfactory agreement.  However, in
view of the fact that I am considering other possibilities at this time,
I am not prepared to make a final commitment.  Understanding that you must
make some decisions, too, I will endeavor to make a final decision by
_____, and will communicate that decision to you.

                              Sincerely,
```

Sample Letter Searching Out Job Possibilities

```
Dear Mr. or Ms. _____:

    I am writing to you with the thought that your office may be in need
of an associate within the next six months or so, and that I might interest
you.  My resume is enclosed.
    I expect to be in your vicinity during the week beginning _____,
and I hope very much to meet you then.  If possible, I will telephone you
in advance to arrange for an appointment.

                              Sincerely,
```

Sample Thank You Acknowledgement

```
Dear Mr. or Ms. _____:

    This is just a note to thank you for spending so much time with
me the other day.  I enjoyed talking with you and meeting your partners.
    Your office interests me a great deal, and I shall keep in touch
with you.

                              Sincerely,
```

Some employers attempt to exert pressure on applicants to make a quick decision. Smaller firms, for example, may feel that they cannot play a numbers game, making ten offers for five spots on the assumption that they will have only five acceptances. They may make only one offer and will want to know if that candidate is going to turn them down right away.

While the employer wants you to decide as soon as possible, you will want to keep your options open as long as possible. This is a matter for negotiation along with other issues such as salary, benefits, starting dates, etc. But remember that once you know an employer wants you, you are playing a much stronger hand than when the process started.

Negotiating a Job Offer

Many law students fail to think of themselves as negotiators when they get a job offer. They simply take the money and run. While negotiating varies according to issue and employer, many of the terms of employment are subject to negotiation.

Generally employers that participate in fall on-campus interviews and other employers with highly structured personnel policies are more likely to have predetermined what they are willing to offer you. They are less likely to be willing to negotiate major terms like salary and benefits, but may be more flexible on issues such as practice area assignment or starting date. Smaller firms and other employers that do not hire associates on a regular basis are less likely to have a clear idea of what they will agree to give. These employers are more likely to negotiate a wider range of issues.

Many students have taken law school courses on negotiation and should recognize that the principles of negotiation are the same in a job offer situation. A few suggestions may help you negotiate the best possible terms for yourself:

• Figure out what you want out of the negotiation. What would you like to get ideally? What would you be willing to accept as a fallback position? Which issues are critical (non-negotiable) and which are you willing to concede in order to reach an accord?

• Figure out what the employer wants out of the negotiation. What is the maximum you can expect? Which issues are critical to the employer?

• Construct an agenda for the negotiation. When you sit down

Chart 21
Negotiating an Offer – The Bargaining Range

Even though salary expectations differ, both employer and prospective employee are able to negotiate when their bargaining ranges overlap, as in the first example below. In the second one, expectations are so widely apart that there is no common ground on which to negotiate.

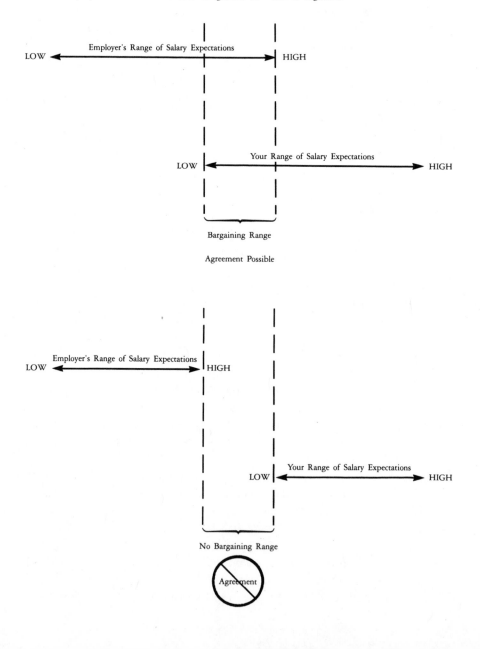

to talk about terms have a plan for attaining your objectives. Employers hiring to fill a single position are more likely to negotiate terms than employers hiring two or more since it may be awkward (or illegal) to start different lawyers with comparable qualifications at different rates.

• Keep in mind your bottom line. Both you and the employer have a bargaining range (See Chart 21). Do not expect the employer to go outside its bargaining range to accommodate you.

Try to make this a win-win situation. Both you and the employer should walk away happy. Some of the specific areas that you may be able to negotiate include:

• Starting salary.

• Benefits. Health insurance may be fixed, but professional benefits (e.g., bar dues, CLE allowances, club memberships) may be subject to negotiation.

• Incentives/bonuses. While signing bonuses are uncommon except for genuine superstars, many smaller firms are willing to give associates an incentive to produce work or bring in clients (e.g., a percentage of the fees from all new clients brought to the firm by the associate).

• Practice areas. This is the most commonly negotiated term of employment.

• Working conditions. Support, office space, expectations.

• Special arrangements. Child care, part-time status, tuition for LLM program.

• Time off. Vacations, National Guard, maternity leave.

Your own marketability can also be a factor. Does the employer want you because of your Ph.D. in genetic engineering? Are there other comparably qualified candidates in the wings who would take the job if you said no? How close is it until the time when you plan to go to work? How many other offers can you expect to receive in the near future? You should not hesitate to ask for specific terms once the employer has formally extended you an offer. Do not wait until after you start work to clarify terms and conditions of employment.

Making a Decision

Whether you receive a single offer or have several to choose from, take time to assess options in order to reach a sound decision. Develop a list of the advantages and disadvantages for you in any position. Then on a scale of one to five (1 = ideal; 5 = unbearable), rate the offer you have received according to the factors you have listed (See Chart 22). Use this rating system to help clarify your thinking about the offer.

Ask yourself: Is this the type of practice I have been seeking? Will my family and I be happy in the community? Do I possess the requisite skills for the job? Does the management style of the employer seem consistent with my working style? Will my peers be the types of lawyers I find interesting and congenial? Is the money offered satisfactory?

While salary is important, especially for those with financial obligations, it should be weighed against a number of factors that receive your careful consideration. Only a relative handful of graduates can be expected to see the top dollar figures being quoted in newspapers and periodicals. For most applicants this is simply being unrealistic.

Because the first few years of practice represent an apprenticeship or internship, and the beginning lawyer is learning how to practice law rather than generating a profit, starting salaries for new lawyers may not reach the impressive levels indicated by the legal press. On the other hand, economic surveys show that you can expect your income level to grow year after year, reaching the top income figures after about 20 years of practice. Thus, initial salary and benefit packages are important, but these are only part of the overall picture.

Before you total up your ratings for the positions you are evaluating, take a second look at the list of disadvantages. In contrast to the pluses, the disadvantages are often thrust to the back of one's mind. On a day-to-day basis, however, they can tarnish even the advantages most eagerly sought.

What if you are not really comfortable with your office peers? Will you be excluded from the informal discussions at lunch or other moments of relaxation that contribute so much to your professional growth? Will advice and counsel be freely provided by those who have performed similar tasks before? Some disadvantages are merely inconveniences, but others can have truly inhibiting effects upon your professional life.

One additional factor deserves special consideration: How will accepting the position influence your future?

Chart 22
Offer Rating Sheet

Offer	Pros	Weight 1 to 5	Cons	Weight -1 to -5
1.				
2.				
3.				
4.				

In *The Making of a Public Profession,* Frances Zemans and Victor Rosenblum point out the importance of the selection of a first position on future potential. Reviewing their survey results, you cannot help but be impressed by the importance of your first position to your entire future career. Your potential for specialization is determined. Upward professional mobility is developed. Lateral mobility is defined.

Your question, therefore, is simply: What limitation will this first position impose if all does not go as well as you hope? If a chance for a partnership does not develop, how saleable in the legal marketplace will be the skills you acquire? Will your skills be easily transferable to another area of the country? How closely tied to your present community will you be by your clients, your business, and professional contacts, or the specialized practice experience you have acquired?

Should you have to choose from two or more offers, it may help to make lists of the pros and cons of each offer. But although a ranking may help you to review your own objectives, it may not answer the question of which offer is most likely to satisfy you. You might play out a worst case scenario and imagine where you will be if the job does not work out.

In the end, it is frequently a subjective rather than objective decision. Carefully assessing an offer means considering personal feelings not just attempting to quantify advantages and disadvantages. Ultimately, you make a choice and go forward.

Finding Satisfaction

A number of different surveys of young lawyers report that for many their present work failed to meet their expectations for personal satisfaction. Those who are not happy frequently experience frustration either because of unrealistic expectations or because they chose the wrong type of position to meet their goals.

For many new lawyers, the biggest dissatisfaction is the amount of time spent on trivial matters. This is not surprising. Most clients have problems that loom large in their eyes but which to the trained professional are routine and simple.

Some offices are involved in large cases with millions of dollars at stake. A virtual army of attorneys may be involved for days or months in compiling data and citations and cataloging a myriad of documents. Many of the lawyers involved in such tremendous compilations will not be around to see their contribution to the final outcome. They may not know the overall objectives of the client representation for which they work so diligently. Although this situation is highly frustrating, young lawyers should be aware that this kind of data collection work is typical in firms where large issues are a way of life.

Dissatisfaction can also arrive after two or three years of practice when lawyers begin to feel they have mastered the skills of practice and that responsibilities are increasing more rapidly than compensation. Still another type of annoyance to many young lawyers is the administrative detail that the operation of any office requires but particularly larger firms. It is frustrating when there does not seem to be enough time to deal adequately with the challenging legal matters at hand.

New lawyers also may complain that they have insufficient time to do an adequate job on their assignments. The fact is, you cannot spend $2,000 worth of time on a case that will bring only $200. A new lawyer may also have several assignments from different partners or senior associates and feel they cannot all be completed within the time frame allotted. Or there simply may be too few lawyers to handle the total case load.

Lack of feedback or evaluation from superiors represents another source of dissatisfaction. This is perhaps the most serious problem because it limits professional growth and development. It is also the most difficult to remedy because training must be initiated from the top to be truly successful. Forward-looking offices seek ways in which to improve the skills of both new lawyers and more experienced ones.

On an encouraging note, job dissatisfaction seems to dissipate after the third year in practice. As new lawyers gain experience, they develop a more realistic outlook on practice and better means of coping with its many irritants.

Although a certain amount of frustration is inevitable in the transition from law school to the real world, long term career dissatisfaction is often avoidable. If you match your skills and goals to the best position available, you are more likely to achieve satisfaction in your work. Seek out the possibilities, rather than accept whatever comes along, and take time to weigh the advantages and disadvantages of any offer. Negotiate to get the best employment package and choose the position which offers the best opportunities for personal and professional growth. If genuinely torn between career choices, use contacts in your network to help you decide what's best for you.

16
Reassessment

You have spent the weeks following your office visit in a state of anxious anticipation. Then, one day the mail brings a law firm envelope. Instead of seeing the words of welcome that you expected, it begins with the conciliatory "We certainly enjoyed having the opportunity to talk with you. Unfortunately..." Suddenly, you are aware that your job search is not over yet.

Not every letter and resume you send out will get a response. Not every interview will come to a successful conclusion. These two facts of life tend to result in a discouraged frame of mind—the rejection syndrome.

Coping With Rejection

There are many reasons for such disappointments, many no fault of your own. If, after the first few weeks, your job search has not yet produced results, you may begin to wonder: Did I learn enough about the prospective employers? Were my cover letters as personalized as I could make them? Did I present myself effectively in the interview? Such self-analysis and criticism should not disintegrate into self-castigation. Your need is to overcome feelings of personal rejection because they produce an attitude that is virtually self-defeating.

One way of dealing with this attitude is through a program of rewards to yourself in an area that is specifically under your control: your job campaign. Establish benchmarks of achievement in your campaign: so many offices added to your files, so many personalized cover letters written, an interview obtained, and so many acknowledgments made. When you reach each benchmark, reward

yourself. The reward need not be expensive. It may be the allocation of time to read a special book or article. It may be seeing a
movie you have been longing to attend. It may even be a sinfully
fattening sundae. When you do a good job, treat yourself well.

It has been said that a good trial lawyer is not unlike a good
prizefighter. Both step into the ring knowing someone has to lose.
After a loss the best lawyers and prizefighters share the ability to
rise confidently for the next fight. Rejection gives you an opportunity to hone an important professional skill.

The difficulty lies in learning to swallow this rejection and go on.
For many law students, dealing with rejection can pose a major
problem because they have not had much experience being rejected, having succeeded at nearly everything they have tried.

So how does someone who has always been a walking success
story cope with the "rejection blues?" The answer is simple—by
preparing emotionally and mentally beforehand.

Perhaps the best way to deal with rejection, is to build a list of
specific options before the interview process even begins. As some
options do not work out, others can be added to the list. It is
important never to allow the list of alternatives to become exhausted. (See Chapter 7.)

It is important also to understand the meaning of rejection. First
of all, everyone, even a walking success story, must understand that
no one goes through life with out facing rejection. So rejection is
not necessarily synonymous with failure—it is merely a setback,
and should be viewed as such. In baseball, a good batter gets a hit
three out of ten times at bat. In business, a successful entrepreneur
frequently experiences many business failures before finding a successful combination.

Secondly, remember that your response to rejection is influenced
by several factors, such as the number of other rejections already
received, the amount of energy and desire you invested in getting a
particular position, and your basic orientation to the job-hunting
process. The response may vary from situation to situation, and
from person to person.

If this particular job was a big deal, i.e., you invested a lot of
time and energy into getting it, then by all means, allow yourself to
go through the "grief" process. Grief for a lost job opportunity does
not differ all that much from the grief following any significant loss
in life and you may experience stages of denial, anger, bargaining,
depression, and finally acceptance. It sometimes helps to have

someone with whom to share these feelings, and with whom you can work the problem through to the point of acceptance.

This might be a good time for self-evaluation as well. Determine whether there are areas over which you have control. Consider how much you can change. Get a handle on your basic abilities and goals. Try to generate some new alternatives for yourself. Ironically, the rejection period can be a very creative time. The road to acceptance should be one of growth. You should learn about yourself and change. Ask yourself how the situation could have been different. Ask what you can do in the future to avoid a recurrence. The most important thing is to get in touch with the positive side of the experience.

Do not take too long "getting in touch" or you will lose possible advantages and opportunities that have come up in the meantime. Do not let your job search grind to a complete halt. Sometimes students who do not get job offers in their first attempts do nothing more until after graduation or even after the bar exam. In such cases, the passing of time forecloses many options, and the pressure to get a job only becomes more intense.

Building Skills

Sometimes coping with rejection will lead you to reevaluate your position in the market. You may want to look at other alternatives. Or you may decide to press forward in the same direction and hope that fortune will smile on you soon. You may, however, conclude that in order to move forward or to change directions you need to strengthen your skills.

If you have evaluated your skills already, you may be able to identify problem areas. If not, you should look back to Chapter 5 for help on identifying career skills. Either way you should attempt to identify not only a picture of your shortcomings but a plan for overcoming them.

In some situations you may be able to make adjustments, either academically or experientially, while you are in law school. In other cases you may need to consider post graduate solutions.

Graduate Law Study

Many law schools offer master of laws (LLM) programs. These vary from general studies to highly specialized curricula. Probably the most common LLM is in the tax area, because of the unique aspects of tax practice. Many other areas, such as environmental law, are covered by LLM programs as well. For some fields such as law teaching, an LLM at a prestigious law school can add luster to the resume of a candidate from a regional institution. As a rule, however, an LLM program is not the place to go to avoid the job market for another year. It should be utilized to enhance your skills and credentials when you have a good idea where you are going.

Graduate School

Some students believe that by combining different degrees, they can qualify for jobs in which they would otherwise not be considered, including both specialized legal jobs and nonlegal jobs for which a JD would be an asset but not a qualification. Although many students do graduate work before law school, some choose to do it afterward.

Among the most common graduate programs for law grads are the MBA, MPA/Public Administration and Ph.D. As with the pursuit of an LLM, you should seek other advanced educational degrees only when it is consistent with your other career goals, not just to escape reality.

Fellowships

There are also a number of post-graduate fellowships available. Some of these are well-known, and others less recognized. The competition for all is stiff but the benefits can be great. Details about available fellowships can be found in your placement office.

For example, consider the White House Fellowship program. The purpose of the program is to give the fellows first-hand, high-level experience with the workings of the federal government and to increase their sense of participation in national affairs.

The fellows are younger men and women, age 23 to 35, chosen from business, law, journalism, the universities, architecture, or other occupations. Fellows are assigned to the office of the vice-president, to cabinet officers, and to members of the White House staff. In addition to their daily work, the fellows take part in seminars and other activities especially planned to advance the purposes of the program.

There are a number of similar post-graduate fellowships and research grants each year. Because most lawyers tend to be highly goal-oriented most move directly into positions with law firms and other legal employers. Law placement offices often do not publicize the availability of many fellowships because so few lawyers pursue this route. For some students, however, such a move might make sense to develop their skills and marketability.

17
Job Hunting Nuts and Bolts

Much of the literature in the career planning and placement field fails to offer alternatives to traditional job hunting techniques. Creative approaches to the process are seldom suggested even by experienced career counselors. But the truth is that not everyone will succeed following the traditional paths.

Not everyone went to Harvard. Not everyone made law review. Not everyone has a daddy who will hire them no matter how poorly they do in school. In other words, something should be said for the benefit of the other 90%.

What problems do you face when you begin your job search without an instant network of relatives or pre-existing contacts? For you, the task is to create contacts on your own. You have to work harder, longer, and smarter than your more fortunate classmates.

One of the most difficult problems a job seeker has to face is how to make contacts with prospective employers when he or she has no certain knowledge about what jobs are available. In such a situation, the individual must find the opening, or in some cases even create the demand.

This method of job hunting variously known as "pounding the pavement" or "beating the bushes" can be frustrating and dehumanizing. The percentages drop as soon as you go from jobs you know are available to those you think might be available. Still, much of the headache can be avoided by following a few simple rules.

Plan—If you have some idea about what you want, some priorities, and some system for your search, you will have overcome the major hurdle. Too many people start looking first, and ask questions later. This not only cuts down on efficiency, but also increases the likelihood of accepting a personally dissatisfying position. Your research and evaluation before you ever start to look for a job should be painstaking and thorough.

Persevere—Recognize the fact that you may not meet with instant success. Prepare contingency plans and keep looking. Retrace your steps from time to time, especially in areas with large lawyer populations. Whenever you get a lead from one source, follow it up. In fact, you should attempt to find leads even when your discussions with employers are otherwise unproductive.

Pick and choose—Blanket applications usually are not the best way to apply for jobs. Carefully drawn personal letters to employers are usually more effective.

Pull all your strings—Crass as it may sound, always try the easiest route—ask for help from family, friends, or acquaintances who are practicing attorneys. If you have an ice breaker, or a recommendation, do not hesitate to use it.

Work cooperatively—The idea of group and team interviews is more revolutionary. In the group interview, more than one person meets with a representative of a legal employer at the same time. Using a team approach, you and one or more other persons interested in the same type of practice go to a city together, but interview separately avoiding overlap. By comparing notes at the end of an interviewing day, the amount of territory you can cover will be multiplied. It is essential that you lay the ground rules beforehand, and start out with an attitude of cooperation.

Be creative—These suggestions do not exhaust the job hunting possibilities. To paraphrase the old Star Trek motto, go boldly where no one has gone before. The greatest asset one can have in job hunting is a creative and fertile imagination.

Applying Long Distance

Most law graduates enter practice in the state or area where they went to law school. For graduates leaving the area after graduation, contacts with outside lawyers may seem limited.

Actually, the limitations only depend upon the amount of time and effort you are willing to spend. Applying long distance will require more research because you must base your decisions upon where you would like to live as well as with whom you could work.

The following comments suggest ways you can go about researching, finding, and applying for such positions:

• Research desirable areas to live. Get newspapers and magazines from different cities. Write to the Chamber of Commerce. Find out about the economic, political, and environmental conditions in the area and then ask yourself if these conditions will be agreeable to you.

• Contact local bar associations. A state bar will have addresses of local bar associations and their officers. Many times these people can help.

• Read the bar journals. Almost every state has a bar journal, and many of these have a placement section.

• Research some more! Try to find out who the legal employers are and how you can find potential openings. Even if you have lived in the area before, you have probably never looked for a legal job there. Check your placement office files. Check the *Martindale-Hubbell* to locate other graduates from your law school or your undergraduate alma mater. Watch the current job listings on your schools placement office bulletin board.

• Establish personal contacts. Even if you do not have contacts within the legal community, you might know someone who does. Check groups with professional interests similar to yours, and if you have an interview that does not result in a job, always ask for other possible leads.

• Apply for temporary jobs. It is easier to look for jobs if you live in an area than to try to do it long distance. Also consider positions like judicial clerkships to get you there.

• Use letters of introduction. Some students have firm ideas about where to begin looking for a job upon graduation, but have no idea how to begin looking. When they arrive at their destination, they discover that a strange city can be an imposing obstacle to even the most daring individual. Many placement offices will provide a letter of introduction to placement offices at other schools in the area requesting that they provide names of persons who might offer employment or help you to get some feel for the local employment market.

• Go there. Everything is easier when you visit a place personally. Despite the cost, an interviewing trip will demonstrate your interest. Many students, make the ultimate commitment: Move to the area, take the bar exam, and keep looking until they find a job.

Where Are the Lawyers?

Lawyers often attend conventions, conferences, and institutes that focus on their specialty. If you are interested in a particular area of practice, go where the lawyers are. Many continuing legal education conferences are offered free or at reduced rates for law students. This approach may require you to be assertive in meeting people and arranging interviews or can offer informal opportunities to talk during breaks or discussion groups.

Pitfalls for the Unwary

Although this book urges you to assert your individuality, assess your talents and interests, and take control of the job search process, there are those who give you advice to the contrary. Three particular approaches to the job search deserve attention because of their ineffectiveness. These are the hat-in-hand approach, mass mailings, and putting all your eggs in one basket.

Hat-in-hand. This approach begins with a mental attitude that you will be lucky to find a job, any job. If you have to take what you can get, there is little reason to devote much attention to what you have to offer.

In the end you will probably find a job based upon a fit between your skills and the employer's needs. The hat-in-hand approach, however, can divert your attention to many openings for which there is no fit, and little prospect of getting hired. A hat-in-hand mentality also tends to cause you to undersell yourself. Rather than starting with the best possibilities and working down a priority list as this book suggests, the hat-in-hand approach leaves you at the bottom of your list.

Mass mailings. Sometimes a corollary of the hat-in-hand approach, mass mailings represent an attempt to get a job by playing a numbers game. In commercial advertising, a direct mail ad campaign may go out to thousands of recipients. Most of these will not respond, but a small, predictable percentage who do will make the campaign profitable. A response rate of 0.5 percent is considered good, so 200 letters might result in one interview, 400 might result in two, etc. It is not just a question of financing such a campaign, but rather who will respond to a mass mailing. See Chapter 14 for a discussion of better ways to contact employers.

All your eggs in one basket. Some law students want one job so much that they pursue only that position. Some students count on a part-time job developing into permanent employment. Others have received assurances that a job would be available for them when they graduate.

Not a year passes that virtually every placement director in the country encounters at least one desperate graduate whose plans have fallen asunder. Do not be caught in this situation. Even if you have a strong possibility for employment, check out others. Maintain alternatives in case your first choice falls through.

Timetable for the Job Search

The job search is made more difficult by the fact that the timetable for job applications is a complicated one. In fact, there are many different timetables for the job search. This is because different types of legal employment may require you to contact employers, interview, and make decisions at different points in time.

These scheduling anomalies can catch the inattentive law student by surprise. If you overlook critical dates, you may foreclose many job opportunities. Chart 23 provides an overview for many of the critical dates in the job search process. You should use this chart in structuring your own personal job search. In addition, the following generalizations pertain to specific job markets:

Large Firms and Corporations

Large firms, corporations, and other employers that participate in the fall on-campus recruitment process at law schools typically do most of their hiring through campus interviews. This is true whether the firm visit your campus or not. They interview for summer clerks during the second year of law school, make offers to clerks at the end of the summer, and interview third year students for positions only if they do not fill all openings from the ranks of summer clerks.

This process takes place each fall and the dates can be affected not only by the particular schedule set up by your law school placement office for conducting interviews, but also by NALP guidelines concerning the acceptance of offers by employers participating in fall on-campus interviews. If you want to get a job with

Chart 23
Job Search Timetable

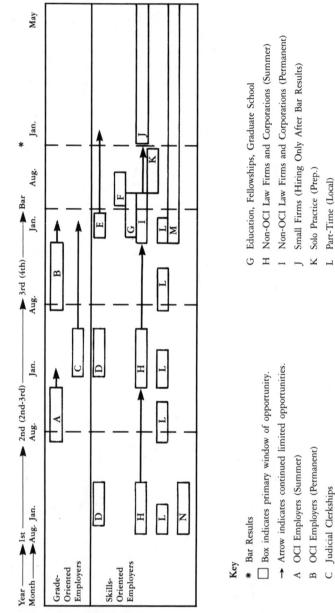

Key

* Bar Results

☐ Box indicates primary window of opportunity.

↑ Arrow indicates continued limited opportunities.

A   OCI Employers (Summer)

B   OCI Employers (Permanent)

C   Judicial Clerkships

D   Non-OCI Government and Public Interest (Summer)

E   Non-OCI Government and Public Interest (Permanent)

F   Government (End of Budget Year)

G   Education, Fellowships, Graduate School

H   Non-OCI Law Firms and Corporations (Summer)

I   Non-OCI Law Firms and Corporations (Permanent)

J   Small Firms (Hiring Only After Bar Results)

K   Solo Practice (Prep.)

L   Part-Time (Local)

M   Non-Legal Business and Miscellaneous

N   1st Year Summer Volunteer

an employer that recruits through campus interviews, you must keep this timetable in mind, even if you do not go through the interviews themselves.

Small Firms

Small firms tend to hire new lawyers when they need them. Frequently when they need someone is yesterday, so the firm will require candidates to have taken and passed the bar exam.

Other small firms recruit almost exclusively from the ranks of part-time (as opposed to summer) law clerks. Thus, there is no magic time frame for small firm hiring, other than some early in the first year of law school until several months after graduation.

Clerkships

Most federal district and appeals court judges begin the clerkship selections process early in the spring semester of student's second year (third year for evening students). Although the interviewing process may extend through the summer and even into the next fall, many judges have completed their selection by early March.

Your school undoubtedly will have special procedures for applying to judges for clerkships and should you miss this window your chances of getting hired are diminished considerably.

Clerkships for state judges generally lag behind federal clerkships. Consult the court in the jurisdiction where you will be applying.

Government Agencies

Government agencies are often influenced by budget cycles which run for a year beginning in September or some other annual date. Even agencies that try to recruit through on-campus interviews do not know how many openings they will have until the following spring or summer.

The armed services, foreign service, FBI, as well as graduate law programs have their own application deadlines and beginning dates for training/educational programs. Check with your placement office or the ABA Career Series annual reference book, *Now Hiring: Government Jobs for Lawyers*.

It is important to look for application deadlines and hiring patterns whenever you conduct research on legal employers. Be sure and note this information on your file cards or database.

Many students ask how long the job search should take. Of course, the answer depends on many factors. Assuming that you have done all the necessary background research, prepared a resume and committed time to the job search, you should plan on several weeks of sending out applications. This assumes that you will be doing things other than looking for a job, and that you will not send out all your applications at once. You will be responding to old applications as you send out newer ones.

As a rule of thumb, you should expect to hear from employers about two weeks after you send your letter. If you have not heard anything after four weeks you might want to follow up with a second letter or phone call. If you have not heard anything within six weeks, you probably will not. Unfortunately, some employers lack the staff or simply the courtesy to respond to students who contact them.

If your initial efforts are not successful, this stage of the job search will continue. Weeks can easily turn into months. As a rule, if you have actively pursued legal employers for three or four months without a positive response, you should probably go back to the drawing board. Your career counselor may be able to pinpoint problems that hamper your success.

When an employer becomes interested in you, the next step is to schedule a screening interview. It normally takes two to four weeks to contact you, schedule the interview, and conduct the interview. Even where the law school placement office serves as a facilitator for the interview scheduling, there is some delay between the time you first sign up for interviews, and the interviews are held.

Since you may be talking to a number of employers on different dates, this stage of the process normally lasts for several weeks. Most law students find that there is a natural limit to the number of interviews they can endure when not pressed to do so by necessity. If they begin to receive positive responses to their first interviews, many law students cease contacting new employers until their initial interviewing is completed.

After the screening interview, you can expect to wait two to three weeks before hearing from the employer. The time frame may be extended if the employer conducts a national search with many applicants or reduced if the search is limited to two or three individuals. Allowing another two to three weeks for employers to make decisions, you should expect to have offers in hand within three to four months after you started the process. So if you plan on going through fall on-campus interviews, the process will start in mid-August and you should be finished by mid-November.

After you receive one or more offers you should have some time to make a decision. Since employers want you to decide as soon as possible, most students want to extend the time frame to maximize their options. With respect to on-campus interviews, NALP suggests that employer offers to summer clerks be held open until November 15th, and offers made to students interviewed during the fall until December 15 (*See* Appendix.) Some employers expect an answer on the spot. (Federal judges are famous for this.) Although these matters are generally subject to negotiation, a sense of fair play and reasonableness on the part of both employers and candidates should put limits on the time frame for making decisions (See also Chapter 15).

You may find yourself cut out of the process at a number of different points. If you have not taken the time to initiate new applications before older ones are rejected, you may find yourself at some point back to square one facing another three or four months of job search. It is probably fair to say that your job search will not go as well as your wildest hopes, but will go better than your gravest fears. A job search of three to six months is not unusual; one extending beyond nine months is atypical.

The timetable for part-time job searches, because of the temporary nature of the employment and the quick turnaround of the openings, is generally abbreviated. And a job search for a highly technical or specialized position may last a year or more.

For the substantial number of law students who go through the on-campus interview program at their school to find a permanent job, the process takes a good portion of the fall during the second and third years of law school (third and fourth for evening students). Although it is possible to skip second year interviews and look for a permanent job during your final fall in law school, a majority of positions offered through on-campus interview programs are the result of summer clerkships obtained during the second year.

Conclusion

Different legal jobs as well as law-related jobs can be expected to follow different cycles. Small firm hiring does not follow any cycle at all. Your research into potential employers should include the timing of the application process. If getting a job requires being in the right place at the right time, you can significantly enhance your chances by figuring out when the right place and right time will occur.

Part III

The Market

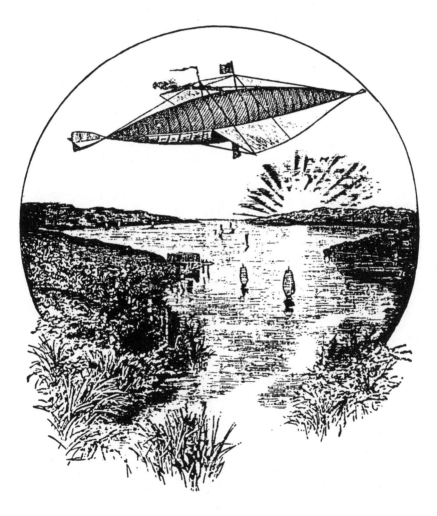

For every thing there is a season,
And a time for every purpose under heaven.
Ecclesiastes

18
The Legal Job Market

Who has not heard that there are too many lawyers? The statistics are plain enough: there are over 800,000 lawyers in the United States, and projections indicate that the profession will reach 1,000,000 before the year 2000. This will represent one lawyer for every 250 people in the United States. Approximately 40,000 new lawyers pass the bar each year. These figures have led some to conclude that there is an oversupply of lawyers and "the job market is glutted."

In 1961, the American Bar Association created a Special Committee on Lawyer Utilization to study the question of whether there were too many lawyers. That committee concluded that although the profession was growing rapidly and that many graduates might not find their ideal job, there was no evidence of an oversupply of lawyers in the foreseeable future.

Despite the ABA findings, the idea of a lawyer glut has been popular in the press, creating a myth that there is an oversupply of lawyers. It has been fueled in recent years by a downturn in the national economy. And yet, year in and year out, most graduates find jobs.

Part of the reason that the legal job market has continued to expand may be attributed to the increasing complexity of society and the concomitant demand placed upon it for legal solutions to problems. There also seems to have been a pent up demand for legal services, as shown by a study from 1977, *The Legal Needs of the Public,* in which researcher Barbara Curran suggested that there were tremendous unmet legal needs from individuals to small businesses that typically did not use lawyers in a preventative way. Another part of the explanation may be found in a variation of

Parkinson's Law that the amount of work has expanded to meet the size of the work force.

Finally, the job market for lawyers has expanded as lawyers have moved into non-traditional but law-related fields. Although lawyers have always worked for trust departments, title companies, accounting firms, and educational institutions, the interest in the legal talent from these other quarters has mushroomed. Interestingly, the rapid increase in legal salaries among large New York law firms was fueled by competition for legal talent with investment banking houses during the heyday of mergers and acquisitions practice.

Because the job market has fractionalized over the years, there is not one job market for lawyers today, but many. The job market for lawyers entering private practice may be the predominant market, but it is not the only one. All this makes job hunting significantly more complicated, although ultimately it means more opportunities for more people.

What are the prospects for the 1990s? Is the job market infinitely elastic?

There is evidence that certain segments of the market already may have become saturated in some geographical areas and some areas of practice. There is also evidence that the increased size of the profession has increased competition and reduced law firm profitability.

This means that less successful practitioners may be driven from the market because they cannot make a living practicing law. In addition, the market may contain an underbelly of marginal practitioners and underemployed young lawyers. Again, evidence exists that such an underbelly will persist in the 1990's, and that underutilization of lawyers will create special image, professionalism and ethics problems for the legal profession.

Aside from the question of how the legal profession should deal with these developments, there is a more personal question of how you should cope. Some individuals who have difficulty finding a job, may use the job market glut as an easy excuse. The reality is, however, that despite many problems you *can* find a job. The simple answer is to plan carefully and remain flexible. This theme is repeated throughout this book. Beyond doing homework, however, you must have confidence that hard work and competence will pay off in the end.

Note that there is a difference between naive doggedness and savvy dedication. More than a few lawyers have learned the hard way that long hours and blind loyalty do not assure success. In these volatile times, a constant self-awareness and sensitivity to the external environment are prerequisites to long term success.

The following sections briefly describe some of the more important job markets for lawyers. They represent jumping off points rather than final words on the topics covered.

Private Practice

The broad heading of "private practice" encompasses work in organizations that provide legal services to clients, from sole practitioners to firms of over 1,000 lawyers. The most recent NALP Employment Survey indicates that 62.9 percent of law school graduates who responded to the survey chose to enter private practice in 1990.

Within this category of law firm employment there are numerous variations, such as small, medium, and large firms, as well as sole practitioners. Given such diversity, the advantages and disadvantages of each group must be assessed separately. Each private law office, however, is an entrepreneurial venture and it must be profitable to be viable.

Small Firms

Small firms of two to ten lawyers often attract graduates who hope to avoid the pressures and impersonal demeanor of larger firms. The 1990 NALP Survey shows that 26.6 percent of law school graduates who enter private practice choose a small firm. They are attracted by the chance to be their own boss, set their own hours, and handle their practice in the way that they deem most satisfactory personally. Smaller firms can be found in metropolitan areas, and while they almost certainly promise lower initial income than the larger firms, they may offer more freedom and variety in terms of practice area for many graduates.

The small firm also has lure for those who are tired of the problems and inconveniences of urban life, and prefer living in small towns or rural areas. Whether or not this is an attractive option for you will depend on several factors. Whereas some individuals might consider small town life to be appealing, others might feel stifled by the lack of cultural opportunity or professional recognition. Clearly, the type of legal work that you would handle in a small town would differ markedly from the work you could expect in an urban setting.

Many small firms are not able to specialize because the available clients require a more general service. Generally speaking, smaller firms lack adequate resources to sustain a specialized practice. Some small "boutique" firms, however, have successfully achieved such narrow specialization.

Just as it is difficult to define a small firm by size, so is it by organizational structure. A small firm may be a true partnership with a written agreement. Or it may be a handshake partnership, often resting on a longstanding and well-understood relationship. It may be a group of sole practitioners sharing offices and such expenses as secretarial assistance, libraries, and legal assistants, with each practitioner keeping his or her own clients and retaining fees on an individual basis.

Generally the small law office does not recruit on a regular or even on an annual basis. Small firms recruit most often when a specific need for additional help arises. As a result, recruiting efforts are likely to be more casual, and openings likely to arise at times other than traditional recruiting schedules (the on-campus interviewing season). It is not unusual for a small office to contact the placement officer of a law school three or four months after graduation and ask for assistance in locating a graduate for a position that has suddenly developed. It is therefore important to stay in touch with the placement office of your law school if you do not have a position when you graduate.

There are two special aspects of small firm recruiting that students often fail to address. First, it is often essential for the candidate to be admitted to the bar. The potential for full utilization of the lawyer from the first day of employment is often a vital consideration, so do not be surprised if you are not a viable candidate until you have passed the bar exam. That is an economic dictate, not a rejection of you personally.

The second consideration, one that both you and the employer share, is the high degree of visibility in a small firm. If you and your colleagues are not compatible, there is no back room in which you can hide. Being aware of this fact, small firms are extremely careful in their selection of new lawyers. You owe yourself the same carefulness.

The very closeness of a small office, however, also provides distinct advantages for a graduate. Because of your high degree of visibility, you will meet clients earlier than you would in a larger office. As you prove capable, you will receive additional responsibilities. It would be a mistake to make generalizations about small firms without knowing specifics. Young lawyers whose professional goal is intellectual stimulation sometimes assume that it can be found only in very large firms. They eventually may realize they have misjudged the situation when they spend time in the real world.

Sole Practitioners

In the professional use of the term, a sole practitioner is a lawyer who practices entirely alone with only secretarial or legal assistants in the office. As soon as an associate lawyer is added to the office, the lawyer cannot be said to be practicing alone. This situation becomes confusing because of office sharing arrangements, and work for space agreement. The ratio of sole practitioners to the total lawyer population has decreased steadily from 70 per cent in 1950 to less than 40 percent today. There has been much speculation as to why this trend has developed and why it continues.

Hanging Out a Shingle

Some brave souls would argue that the most effective way to achieve valuable experience in actually practicing law is to plunge into private practice immediately upon graduation from law school, and hope that experience will indeed be the best teacher. This has both rewards and inherent problems, both of which should be given careful consideration.

"Hanging out a shingle" is certainly not the path for the faint-hearted or for those who must rely on a steady income to provide for their family or repayment of law school debts.The NALP Employment Survey, indicates that less than 1% (down from 8% in the late 1970s) of the graduates choosing private practice become self-employed.

One answer may be the rise of institutional law firms that offer more jobs than in the past. Why have more and more lawyers chosen to practice in larger and larger firms? And what lawyers are more likely to be happy as individual practitioners than as employees or owners of a law firm? First, large law firms have grown up to meet the needs of clients. Individual practices serve individual clients. Larger business organizations frequently have a large volume of complex legal problems that cannot be dealt with by a single lawyer. A very large firm essentially serves the legal needs of very large corporations. Smaller firms serve smaller business entities. It is no accident that more of the lawyers whose work involves representing individuals choose to practice by themselves.

A second factor that has promoted law firm development has been economics. Economies of scale work in the legal services industry the same way they do in other businesses. The economical practice of law more and more requires the use of sophisticated equipment, which represents a substantial capital investment for a sole practitioner. Overhead has taken an increasingly large percentage of firm profits in recent years for all firms, but the bite is particularly painful for individual practitioners.

A third factor is specialization. The renaissance lawyer is dead. Lawyers increasingly must become experts at one, or at most a few areas of law. In order to offer potential clients a full range of legal services, it is increasingly necessary to bring together a group of lawyers with different specialties in order to have a full service law firm.

Some law school graduates are more likely to succeed opening a practice than others. Desire and determination are not the controlling factors.

Probably the most apparent factor in succeeding as a solo is competence. Although competence is difficult to define, it is clearly more than legal knowledge. The Model Rules of Professional Conduct define competence as "sufficient knowledge, skill, preparation and thoroughness to adequately represent the client." It is often said that when you pass the bar exam you know more law than at any other time in your professional life. Yet, those contemplating solo practice often express fear about their competence. This fear may be rooted more in the absence of necessary skills to practice competently than the lack of substantive legal knowledge. When you practice alone, you can look up the law if you are unsure of something, or associate with another attorney if you lack expertise. But knowing how to handle a case, run an office, and collect your fee are much more elusive skills which are generally not taught in law school.

The prospective solo practitioner should have experiences in two distinct areas: running a small business and working in a small law firm. The principles of running any business are similar, and the skills transferable from one experience to another. If you lack business acumen built upon practical experience, you should be wary of opening a law office. You also should have experience working in a law firm that handles cases like those you will encounter as a practitioner so you can develop a working knowledge of how to handle legal matters from start to finish.

For the first few years, it is almost essential that the self-employed lawyer have a professional mentor to turn to for advice and counsel. Those who choose this path have no more knowledge of how to practice law than any other graduate, and the guidance and instruction provided by a mentor may substitute in part for that provided by the more senior members of a law firm. The problem is that the majority of lawyers today may not have experiences of practicing alone themselves, and, therefore, cannot serve as role models for younger lawyers who choose solo practice.

A second factor in the equation is financing. Law firms tend to be under-capitalized, in part because law has not tended to be a capital-intensive business in the past, and in part because of the prohibition against investment in law firms by nonlawyers. Inadequate financing is probably responsible for more new practices failing than any other cause. If you open your own law office, you should not plan to take anything out of the practice for the first year, and you should have sufficient reserve to cover inevitable cash flow problems in the early months of the practice.

Even if a client walks into your office the first day you open your doors, you may not see the fee for several months. During this time you still have bills to pay. Jay Foonberg, author of the classic *How to Start and Build a Law Practice,* suggests that you set aside living expenses for one year before attempting to start your practice. For some people this may not be a problem. They have a working spouse; they will retire from another job with a good pension when they graduate from law school; they are independently wealthy.

For other graduates, the solution must entail obtaining loans. Whether you go to family or a lending institution, the lender will want to be convinced that you will repay the loan, i.e., that your practice will be successful. You will need to show more than good intentions. To convince a lender that you are a good risk you will need a good credit history and a well thought-out business plan. You can take steps to solidify your credit rating long before you go to ask for a loan. Aside from paying your bills, you should attempt to develop a relationship with a banker in the area where you hope to practice, and take out smaller loans which you pay back promptly.

The business plan is a key part of the third factor related to successfully opening up practice—planning. Not only do you need a business plan for the bank, you need it for yourself.

First, you should conduct a market analysis. Look carefully at the area you plan to open your office. What are the demographics? Where do people live and work? Who are your potential clients? What drives the economy of the area? Where are the banks? What are the opportunities for business growth? Who is your competition? How many lawyers practice in the area, and what do they do? Do nonlegal institutions provide any law related services?

Then you must figure out where you fit in. What is your market niche? What clients do you hope to attract and how? What services will you provide? Where will you locate in order to assure that potential clients reach you?

The business plan should contain an organizational plan. Even if the office will just include you and a secretary, that structure should be described. And your long range goals should be addressed briefly also.

Finally, the business plan should include financial projections including anticipated profits and losses, and cash flow. The more realistic your budget, the more likely that it will impress a lender as well as serve you in your practice.

Opening a law practice may be a legitimate career option for some people, but a disaster for others. Entering a solo practice right out of law school should be an affirmative choice and not a selection of last resort. For the right kind of person, however, hanging out a shingle remains as a viable option.

Medium and Large Firms

About 28.1 percent of the surveyed by NALP graduates who entered private practice in 1990 joined very large firms of more than 100 lawyers. Approximately the same percentage went to work for firms of 10 lawyers or less.

The patterns of practice at larger firms have been well documented in a number of books, both fiction and non-fiction. Some discussion concerning the recruitment practices of very large firms, however, may be helpful.

. These firms recognize that their continued growth and vitality depend upon the recruitment of highly capable people. Consequently they undertake sophisticated recruitment programs that include on-campus recruiting, deadlines for offers, a careful selection of schools for maximum potential results and the use of recruitment coordinators.

Large firms are aware that they must hire far more associates than can possibly be expected to become partners. Such firms, however, are also aware that the training they provide and the standards they require are such that those who do not attain partnership within the firm are sought after candidates in other firms.

Larger firms tend to provide greater opportunities for specialization, and also, of all the legal jobs, it is probably the large firms that provide the highest initial starting salaries, and provide not only a sense of security but also a chance to practice law with other attorneys who are generally quite competent, and therefore able to provide the benefit of valuable experience.

The problems of being an associate with a big firm cannot be overlooked either, and in recent years these problems have been a source of increasing concern to law school graduates who want freedom in both the hours they work, and the kind of clients they handle. The decision is a difficult one, and the advantages and disadvantages must be weighed carefully.

Medium-sized firms are in a sense transitional organizations. When a firm reaches a size of about 10 lawyers, it begins to become institutionalized: it hires more regularly; it departmentalizes; it becomes more structured administratively. Such a firm will become more and more like a large firm as it grows, even though it may try (usually unsuccessfully) to retain its small firm attributes.

Business Organizations

The number of attorneys employed by a corporation will vary widely with the size and type of the corporation. Many smaller and some larger corporations farm out all their legal problems to private law firms. Many others have in-house counsel for only certain matters. Other corporations have a legal staff large enough to handle most legal problems in-house.

In a small corporation an attorney may have responsibilities other than the legal affairs of the business. An increasing number of corporations are seeking young lawyers to handle legal problems and assume management duties, as well. If there is a legal department or a full-time lawyer employed by the corporation, the individual is often referred to as the general counsel.

Some corporations hire lawyers outside their regular legal departments. Oil companies typically have exploration or land departments totally distinct from their legal departments. Some companies hire attorneys in tax departments, in research and development, and in other capacities which require an ability to deal with the law.

The starting salary in corporations tends to be higher than small firms but less than the highest paying large firms. Also, an attorney's first year in a firm may necessitate working 60 or more hours a week where a corporation may follow a typical 8 a.m.–5 p.m. schedule. Finally, the fringe benefits and working conditions are often more generous in a corporation than in a firm.

In business, as in government, many management decisions such as those involving the number of lawyers and salary ranges are made outside the legal department. Top leadership has relatively little turn-over, so variations in form and procedure remain relatively stable.

Once again, however, there is a wide range of opportunity, depending upon the nature of the legal work of the individual organizations. Although form and structure may be dictated by outside forces in both government and business, each legal department nevertheless has a unique personality formed by the individual viewpoint of the general counsel and senior staff of the department. The last part of this chapter gives a summary of nonlegal positions in corporations.

Government

The tremendous variety of work found in private law offices is not nearly so evident in government employment. Many of the rules, not to mention the budget, are decided upon by a legislative body rather than those within the immediate office. Differences among government agencies depend upon the scope and jurisdiction of each agency. For example, work in a district attorney's office will provide early exposure to criminal litigation, while work in the Office of the General Counsel of the Environmental Protection Agency offers exposure to environmental litigation.

Federal Government

Opportunities with the federal government are as varied as the department themselves, and the departments are as varied as the problems facing the country today. For almost every facet of American life there is a government agency designated to deal with it. Within this framework, the opportunities for employment are virtually endless.

The diversity of activities within the broad scope of "government service" necessitate the careful investigation of each individual department, as each is a unique entity with its own particular advantages and disadvantages. The same person who would not be at all interested in dealing with laws of consumer protection and anti-trust law with the Federal Trade Commission, or the Tax Division of the Justice Department might enjoy dealing with the problems of rural America in the Department of Agriculture.

Although many would criticize the federal government for its "bigness," this is, in terms of employment, not always an accurate perception. Each department retains a certain degree of autonomy and self-sufficiency with a group of people all working in the same general direction within a department, whether it be admiralty, tax, transportation, communications, anti-trust, banking, patents, communications, labor, or an almost infinite list of other possibilities.

Your placement office may collect pamphlets and brochures from many of these different agencies. Some federal agencies interview on campus, but you must contact the majority of them directly.

State Government

For graduates seeking jobs with state agencies, the road to employment may seem strewn with obstacles and at times impassable. A plethora of agencies exists in each of the fifty states. In many states there is no centralized organization or bureau, such as the U.S. Civil Service Commission, which coordinates the hiring of personnel. Yet, despite this, it is possible to traverse the course and find the way to gainful employment.

The key to success may well lie in the right combination of luck and perseverance. Many state agencies hire someone when a position comes open, unlike large law firms that know in any given year how many new attorneys they will need. Thus, retracing ground may well be necessary. The hiring offices of some of the state agencies are not too well-coordinated, and you should not become discouraged if your initial efforts do not meet with success.

Local Government

Jobs with governmental entities below the state level are often hard to find because there are so many potential places to look. District, County, and City Attorneys' offices often hire recent graduates. In larger cities, these offices have regular openings as well as more coordinated hiring policies.

There are also many opportunities in fields such as land use planning, utilities law, etc., in departments within city government and in special districts (e.g.—water, school, regional planning). Local government agencies are more likely to recruit from the local bar than to solicit applicants from law schools. Since there is no comprehensive list of such local government jobs, you should discuss your plans with a member of the placement staff for personal guidance.

Military Service

Each branch of the military service has its Judge Advocate General's Corps or equivalent. The salary, benefits, and relative security of military life may be attractive to many graduates.

Significantly, the military services represent one of the largest employers of law graduates in the country, and despite the fact that the military legal system is different from the civilian one, military legal alumnus testify to the excellent preparation for law practice that they receive.

Judicial Clerkships

Because of the unique opportunities judicial clerkships offer, these positions are prized not only for their current value but also for their worth in providing valuable experience for future positions. Because clerkships are of limited duration, they are not generally considered as career paths in and of themselves but as gateways leading to future career options.

Perhaps more than any other type of legal position, a clerkship, in terms of the quality of the experience, is strongly related to the personality and values of the judge with whom it is served. Rare is the judicial clerk who does not find the experience a rewarding one.

An increasing number of students are taking advantage of opportunities to serve as clerks to federal as well as state judges. Former clerks almost always remember their days working for the judge with fondness, as a time of growth and learning and often an opportunity to develop a close relationship with another person. Clerking may not be the ideal job for everyone, but if you think that you might be interested, you should begin to investigate the possibilities early.

When preparing the application, remember the criteria that a judge is likely to use: reputation of the law school, academic record of the applicant (practical employment experience may compensate for lack of journalistic endeavors), and personality of the applicant.

To avoid becoming lost in the endless pile of resumes, try to arrange an interview with the judge. Some judges select their clerks without conducting personal interviews, but you should make every effort to schedule a face-to-face meeting anyway. A follow-up thank you may well provide a valuable reminder of who you are.

If you are interested in learning something about what a law clerk will be doing, it might be beneficial to contact graduates presently clerking or talk to a faculty member with fairly recent clerking experience. Many placement offices offer programs on what to expect and how to apply for clerkships.

Letters from judges seeking clerks may be posted at your placement office or funneled to a faculty clerkship committee. Many judges do not send out letter soliciting resumes, and so you would be well-advised to make contact with judges early.

The hiring process begins in the spring semester of the second year for many federal judges and extends into the third year for some state court judges. Except in rare instances, clerkships begin on September 1 after graduation.

Several members of your faculty undoubtedly have very good contacts among the judiciary. If there are judges you are particularly interested in, you may request faculty members to write a personal letter on your behalf. On the other hand, if you are sending letters to a large number of judges, it may not be wise to ask faculty references to send out mass recommendations.

Federal Courts

Federal judges may be contacted by writing to them at the United States courthouse in the city where their court is located. A listing of federal judges is available in the front of each bound edition of the *Federal Reporter.*

A clerkship for the court of appeals tends to involve less action and more scholarship than a clerkship for a federal district court. A major portion of an appellate clerk's time is consumed in research and writing. When a case comes to the court of appeals, most of the routine questions already have been ironed out in the district court, and the difficult questions are left for the appellate court to consider. Thus, the appellate clerk is afforded an opportunity to study fewer questions, but more in depth.

The range of legal problems encountered in a federal court of appeals is quite wide. A sampling would include *habeas corpus,* criminal law and procedure, labor, administrative procedure, tax, admiralty, antitrust, securities, bankruptcy, civil rights, poverty, Social Security, and welfare.

In addition, because of the federal court's diversity jurisdiction, a federal court encounters the normal range of common law matters, including contracts, torts, and occasionally real property matters. The clerk always attends oral argument, and therefore learns a great deal about what to do and what not to do, as a lawyer presenting a case orally to a judge.

While an appellate clerkship does not offer much direct contact with trial practice, it does provide opportunity to pick up a great deal of information about trial practice from the study of trial records which are always included in an appeal. By reading all the motions and pleading filed in the trial court, and studying the trial transcript, the clerk learns how to prepare a record for appeal.

The duties of a clerk for a federal district judge are somewhat different and quite varied. Individual judges utilize their law clerks a valuable adjunct to the judicial decision-making process.

There is much activity outside the courtroom in connection with pre-trial motions and memorandum opinions. The law clerk examines all of the pleadings and briefs and prepare memoranda for the court. Active discussion may ensue between the court and the law clerk concerning the positions taken by the respective parties and their merits.

A law clerk is a valuable sounding board, against whom the judge can "bounce" legal theories offered by the litigating parties, legal concepts overlooked by the parties, and the consequences of a decision to be rendered.

State Courts

Although much of the attention at law school is placed on federal judicial clerkships, at least in part because the faculty considers such appointments prestigious, every jurisdiction has a system of state courts that utilizes judicial clerks to some degree. Some states only provide funding for clerkships at the appellate level. Others offer trial court clerkships just like the federal system. In either case, state courts offer an excellent opportunity for graduates interested in judicial clerkships, but who may not be successful finding a position in the highly competitive federal system.

The procedures for applying to judges at the state level are similar to those in the federal courts, although the specifics will vary from jurisdiction to jurisdiction. The timing for applying to the state courts is generally, but not always, later than for the federal courts. If you are interested in a state court clerkship, consult with your placement director or the court administrator in your state.

Administrative Courts

Students who want clerkship experience should also consider opportunities in the administrative courts, including the Tax Court, Court of Claims, Court of Patent Appeals, to name a few. The number of applications for these positions is often less then for the regular courts because not as many students think about them, but you should keep the administrative court in mind as one of the possibilities for clerkships.

Academic Positions

A relatively small number of law school graduates enter academic positions as teachers, administrators, librarians, or editors. The ranks of academic lawyers increase somewhat for experienced lawyers. These positions, however, retain an aura of exclusivity and appeal to many, in part because lawyer career satisfaction surveys have found this group to be the most satisfied in the legal profession.

Law Teaching

Law school teaching tends to be very exclusive, and entry into this profession, difficult. Although this varies from school to school, recent graduates are invariably law review editors, number one grads, U.S. Supreme Court clerks, and the like. For those not so fortunate as to possess these credentials there are two basic ways to find a position.

The first is to develop expertise or recognition in some field, to be considered a leader in that field. This recognition typically takes ten years or so to gain, but not necessarily.

The second is to do graduate law work at a school which has a program oriented toward teacher training, like NYU, Harvard, Columbia or Yale. The better programs have seminars on teaching law. You also have the opportunity to continue to write and develop your professional area. Many schools use LLM candidates to teach the first year legal research courses.

The Association of American Law Schools (AALS) sponsors both an employment register and an annual recruitment conference. If you are interested in law school teaching, however, you should speak candidly with your dean or a member of the faculty about your chances.

Teaching Law-Related Subjects

Teaching legal subjects extends far beyond teaching in law schools. Universities and colleges, community and junior colleges often offer legally-related courses like business law, jurisprudence, individual rights, paralegal training, law enforcement, and others.

Often individuals find jobs by going to the college and selling themselves as teachers for these legal subjects. You may want to write the American Association of Community and Junior Colleges, One DuPont Circle, Washington, DC 20036, or one of the business professional associations. These various professional associations in the academic world handle recruitment of new teachers in their area just as the AALS does in law. These associations should be contacted directly if you have a specialty. In addition, your placement office may post jobs, and the *Chronicle of Higher Education* lists openings in the teaching field.

Administration

Many lawyers assume responsibilities in the areas of educational administration, student personnel administration, financial aid, placement, admissions, and legal advisement for school districts, colleges and universities, as well as law schools.

The administrator, even though he or she does not actively practice law, is called upon almost daily to deal with legal questions. In areas such as equal employment opportunity, educational privacy rights, and countless others, legal training is invaluable.

Law Librarianship

Continuing accumulation of court decisions, rapid expansion of government regulation at all levels, and new legal problems caused by social change have produced a need for legal information management specialists. Law librarians must possess both knowledge of and management skills regarding the materials that are the lawyer's basic tools. Computer science, too, is having an impact upon libraries, both in management and research aspects of library service.

Law library positions exist in courts, bar associations, law schools, international agencies, law firms, government offices, and businesses. The American Association of Law Libraries also has a guidebook on careers in law librarianship as well as information about placement assistance.

Legal Research, Editorial, and Publishing Work

Editors are in short supply for such publishing firms as Shepard's Citations, West Publishing Co., Commerce Clearing House, and the Lawyer's Cooperative Publishing Co. Interested students should contact these publishers directly for further details.

Public Interest

The term *public interest* means many things to many people because there are many visions of what constitutes the public interest. Traditionally, public interest positions include legal services programs for indigents, and the law reform activities of civil rights organizations. In recent years, the definition of public interest law has broadened to include private associations with broad social or political agendas, as well as special interest groups.

Legal Aid

Legal aid and social services will not bring you wealth or fame. If you choose to practice in this area your primary rewards will be personal. There is a great need, however, for legal services lawyers because those who enter this type of practice are in short supply.

Legal services programs seek to provide representation to persons and groups who could not otherwise afford it. The category includes legal aid and public defender work, as well as the broad area of law reform.

Not all legal services programs are involved in all these areas. Funding comes primarily from governmental and private foundation sources. Although the opportunities in the poverty law area have diminished since the mid-sixties, there is still a great deal of need to attract motivated, competent individuals to practice law on behalf of the poor. Because ethnic and racial minorities constitute an inordinate percentage of the poor, minority lawyers who can communicate effectively with minority clients are in great demand.

As a legal services lawyer you have the ability and training to contribute significantly to the public interest, but such dedication involves some sacrifice in terms of your own personal comforts. The degree to which you dedicate yourself to solving these problems could range from an entire career devoted to legal aid, to occasional pro bono work while engaged in private practice.

Work in a legal services program can be frustrating but it is ultimately rewarding professionally (if not financially), and is always excellent training for young lawyers. The question is, are you willing to sacrifice a lucrative position in private practice for the satisfaction of doing something that must be done? It is eventually a question of ordering priorities in an effort to determine what it is that you want from your career. Since your profession has prepared you for a vast range of other alternatives the decision to pursue a career in legal services is an extremely difficult one.

Private Associations

Citizens in the United States in recent years have begun to view the law as a vehicle for promoting the public interest instead of a tool of special interests. Or one could say that new special interests have evolved to represent groups that have not tended to use the judicial system to protect their rights in the past. No matter which view one takes, the fact remains that more people than ever before are getting involved in the legal process.

Some of the areas that have aroused considerable interest are consumer protection, environmental law, land use planning, communications, governmental responsiveness, and ethics. Whenever a group of concerned citizens attempts to assert or defend its rights, lawyers are likely to be involved.

Funding for public interest representation has come to a certain extent through the government and charitable sources, but a large part of the burden has been shouldered by the citizens who are represented.

Just as in legal services, public interest law may involve legal advice and representation or law reform. Groups may secure someone in a law firm to represent them, hire a staff counsel, or rely on volunteers to handle their legal work.

Lack of government support, tighter foundation budgets, and economic woes on the part of ordinary citizens have combined to make good-paying jobs in the public interest field scarce and competition fierce. But for persons willing to make the commitment, the need is there. It is exciting to view the significant numbers of good law students who find the problems impossible to ignore.

Non-Traditional Alternatives

Increasingly, traditional types of practice are to be found in areas that have not employed lawyers in the past. Among these new employer groups are such organizations as foundations, labor unions, trade associations, bar associations, universities, consulting firms, and other organizations that have found that having a lawyer on staff is sound business.

The phenomenon of lawyers in nonlegal positions emerged without fanfare. Apparently it grew out of the need of business and industry to have people with legal training in strategic positions, where potential problems could be spotted long before they became major issues.

For example, an advertising account executive with legal training can alert management and the agency's counsel that certain ads under preparation pose probable legal problems long before they reach media distribution. A contract administrator with legal training can more easily spot the failure of a supplier to meet contract specifications long before expensive problems and delays develop.

Many law students either do not want to practice law upon graduation or have serious questions as to whether they would really enjoy doing so. Unfortunately for these students, placement offices often are not geared to handle their needs because the great majority of law students seek legally-related jobs.

Students should consider nonlegal career options if they have made a careful self-analysis, and really want to go that route. By the same token, students should not refrain from considering nonlegal employment just because a majority of their cohorts choose legal alternatives. There are literally thousands of job titles recognized by the Bureau of Labor Statistics. The terms *nonlegal* and *law-related* refer to positions where legal training is a special asset. Although not practicing law per se, law graduates, by virtue of their legal training, may have a distinct advantage over other applicants in nonlegal positions, and find their knowledge of the law to be a valuable asset on the job. Pre-legal training combined with a legal education may provide special qualifications for young attorneys. If additional training or experience would be necessary in order to be considered for such positions, students should not hesitate to obtain these qualifications.

The first group of nonlegal jobs includes that broad category of things we generally term as business. The most logical place to go to get information would seem to be a business school placement office. This is both true and untrue. First there are a number of areas where the law school has some information. Secondly, business placement offices may be unwilling or unable to assist law students.

As in the case of legal jobs, there is an over representation of corporate giants, conglomerates, and so on, forcing those who would choose a small business enterprise to look on their own. Some of the areas in which law students have expressed an interest include the following:

- Accounting
- Banking
- Entrepreneurship

- Insurance
- Business planning
- Management
- Real estate
- Securities
- Titles companies
- Systems analysis

There are many nonlegal government positions for which legal training would is an asset, including federal, state, and local positions. Federal jobs can be investigated through the *U.S. Civil Service Commission* and the *U.S. Government Organization Manual.*

For state employment, try to contact a placement office in that state or write the governor's office. Due to the myriad of local governments and special districts, local jobs must be researched individually. Government-related work includes:

- Research
- Land use planning
- Police work
- Administration
- Politics, campaigning

Communications is yet another area where lawyers are apt to do well with their verbal and cognitive skills. In fact, a perusal of the biographies of famous authors will show that a significant number were or are attorneys. Here, as in the education field, specialized training may be necessary. Communication includes:

- Advertising
- Creative writing
- Journalism
- Law-related publication
- Radio-Television
- Film

The graduate who pursues a nonlegal path, however, must realize that there may be no return. As nonlegal skills are acquired, and as the distance from day-to-day legal practice increases, it becomes virtually impossible to match current earnings with salary levels of law graduates in their first positions.

Professionally speaking, it is back to square one. There are exceptions, but no return remains the general pattern for nonlegal careers. For more information on this topic, see the ABA Career Series book *Non-Legal Careers for Lawyers* by Frances Utley and Gary A. Munneke.

The Hiring Process

Law students often ask what employers want in a candidate. This question underlies most student concerns about resumes, interviews, preferred courses of study, and the like. Since no two lawyers are alike, and different types of organizations have different hiring practices and needs, it is difficult to generalize about what they want. The hiring process, however, is not without clues.

The Need

An employer must first be sure that the work load in the office requires additional assistance. The exception is when qualifications of an individual trigger a response to needs not fully recognized by the employer. A job seeker could, for example, convince an employer that his or her special qualifications could match unmet needs in the organization. Generally speaking, however, if an employer does not feel that additional assistance in the office is essential, it will not initiate the hiring process.

Recruitment Costs

Few law students realize the economic costs to a firm of hiring an associate, but employers must evaluate the economic considerations before deciding to hire a new lawyer. One consideration, for example, is where to put a new lawyer. The cost of office space is considerable. In 1990, standard office space in the major metropolitan areas was renting for from $30 to $50 per square foot per year. An area of 100 square feet for a desk and chair will cost a firm $3,000-$5,000. This figure does not include the cost of furnishing and maintaining the new lawyer's space, or the additional space required for secretarial support.

There may simply not be space available to to accommodate an additional person. It is not unheard of for new lawyers to find themselves occupying the library, sharing space with several others, or even working in a basement file storage area. An employer knows that this is far from ideal, but sometimes the work demands precedence over the environment.

Not only does the new lawyer occupy space, but also he or she requires support services. Secretaries, legal assistants, file clerks, billing functions - all take up precious room. It may be possible to absorb a new lawyer into an office without additions to the support staff but if any are necessary, an employer must plan for space for these individuals as well.

The list continues. The costs of such office equipment as telephones, typewriters, computers and software, dictating units, and file cabinets must be included. In 1990, annual overhead costs for a new associate, not including salary, may run from $30,000 to $80,000. A simple formula many employers use in estimating the cost of adding an associate to the office is called the rule of thirds. Salary represents one third of the cost, overhead counts one third, and one third of the expense is eaten up in partner training and review time.

No matter what the size of the law office may be, the decision to add an associate will also involve recruiting costs. It may cost a firm $50,000 to recruit one associate. If ten lawyers are to be employed by a larger firm and extensive on-campus recruitment is undertaken, the direct and indirect costs of such a program can amount to $500,000 or more. The major part of this expense is from partner and associate time involved in interviewing.

Even the smallest office, planning to add only one associate, faces a substantial investment of time and money in the recruitment process. Every minute of reading resumes, making phone calls, writing letters, and interviewing candidates is time away from client work. It may seem more convenient for you that the employer come to your campus, but if the number of people from your school interviewing an employer is small, it may be much more cost effective for the employer to interview at the law office.

Another consideration is the per capita cost of hiring a new lawyer. If a 100-lawyer firm adding ten lawyers invests $50,000 per person hired, or $500,000 total, that cost divided by all the lawyers on staff equals $5,000 per lawyer. The sole practitioner who makes the same investment to recruit one associate will have to take $50,000 out of his or her wallet. In practical terms, small firms are less likely than large ones to use campus interviews, summer clerkship programs, or high starting salaries as a recruiting strategy.

A final consideration is the cost of losing an associate. If you and the firm decide to part company, the loss is more easily absorbed by a large firm which generally anticipates a certain turnover among associates. But for the small firm, losing someone after spending time and money on recruiting and training can be disastrous. There is a pressure to make the right decision the first time. At the same time the small firm may lack the resources to conduct a thorough recruiting program.

Your best strategy is to let the small firm know you want to work for them. Be willing to assume some of your own interviewing costs, and expect to make less money when you start. Work really hard during the first year of employment—it is more critical to do this in the small firm than in the large firm.

Economics of Hiring

In addition to recruiting costs and overhead costs, many other economic factors go into the decision to hire a new lawyer. Learning a few basic principles of law firm management will help you understand the very different hiring patterns for different employers.

First, hiring is an economic decision for a law firm. If you as a new lawyer do not carry your weight, your stay with your employer may be brief.

Second, it is easier for a large firm to predict its needs in advance, recruit effectively, and bear the cost of training new associates than it is for a small firm or sole practitioner.

Third, understanding the economics of law firm hiring will give you an advantage in the interviewing process, whether it be on campus or in the law office.

The income in a private law office is determined by fees charged to clients and the decision to hire is inextricably linked to that fact. The amount of the fees and the method of their calculation determine the compensation that the employer is able to offer.

In most firms, all the lawyers in the office who work on a client's case keep time records. Each lawyer will have an assigned dollar rate which the client will be charged. Charges are also recorded for legal assistants and secretarial work, photocopying, telephone calls, travel time, court time, and so on. Normally, the client will be sent an itemized bill on a monthly basis for all of the charges incurred.

How the hourly billing charges for lawyers are calculated is of primary interest to you. Partner rates are based on such factors as who developed the business, who did the work, and the degree of expertise required. Associate rates are based on quite different factors, and these are more important for your consideration.

Usually hourly rates for associates, determined by the number of years they have been admitted to the bar, will be fairly uniform for associates at the same level within an office. Figured into the hourly rate is the associate's salary, share of overhead, employee benefits, and other costs that cannot be charged directly to a client.

To keep track of time spent on various client matters, each law firm employee keeps detailed time records, usually expressed in six minute units or 0.1 hour. Phone calls, photocopying charges, and similar expenses are also noted. Many associates are unpleasantly surprised to find that the law office expects 1,700 annual billable hours from the associate, and some firms actually require associates to bill over 2,000 hours each year.

Those 1,700 billable hours may not seem extreme if you assume that you will work just 34 hours a week for 50 weeks a year in order to meet that criterion. Unfortunately, much of your time will not be billable. A beginning lawyer may take 24 hours to draft a contract, for example, while an experienced associate could have completed the matter in 8 hours. The client cannot be charged for the additional 16 needed by the new attorney nor time spent by a partner or senior associate redrafting the contract if the beginning lawyer's work was deficient.

Furthermore, associates cannot bill time spent on administrative tasks, training, evaluation, or talking informally to colleagues. In actuality, many associates discover that they can bill little more than one-half of the time spent in the office to client matters. Thus, to bill 34 hours to clients each week, an associate may spend 65-70 hours in the office or 11–12 hours per day six days per week.

What does this have to do with hiring? If the average law practice grows at a typical rate such as 7% per year, and the average annual billable hours amount to 1500 per attorney, a sole practitioner will have 105 new billable hours of work in a year. A firm of ten will have 1,050 such hours, and a firm of one hundred, 10,500 hours. The predicted number of new billable hours will determine how many new lawyers can be hired in a given year.

You are unlikely to bill any hours to a client during your first day with a firm. During your first year, you may bill less than 1,000 hours, and the costs of hiring, training, and supporting may exceed by far the income you bring into the firm. As time passes you will become more productive, and at some point you will produce as much as you cost to keep. After another period, your income (for the firm) will recoup the losses from your first few months. Then there will be a period of clear profit for the firm before you are made partner and begin to "share in the pie."

Thus, a ten-lawyer firm with its 1,000 growth hours ought to be able to hire you. The 100-lawyer firm will be able to hire you and nine classmates. For the sole practitioner with only 105 new hours, however, the only way to hire you is to have a phenomenal growth year or to take the money out of his or her personal income to pay your salary.

Firms of ten lawyers or more can predict their needs. Smaller firms usually cannot—at least not a year or more in advance. Therefore, smaller firms are destined to be more sporadic in their hiring.

Corporate and Government Budgets

Corporate or government employers face a situation substantially different from that found in the private practice of law. A budget for a corporate legal department or government agency is established considerably in advance of the year it is to cover. The degree of involvement of the general counsel in the budgeting process varies from organization to organization. Each employer must cover the cost of any new additions to the staff within the budget guidelines. Although there may be procedures available for supplementary appropriations in emergency situations, frequently these funds are not disbursed liberally.

The corporate legal department or government agency must incorporate its budget for new staff into the total organizational budget. The larger the organization, the more precise is the structure needed to provide equity for all. That fact may curtail the freedom of the general counsel to add lawyers to the staff or offer higher salaries than the budget dictates. For this reason salary bargaining by the candidate is seldom a practical approach in the corporate or government environment.

Work Assignment

Assigning cases in a law firm is a delicate balancing act. The client obviously prefers a senior partner to be visible. While having an associate do the work is more economical for the firm, a partner or senior associate must review the new attorney's work until an office has complete confidence in the beginning associate's work. This subtle factor leads many law firms to conclude that no associate carries his or her own weight for at least two years.

Another factor in the selection of an associate to work on a particular project is the lawyer's expertise. For example, an associate assigned to an environmental case will acquire a good deal of knowledge about the issues involved. When a similar case arises in the office, it will be more economical to assign the case to the same associate to make use of the knowledge already gained.

This process of gaining expertise by accretion produces de facto specialists in the law. New lawyers should be cognizant about how work assignments will affect their present value to the firm as well as long-term marketability.

Productivity

Abraham Lincoln said: "A lawyer's time is his stock in trade." Productivity or the amount of work accomplished in one hour is a major concern to the employers of new lawyers. Compensation rates for new attorneys today are much higher than those in the past and current rates are in turn reflected in the fees charged to clients. An employer cannot be satisfied simply because a goal of 1,700 billable hours was attained by an associate. At what rate was the work produced? What revenue was realized from the work? What was the caliber of the work product? To what degree was a learning process involved? How efficiently were information sources tapped?

The productivity concept, which came out of experience in industry, has subtly but radically changed the evaluation of the work of lawyers. Some law students find it distressing to think that such pedestrian concerns as productivity and profitability seem paramount to service ideals in a professional setting. Unfortunately this aspect of practice is unavoidable. Productivity also exercises an important influence on many employment decisions.

For example, an older law school graduate who has developed special skills in a nonlegal area, is still an unskilled lawyer at the beginning of practice, and will require training and experience to become productive. It is difficult, if not impossible, for an employer to offer such a lawyer the same kind of salary he or she earned in the nonlegal position. On the other hand, if an individual's pre-legal skills have direct application to the law firm's practice, the associate's learning curve will be accelerated and productivity increased. In some cases, therefore, the law student with more work experience may have an advantage.

While a special background may permit rapid growth and lead quickly to the compensation levels of more experienced attorneys, there is still a possibility of economic hardship for the individual in transition from another field to law. That is probably why many experienced people use their legal education to enhance their positions in their current fields of expertise rather than starting all over again as a new lawyer.

Hiring a Lawyer vs. a Legal Assistant

The question of productivity also is important in an area that has troubled law students for the last two decades: the imagined competition with legal assistants for available positions. Actually, in the mind of the employer, the choice of a candidate involves an evaluation of current productivity as related to future productivity.

An employer who hires a legal assistant hires someone who will perform a limited number of specific duties over a substantial period of time. On the other hand, if the choice is made to hire a law graduate, the employer anticipates that the graduate will develop skills and assume an ever-increasing range of legal responsibilities. While a law graduate can perform the duties of a legal assistant, a legal assistant can never perform all the duties implied by the term lawyer.

Conclusion

In deciding whether ot hire and whom to hire, an employer looks at basic issues such as evaluating the work that needs to be done, both now and in the future, and the matters of space, support services, training, and productivity.

During the interview process and while working, you should be sensitive to these business aspects of practicing law. Your employer may not expect a new lawyer to know a lot about the economics of law practice, but will appreciate your being willing to learn.

Clerkships

Clerkships are increasingly being used as a recruitment device. Second year clerkships are more common and easily obtained than first year clerkships for law students.

Whether it is a part-time or summer clerkship, the student has an opportunity to see firsthand how a law office operates, the interaction of office personalities, the degree of organization, and many other factors. In turn, the employer can see the student in action on a day-to-day basis and better assess the individual's abilities than in a single interview. Thus, everyone can avoid the problems and miseries that can occur because of a hiring mistake based on too little contact.

If it is impossible to obtain a clerkship experience because you are otherwise employed full-time, consider whether you can demonstrate your qualifications to a potential employer through volunteer work, piecemeal research, or law school externship programs. The idea is to create situations where the employer can observe your work directly.

Who Decides?

Unlike corporations where personnel managers are permanent fixtures, the hiring partner or a hiring committee in a law firm is appointed by the senior management to serve for only a limited period of time. Thus, it may be difficult, if not impossible, for the graduate to determine where the hiring decision finally rests.

In some cases, associates are part of the hiring committee. For larger firms, the recruitment administrator will be included in the hiring process. And in many small firms, the hiring decision is actually a group effort.

Difficult as it may seem to sort out, you should strive to identify the individuals who will be deciding your fate. Questions about salary and benefits, as well as other factors to be negotiated, are best directed to those responsible for hiring decisions.

20
The Real World

The world of work, often referred to in law school as "the real world" (as if law school were some kind of fantasy world!), is complex, varied, and frequently confusing to the job hunter. Careful preparation beforehand can do much to make the trek through the job search minefield less treacherous.

This section deals with four areas which should interest the job seeker: (1) the distribution of lawyers, (2) future trends, (3) employment and salary patterns, and (4) hiring issues for women and minorities.

Distribution of Lawyers

The choice of a place to practice law may depend on where jobs are available. Some places are glutted with lawyers, giving rise to the view that the job market is tight everywhere.

This simply is not true; some areas are very short of attorneys. San Francisco, Boston, and other large cities which are attractive geographically or have a number of law schools tend to be crowded. Smaller cities, with only one law school may have the same problem.

Research indicates that a population/attorney (P/A) ratio of 1000:1 is normal, excluding commercial activity. Increased commercial activity will reduce the ratio substantially because business seems to increase the amount of legal work. Thus, major cities typically have a ratio of around 250:1 or less. An interesting question is: how many lawyers can the market bear? Chart 24 indicates the ratio for various population categories.

Chart 24
Lawyer Population Ratios

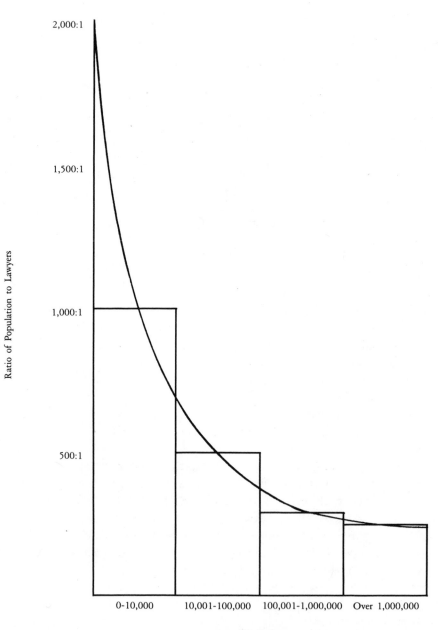

Future Demand for Legal Services

In what fields will the biggest demand of lawyers be in the next twenty years? Where will lawyers be needed in the future? Will there be too many lawyers? Too few? These and similar questions arise every day.

The medical profession has a much easier time predicting future demand. Medical patients, unlike lawyers' clients, are always individuals. Consequently, it is possible to take the projected population of the country, the frequency of various physical affiliations, and even projected problem areas that may arise, and come within a reasonable estimate of the demand for medical personnel.

For lawyers, a similar estimate would begin with determining what the client mix of the future might be—individuals, small businesses, corporations, government and others—and the kinds and qualities of legal services they will require. Then you would need to predict what legislative and judicial decisions will be made in the future. Of course, it is more difficult to foresee what Congress and the Supreme Court will do, let alone 50 state and hundreds of local legislatures and lower courts.

Now add into the mix the entire realm of economics. The real estate market goes sour, and suddenly property attorneys face difficult times. The economy takes a downturn, and bankruptcy attorneys do extremely well. Research and development programs by corporations are cut back, and patent attorneys are in oversupply.

Such economic factors touch upon all areas of practice. Fortunately, their impact is usually for a relatively short period of time. But that very uncertainty is the reason every new lawyer should remain flexible in his or her career thinking.

It is no easier to predict where future developments will lead to increased needs for legal services. Who could have predicted in 1960 the opening up of the entirely new field we now know as environmental law? What impact will result from the "greying" of America? Whole new areas of practice may develop within the span of your career to offer challenges no one can now foresee.

Even new uses for old laws may arise. One young lawyer clerked with an elderly attorney who was a specialist in gold-mining law as it was promulgated in 1876. Naturally, the younger lawyer learned much about the field, but he found clients in his own practice had no use for the knowledge he had acquired while clerking. When individuals and corporations later began seeking to file claims for uranium deposits that had to be mined under the old laws, the lawyer was suddenly inundated with a demand that had not existed six months before.

In addition to changes in the economy and profession during your career, there may be political changes which will have an impact on you and your goals. Many lawyers have been subjected to government hiring freezes or to a change in a political party that wiped out the positions they held.

Changes on the professional level may have substantial impact on the future demand for lawyers. Among the more likely of these are the increase in law office automation, legal assistants, affiliated or subsidiary business ventures by law firms in nonlegal fields, de facto specialization, branch office and multi-jurisdictional practice, mandatory continuing legal education, and concerns about professional competency.

Even though many changes cannot be predicted, it is essential that you monitor current events and developments in the profession throughout your career so you are not caught completely unawares. In so unpredictable a world, "adaptability" and "flexibility" become career watchwords that no young lawyer can afford to overlook.

Future Practice Trends

Who will be your clients? The development of neighborhood clinics, group legal services, law stores, and insurance plans will bring substantial demands from middle income clients for a variety of services. Increased appropriations for the federally funded legal services have provided greater access for individuals in low income groups to seek legal assistance in civil and, increasingly, criminal cases.

Some changes will occur in the areas of advertising, specialization, the self-regulation of the legal profession, and questions of competency and responsibilities for giving advice. The adversary system is not immune from the evolution: new methods of dispute resolution are being tried. Old concepts of how trials should be held are being challenged. Arbitration agreements and no-fault laws all lead many to believe that the function of the courts will change dramatically in coming years. Moreover, the Model Rules of Professional Conduct recognize that the lawyers act as counselors and negotiators as well as advocates.

Within the legal profession, the growth of really large law firms with several branches is redefining the law firm pyramid. Assembly-line procedures and other office management improvements, including the use of paralegals is helping to reserve the lawyer's time for more complicated legal work. The expansion of legal departments of corporations and the employment of more lawyers in governmental agencies are affecting the traditional attorney-client relationship. These organizational changes are touching every important activity of the individual practitioner and the environment in which he works.

Why are changes occurring? Many, of course, are brought about by forces within the profession, but often lawyers have waited to *react* to external pressures. Because the profession has changed and will continue to change at such a rapid rate, it is important for students to critically reflect and examine the new directions their profession is taking as well as their role within it if they expect to act as agents of change rather than simply to react to change it occurs.

Employment Patterns

The National Association for Law Placement employment report for each year is based on data from ABA-approved schools. The summary of the 1990 NALP Employment Report in the appendix gives an accurate picture of where graduates go and what they do. Since there will undoubtedly be some differences from school to school, students should check with their individual law schools for a more detailed report or more current data.

Employment statistics do not provide any information about long-term career patterns such as job mobility, or intangibles such as job or career satisfaction. There are over 750,000 licensed attorneys in the United States with some 35,000 new law graduates annually. There are many different career patterns open to all these lawyers. While some are more common than others, the diversity of legal and legally-related jobs is amazing.

Salary Patterns

It may come as no surprise to law students that starting legal salaries have risen along with the cost of everything else. It takes more money to live these days, and recent law graduates feel this as acutely as anyone, especially if they have educational loans to repay.

For potential employers, the question of how much to pay is difficult. Placement directors, frequently hear phrases like "the going rate," "competitive," or "comparable," to determine to some extent by comparison with other employers, but also by using an easy formula. Generally, summer and part-time law clerks can expect to make two-thirds to three-fourths what an employer would pay a newly licensed attorney to go to work. The actual range of these salaries is more like one-half to nine-tenths, but the two-thirds to three-fourths figure is a good rule of thumb, using two-thirds for first-year students, and three-fourths for second-year students. Clerk salaries may be described in terms of hourly, weekly or monthly rates. The highest summer salaries in 1992 are over $1,500 week, and the bottom seems to be very close to minimum wage.

There is no way to escape the escalating cost of hiring legal talent these days. On the other hand, employers must continue to grow to meet the needs of their clients, and many will be willing to compete fiercely to attract the best possible legal talent. Inflation will continue to affect salaries as well, although not as much as during the 1980s. It is worth noting, however, that a law graduate today receives very little more real income than a graduate did in 1969. Check the appendix for a summary of starting salaries for law graduates in 1990.

Women and Minorities

The special problems of women and minority law students in the job market deserve mention. Much of the advice in this book applies equally to men and women, majority and minority law students. That does not mean that all law students will always be treated equally. Nor does it mean that the concerns of all law students are identical.

Although the blatant exclusionary practices that characterized legal hiring in the past have diminished, subtle forms of racism and sexism remain. In fact, many women and minority law students profess concern that discrimination simply has gone underground.

Cases such as *Hishon v. King & Spalding*, 467 U.S. 69,104 S.Ct. 2229, 81 L. Ed.2d 59 (1984), and *Hopkins v. Price Waterhouse*, 737

F. Supp. 1202 (D.D.C. 1990), employers that they are not immune from federal and state employment laws (although many small firms fall below the minimum number of employees to trigger coverage by Title VII of the federal civil rights act). A recent suit, *Ezold v. Wolf Black, Schorr & Solis-Cohen,* continues this tradition of challenging unfair employment practices.

Many law students are reluctant to challenge employment practices they consider improper, or at least they are uneasy about their situation vis-a-vis employers. It is true that women and minority students have special concerns, and they may face career issues that do not impede their majority/male counterparts.

If you have particular questions about their career planning or job search process related to your status as a woman or minority law student, you should discuss these questions with a career counselor at your school. You may also find it useful to share your concerns with fellow students, or to speak with graduates who have completed the job search successfully.

21
Substantive Areas of Practice

No book on career planning and law would be complete without a discussion of substantive fields of practice. As law becomes an increasingly specialized profession, the need to make choices about practice areas will increase.

Law students fall into two major groups when it comes to choosing substantive areas of practice: those who have very definite ideas about their substantive preferences and those who do not.

Students who do have strong preferences often come to law school with such attitudes already formed. They want to practice environmental law, labor law, patent law, criminal law, or some other specific field.

Those who are not so sure about their interest, frequently rank selection of a substantive area of practice below other considerations when they make career choices. These students are often quite flexible about the areas of practice they are willing to consider. Many assume that they can make choices about substantive fields after they leave law school and enter the real world.

Most law firms do not practice in just one field and most lawyers do not limit their practice to just one area. Even lawyers who practice in a discrete specialty often are called upon to deal with other areas of law as they intersect the practitioner's specialty. Unlike those who choose medicine, where a podiatrist may work only with feet or a cardiologist only with hearts, lawyers do not have the luxury of such narrow definition because legal problems seldom arrive in tidy substantive boxes. A client who comes to a lawyer for a will may also bring tax problems, property questions, family law issues, and a variety of other considerations.

Even the names given to substantive practice areas can be deceiving. International law may not mean that you look out of your office window onto the Champs Elysee as much as it means practicing corporate law for multi-national clients rather than domestic clients. Entertainment law may not mean hobnobbing with famous actors and actresses, but rather drafting contracts, leases, and other mundane documents.

A useful discussion of many substantive areas of law would require an entire book. The ABA Career Series publishes a number of different titles covering many of the more popular substantive areas of practice. If you are interested in sports law, entertainment law, natural resources law, or another field covered by the Career Series, you can purchase the appropriate book from the ABA Order Fulfillment Department in the Appendix. See also Munneke, *Careers in Law,* VGM Professional Careers Series (1992).

Certainly, selection of substantive fields of practice is an important consideration not only in terms of your initial career planning, but also in terms of your long term career development. Various economic surveys conducted by bar associations have demonstrated that not all practice areas are equally prestigious, lucrative, or competitive. Neither are all areas equally demanding or stressful. Your earlier work in the area of skills analysis should help you to make decisions about substantive practice areas.

Unfortunately, many students make substantive choices for the wrong reasons. Sometimes students develop an interest in an area of practice because they like the professor who taught the course in law school. Their interest is triggered by the professor's enthusiasm, knowledge, and charisma rather than the actual work involved.

Some students simply fall into an area of practice. They clerk for a lawyer after the first year of law school and work on a few bankruptcy cases over the summer. Armed with this "expertise," they sell themselves to a subsequent employer on the basis of their experience in the bankruptcy field. When they accept a permanent job, they are (surprise!) assigned bankruptcy cases. Pretty soon they are the firm's bankruptcy lawyer. The only problem is that they absolutely hate bankruptcy law.

How do you make choices about substantive practice areas without pinning yourself down? How do you establish priorities about practice areas when you have no earthly idea what lawyers actually do in those areas?

Part of the answer to these questions is that you must simply explore different possibilities. Although you may not make a decision to specialize until you have practiced for several years, or you decide not to specialize at all, you can begin to educate yourself early in law school about various substantive options. While you are still in school, you can begin to narrow the alternatives you are willing to consider.

Since substantive practice areas are often defined by other factors such as geographic location, client needs and, organizational type, as you explore these other questions you will develop insights about a variety of substantive practice areas.

Read as much as you can about what lawyers in different substantive fields do. Talk to as many people as you can: lawyers, professors, classmates, and career service professionals. Explore different possibilities: take the clinical courses in law school, write papers, and look for law-related jobs in areas that interest you.

The technique of conducting information interviews can be particularly helpful in aiding you to form conclusions about what sort of practice interests you. Take notes on your impressions after reading or talking with someone. Try to identify specific skills of lawyers who practice in various specialties and compare these skills to your own. Try to narrow the field of possibilities as your base of knowledge increases. Chart 25 contains a list of substantive practice areas. Go through the list, checking areas that interest you and crossing off areas that absolutely turn you off.

As you proceed through the career choice and job search process add new fields and delete others. If it is possible, try to prioritize your list. This activity, over time, will help you to focus your attention without unduly restricting you.

For those of you who have already made substantive choices, here are a few suggestions. First, give some thought to your reasons for making this particular choice. As mentioned above, many students make choices of specialty for the wrong reasons. Even if you *know* you want to practice criminal law it may make sense to ask yourself in light of what you now know about skills analysis and career planning whether this is the best choice to make.

Second, if you do know what substantive area you want, do everything you can to develop credentials in that area. Take all the courses your law school has to offer. Write papers, gain experience, work for pay or as a volunteer, and find ways to demonstrate your commitment.

Chart 25
Substantive Checklist

Administrative	Human Rights
Admiralty	Immigration
Antitrust	Indian
Appellate	Insurance
Arbitration	Intellectual Property
Aviation	International
Banking	Juvenile
Bankruptcy	Labor
Bond	Land Use
Business	Legal Services
Children	Legislation
Civil	Litigation
Civil Rights	Malpractice
Commercial	Medical
Communications	Mental Health
Computer	Military
Constitutional	Municipal
Construction	Oil and Gas
Consumer	Patent
Contract	Personal Injury
Corporate	Probate
Creditors Rights	Product Liability
Criminal	Property
Defense	Prosecution
Disability	Public
Discrimination	Public Finance
Domestic	Real Estate
Education	Regulated Industries
Elderly	Securities
ERISA	Tax
Employee Benefits	Telecommunications
Employment	Tort
Energy	Toxic Tort
Entertainment	Trade
Environmental	Trademark
Estate	Transactional
Family	Trusts
Finance	Utilities
Food and Drug	Welfare
Fraud	White Collar Crime
Gender	Wills
Government	Women
Health	Zoning
Housing	

Source: National Association for Law Placement

Third, start *now* to develop a network. In one sense, making contacts along substantive lines is relatively easy. Bar associations are often divided according to substantive sections, continuing legal education programs generally have a substantive orientation, directories and law school courses are defined along substantive lines. Even those who choose to be general practitioners have their own section in most bar organizations! Additionally, electronic database searches can be conducted using substantive variables. *NALPline* on *Westlaw* and *Martindale-Hubbell* on *Lexis* permit substantive searching. In short, if you are looking for lawyers who practice criminal law finding them should not be a problem. A *Lexis* or *Westlaw* search of cases in a substantive area will allow you to identify the attorneys of record, whom you can then track down.

While chances are you will probably end up as a specialist in one or two areas of law rather than as a Jack or Jill of all trades, use the time in law school to explore various substantive areas. Keep your options open, but begin to match your particular interests and skills with types of practice that can best use them.

22
Geographical Areas

Much of this book has covered various types of legal employment, from substantive fields of law to various institutional work settings. From time to time the text has obliquely referred to geographic setting as a relevant factor. This chapter takes a closer look at the geography variable.

For some individuals, geographic choice may be the most important element in the career planning process. Many law students are tied to a particular geographic area. They own a house or other property there. They have a working spouse. They have family and contacts in the community. They have an interest or avocation that can be pursued most easily in a particular geographic area.

Many students select a geographic locale for lifestyle reasons. For the most part geographic choices should be factored into your priorities (See Chapter 7). For most of us, geographic choices represent preferences. For some percentage of students, the reasons for particular geographic choice may be so compelling that they represent outside boundaries on the job search. Such parameters will limit inevitably the choices available to you, so try to distinguish strong preferences from inflexible conditions.

The role of your law school in geographic selection is often underestimated. Two-thirds or more of the graduates of virtually every law school in the United States go to work within 250 miles of where they went to law school. This is true of so-called national law schools as well as local ones.

Some of this may be attributed to convenience and the fact that students develop ties to an area when they live there. Some of it may be caused by people selecting law schools in areas where they plan to practice. Much of it is the result of gradual accretion; over the years greater numbers of any school's graduates settle in the region where the school is located, and this in turns expands the opportunities for current graduates. While graduates of nationally prominent law schools may be able to make a move from coast to coast more easily than their counterparts in new or less widely recognized institutions, regionalism is still a reality.

Major Legal Markets

The availability of particular jobs in certain geographic locations is one of the two main considerations in geographic choice. The other, lifestyle, will be covered in the next section.

There are four super-markets for lawyers: New York, Los Angeles, Chicago, and Washington, D.C. The first three of these are the most populous American metropolitan areas. The fourth is the seat of the federal government and attracts a special universe of practitioners.

In addition to these four legal centers, there are a number of other large cities that have leading legal markets. These metropolitan financial or government centers attract and employ large numbers of lawyers.

This suggests a correlation between population and legal activity. In fact, the number of lawyers per capita population tends to decrease as population increases. While the ratio of population to attorneys usually exceeds 1,000:1 in rural county seats, it may be 100:1 or less in the major cities.

In all the leading legal markets, the makeup of the bar is diverse as to organization, substantive practice, and demographic composition. These communities are supported by strong local bar associations, large libraries including those at local law schools, and in many cases a dedicated legal press.

These institutions help to restore some of the cohesiveness that is lost when the attorney population becomes so large that bar members can no longer know all of their fellow lawyers. Such cities frequently have a number of law firms containing more lawyers than can be found in most rural counties in their state.

Secondary Legal Markets

Another group of legal markets include medium-sized cities that have significant lawyer populations and substantial legal activity.

These cities are frequently state capitals, regional commercial centers, and transportation hubs.

The bar in these second-tier cities has frequently lost the camaraderie and cohesiveness associated with small town practice, but may not have developed all of the resources and communication services of the largest cities. The largest firms in these cities frequently approximate the size of medium size firms in the largest metropolitan areas. Law practice and the bar are frequently less diverse than in the first tier legal markets, often reflecting the specific population and economy of region.

Tertiary Markets

Cities which fall within a range of metropolitan population between 100,000 and 500,000 are legal centers within a well-defined geographic area. The economy is frequently dominated by one or several clearly identifiable industries.

In most cases, even the largest firms contain fewer than 50 lawyers, and the bar itself retains some vestiges of a small town legal community. These smaller cities include many state capitals for less populous states, university towns, and business centers in the country. County seats throughout the United States generally under 100,000 population serve as centers of local government and business.

Frequently, the bulk of legal activity in the county is conducted in this city, if only because the courthouse is there. Generally, there is some agricultural economy in the area, as well as some local industry.

Although the practice of law is defined by the population and economy, there are certain common threads that run through law practices in this size town almost anywhere in the United States. The largest firm may contain 20 lawyers or less. The total number of attorneys often will be less than 100.

This means that everyone knows everyone else. A handshake can still bind a business deal. Grievances are frequently handled informally. Reputations are slowly made and quickly lost. Family ties can be as important as legal expertise in developing a clientele.

Lawyers frequently retain a greater degree of the social standing that is sometimes lost in more anonymous urban centers. Their income is often less than it would be in the large cities, but the cost of living is less, and for many people lifestyle considerations more than compensate for the lack of economic advantages.

Small Town and Rural Areas

For lawyers who practice in small towns and rural areas, much of their business involves representing individuals and families. Frequently many of these clients are linked to farming and ranching in some way or another local industry, such as fishing, logging, or tourism.

For these lawyers, going to the county seat may be an excursion. They are frequently on the periphery of the organized bar and may even practice law part-time.

On the other hand, modern technology and the media make it possible for more lawyers to practice outside metropolitan areas. Nationally-known trial lawyer Jerry Spence, for example, practices from a ranch near Jackson Hole, Wyoming.

Suburban Practice

Of the many changes that characterize post-World War II America, none is quite as pervasive as the rise of suburbia. Without discussing the sociological aspects of this phenomenon, the demographic patterns are quite clear. Large numbers of residents of many older cities have abandoned the city center for more pastoral habitats. As newer cities developed, the suburban model became the predominant housing pattern.

In some cases, the suburbs simply assimilated the pre-existing towns and villages. In others, whole new communities blossomed on the sites of farms, ranches and forests. Shopping malls and commercial strips replaced downtown as the nation's number one shopping destination. The U.S. Census Bureau had to invent new categories to categorize the suburban sprawl, i.e.,the Standard Metropolitan Statistical Area (SMSA), and the Consolidated Metropolitan Statistical Area (CMSA). A whole generation of adults grew up in the suburban culture, and, in fact, the chances are extremely good that at some point during your professional career you will make the choice to live as a suburbanite.

The suburbs represent a geographical choice for law students in two different ways. First, there is a geographical option for any lawyer who works in a city: to live in the heart of the city or to live in the suburbs. The tradeoff is often between a house with grass and trees and a formidable daily commute to the city versus the problems and crowds of the urban environment and the relatively easy access to work and cultural events.

While most lawyers in these bedroom communities trundle off to the city each day to work, a significant number practice in the community where they live. Since suburban communities can vary from small towns to cities of several hundred thousand people to vast unincorporated areas, it is difficult to make generalizations about suburban practice. It is in many ways more like small town than big city practice. The clients are basically individuals and small businesses. But unlike the small town that may be a county seat or at least have a distinct identity, the suburban town's identity is merged into both that of its parent city and of its sister suburbs.

First, suburban cities cannot escape their satellite nature. Not only do many of their citizens work in the city, but city newspapers, television stations, and other media and events dominate the culture. The financial and governmental heart of the metropolitan area is inevitably elsewhere. Non–suburban towns and cities seem more like microcosms of larger municipalities. The distinction is hardest to make in towns that pre-existed urban sprawl, especially those on the periphery of the metropolitan area. Second, there is a definite suburban culture that is not small town and is not big city.

The legal business will reflect the particular problems of suburban populations. Courts and administrative agencies are likely to be "downtown." Law offices are more likely to be located in shopping centers and small detached buildings than in large office buildings. The bar will be less cohesive than the small town bar, and lawyers themselves are likely to perceive as much identity with the larger community of lawyers as with the local bar associations.

Conclusion

Making geographical choices can be a complex but enlightening venture if based on careful consideration of how you want to live. Unfortunately, many law students make snap decisions about where they want to practice while they agonize over what to practice.

There is no shortage of demographic information analyzing places to live. There appears to be less information about regional differences in how law is practiced, so you may have to do some research on your own. Local newspapers, information interviews, chambers of commerce brochures, census figures, and other business research data will all prove valuable to you.

23
Where Do I Go From Here?

In the play, *Waiting for Godot,* by Samuel Becket, the two central characters stand, sit, and sleep by the road waiting for Godot, who never comes, to tell them where they should go. The audience learns that the characters must decide for themselves what they are to do or they will stand by the road forever.

So it is with us. No one else can tell us who we are to be, where we are to go, or how we are to get there. We must make educated guesses and go on.

In 1973, the predecessor of this career guide was published by the ABA. The author of that book, *Where Do I Go From Here?,* was Frances Utley, staff director for the ABA's Standing Committee on Professional Utilization and Career Development. She made the following comments about career planning:

Without thought and planning regarding career choices, the lawyer is likely to become a cork bobbing on this ocean of change rather than a skilled oarsman directing his craft toward a specific objective. No one enters the legal profession by chance. A conscious choice was made to undertake the study of law, so each comes to the practice of his profession with individual ideals, goals, hopes and dreams. Over the years the lawyer will be subject to many economic and social factors over which he has no control. His profession will certainly change and adapt to meet new demands upon it. To achieve his own aspirations, whether because of or in spite of these factors, career planning will be a must.

More important, however, are four specific facts of life concerning the profession of today and tomorrow which now make career planning a necessity. The first is the expanded span of professional life each lawyer anticipates-for most it will be at least forty years. That's a long time.

Viewing the changes in society plus the changes within the profession which have been accomplished till now, it is apparent that you cannot leave future career development to mere chance. It will be necessary to adapt to changes. Choices will have to be made. A sense of direction will be vital to challenge the span of the years.

The second factor is that the lawyer is not a duplicate of the business executive. The shelves of libraries are crammed with volumes directing the career planning of business executives. Many are excellent, yet a review of their contents reinforces the impression that the lawyer has special needs in career planning by the very reason of his professional stature.

The businessman is created by capital and/or ability. For him there is no required course of training, no examination to qualify him for the exercise of his duties, and no supervision by his fellows of his methods of conducting his business. Yet all of these are basic facts of daily life for the lawyer.

The law is a profession. As such, it involves a commitment to service in the public interest. At the same time it is a service by which more than 350,000 of our nation's citizens make their living. For lawyer this often means a complexity of career choices unknown to the businessman. Choosing the most impressive title and the largest paycheck does not necessarily satisfy the lawyer's sense of professional commitment.

The third factor bearing on the need for career planning today is the range of choice available to the industrial lawyer within the profession. This range includes not only the various types of practice over and above the more traditional forms such as private practice, corporate employment and government service, but an ever-growing number of areas where a lawyer's services are found to be not only valuable, but necessary. In addition, even within the more standardized types of practice, there are ever-changing and developing new areas of concentration or specialization.

Today when a lawyer chooses to render these services within the traditional patterns, he does so by choice, not because these are the only forms available. Even a brief glance at the future indicates that this range of choice is expanding, not contracting. In today's world and tomorrow's, the lawyer who just "lets it happen" doesn't do right by himself or his profession.

There is a fourth, and very personal, reason for career planning. No one enters the legal profession by chance. A conscious choice was made to undertake the study of law, so each comes to the practice of his profession with individual ideals, goals, hopes and dreams. Over the years the lawyer will be subject to many economic and social factors over which he has no control. His profession will certainly change and adapt to meet new demands upon it. To achieve his own aspirations, whether because of or in spite of these factors, career planning will be a must.

Frances Utley's words ring as true today as they did in 1973, when I read them as a senior in law school. The legal profession has changed so dramatically in the two decades since those words were written. These changes in the profession have, in turn, transformed the way lawyers and law students look for jobs.

At the same time many things have not changed. Large law firms still come to campus in their hunt for the always illusive "top ten percent." Students will face the same pressures in law school under the same challenges to make sound career decisions.

But the fundamental techniques of career planning, and personal marketing have not changed, even if the market itself and the tools to reach it have. And the need for planning is more obvious than ever.

It's funny, but the same question they asked you in kindergarten, "What do you want to be when you grow up?" perplexes the law school senior. It may be a question you have to answer several different times during the span of your professional life.

Compounding the difficulty, the choices involve a number of different factors. These have been presented in the course of this book in different ways. Essentially, however, the career choice and job search processes implicate considerations involving eight distinct but overlapping concerns. These are legal skills, professional values, type of position, type of organization, substantive specialty, type of services rendered, geographic location, and personal lifestyle. The interplay of these variables offers infinite variety to the legal professional.

But choices present their own issues. How do we know when we are making the right choices? Will our choice make us happy?

If there has been one central theme in this book, it is that most of us can do a better job of making decisions about our lives. We may not be able to eliminate the risk of making a bad choice, but we can reduce it. And while we may not be able to guarantee our future happiness, we can improve our chances of finding it.

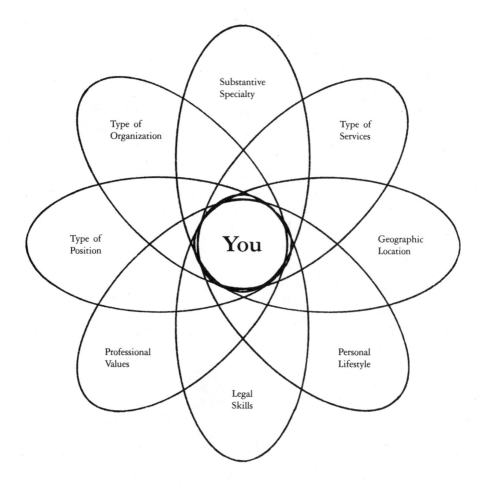

Exploring Careers in Law

The legal profession today is rapidly changing and so are the many different areas of practice within it. The ABA Career Series allows you to examine various fields of law, weighing the advantages and disadvantages of each before you choose a career path.

Use the order form below to indicate which books in the Career Series you would like to order.

Order Form

American Bar Association
Order Fulfillment 511
750 North Lake Shore Drive
Chicago, IL 60611

Quantity	Title	LSD Price	Regular Price	Total
_____	The Legal Career Guide (527-0035)	$12.95	$14.95	_____
_____	Careers in Natural Resources (527-0025)	$9.95	$14.95	_____
_____	Careers in Labor Law (527-0026)	$9.95	$14.95	_____
_____	Now Hiring: Government Jobs (527-0034)	$9.95	$14.95	_____
_____	Nonlegal Careers (527-0028)	$11.95	$16.95	_____
_____	Careers in Sports Law (527-0033)	$9.95	$14.95	_____
_____	Careers in Entertainment Law (527-0032)	$9.95	$14.95	
_____	How to Start and Build a Law Practice (511-0293)	$19.95	$39.95	_____
_____	Careers in Civil Litigation (527-0031)	$9.95	$14.95	_____
		Handling Charge		$3.95
			Total	_____

____ Check or money order enclosed

____ MasterCard   Card Number _____

____ Visa   Exp. Date _____

                       Signature _____

Name _____

Company or School _____

Address _____

City _____

State _____ Zip _____

A phone number will speed your order if we need to contact you:

     (___)_____

30-day money back guarantee if not fully satisfied.

Bibliography

This bibliography includes selected titles that supplement the basic information in *The Legal Career Guide*. It does not purport to be a comprehensive listing of the literature on legal careers, which is always growing and changing. Several good bibliographies appear in the books *Lawyers in Transition, Changing Jobs* and *After Law School*. In addition, NALP and many law school placement offices publish bibliographic information.

Research on legal careers is a process of digging that almost defies cataloguing. At the same time, some books can be characterized as fundamental. Each of the titles here listed provides unique insights into topics covered in this book.

This bibliography includes primarily books of recent vintage with practical value to law students. The bibliography is divided into several sections. Each title is listed once in the bibliography, in the section where it is most relevant, although it may serve as a useful resource in other sections as well.

A. Jobs and Careers

Arron, Deborah L, *Running from the Law: Why Good Lawyers Are Getting Out of the Law*, Niche Press, Seattle, WA (1989).

Bell, Susan J., ed, *Full Disclosure : Do You Really Want to Be a Lawyer?* Peterson's Guides, Princeton, NJ (1989).

Kanarek, Carol, ed., *Changing Jobs: A Handbook for Lawyers*, American Bar Association, Chicago (1988).

Peck, M. Scott, *The Road Less Travelled.*

Terkel, Studs, *Working*, Random House, New York (1974).

B. Lawyers and The Legal Profession

Abel, Richard, *American Lawyers*, Oxford, New York (1989).

Curran, Barbara, *The Lawyers Statistical Report: A Statistical Profile of the United States Legal Profession in the 1980s*, American Bar Foundation, Chicago (1985); Supplement (1988).

Curran, Barbara, *Legal Needs of the Public*, American Bar Foundation, Chicago (1977).

Feferman, Richard N., *Building Your Firm with Associates*, American Bar Association, Law Practice Management Section, Chicago (1988).

Flood, John, *The Legal Profession in the United States*, American Bar Foundation, Chicago (1985).

Freund, James C., *Lawyering: A Realistic Approach to Legal Practice*, Law Journal Press, New York (1981).

Goulden, Joseph, *The Million Dollar Lawyers*, Putnam, New York (1977).

Greene, Robert Michael, *Making Partner*, American Bar Association, Law Practice Management Section, Chicago (1991).

Heinz, John P., and Edward O. Laumann, *Chicago Lawyers: The Social Structure of the Bar*, Russell Sage Foundation (1982).

Hildebrant, Bradford W., *The Successful Law Firm*, Law and Business/Horcourt Brace Jovanovich, New York (1984).

Hoffman, Paul, *Lions in the 80's.*

Johnston, Quinton, and Dan Hopson Jr., *Lawyers and their Work*, Bobbs Merril, (1967).

Kanter, Arnold, *The Secret Files of Stanley J. Fairweather*, Swallow Press, Chicago (1980).

Magness, Michael K., and Carolyn Wehmann, eds., *Your New Lawyer: The Legal Employers Complete Guide to Recruitment, Development and Management*, 2nd ed., American Bar Association, Law Practice Management Section, Chicago (1992).

Mayer, Martin, *The Lawyers*, Greenwood Press, Westport, CT (1987).

Munneke, Gary A., *Materials and Cases on Law Practice Management*, West, St. Paul MN (1991).

O'Neil, Suzanne B., and Catherine G. Spakman, *From Law School to Law Practice*, ALI-ABA, Philadelphia (1989).

Spangler, Eve, *Lawyers for Hire: Salaried Professionals at Work*, Yale University Press, New Haven, CT (1986).

Stevens, Marc, *Power of Attorney: The Rise and Fall of the Great Law Firms*, McGraw Hill, New York (1987).

Stewart, James B., *The Partners: Americas Most Powerful Law Firms*, Simon & Schuster, New York (1983).

White, Christine, and Abbie W. Thorner, *Managing the Recruitment Process*, Law & Business/Horcourt Brace Jovanovich, New York (1982).

Zemans, Frances Kahn, and Victor Rosenblum, *The Making of a Public Profession*, American Bar Foundation, Chicago (1981).

C. The Career Planning Process
Bolles, Richard, *The Three Boxes of Life and How to Get Out of Them*, Ten Speed Press, Berkeley, CA (1987).

Bolles, Richard, *What Color Is Your Parachute*, Ten Speed Press, Berkeley, CA (1991).

Byers Mark, Don Samuelson and Gordon Williamson, *Lawyers in Transition*, The Barkley Co., Natick, MA (1988).

Cardozo, Arlene Rossen, *Sequencing: Having It All But Not All at Once*, Atheneum, New York (1988).

Erikson, Eric, *Identity and the Life Cycle*, W.W. Norton, New York (1980).

Figler, Howard, *The Complete Job Search Handbook*, Henry Holt, New York (1988).

Grief, Barrie S., M.D., and Preston K. Minter, M.D., *Tradeoffs: Executive, Family and Organizational Life*, New American Library, New York (1981).

Hall Francise S. and Douglas T. Hall, *The Two Career Couple*, Addison-Wesley Publishing, Reading, MA (1979).

Holland, John L., *Making Vocational Choices: A Theory of Careers*, Prentice Hall, Englewood Cliffs, NJ (1973).

Isachsen, Olaf, *Working Together: A Personality Centered Approach to Management*, New World Management Press, Coronado, CA (1988).

Levinson, Daniel, J., et al, *The Seasons of a Man's Life*, Ballantine Books, New York (1979).

Scheele, Adele, *Skills for Success*, Ballantine Books, New York (1981).

Sheehy, Gail, *Passages*, Bantam Books, New York (1977).

Sheehy, Gail, *Pathfinders*, Bantam Books, New York (1982).

Sher, Barbara, *Wishcraft: How to Get What You Really Want*, Ballantine Books, New York (1979).

D. The Job Search
Allen, Jeffrey G. and Jess Gorkin, *Finding the Right Job at Midlife*, Simon & Schuster, New York (1985).

Feiden, Karyn and Linda Marks, *Negotiating Time: New Scheduling Options in the Legal Profession*, New Ways Press (1986).

Fisher, Roger, and William Ury, *Getting to Yes*, Houghton Mifflin, Boston (1981).

Fox, Marcia, *Putting Your Degree to Work*, W.W. Norton, New York (1988).

Good, C. Edward, *Does Your Resume Wear Blue Jeans? The Book on Resume Preparation*, Blue Jeans Press, Charlottesville, VA (1989).

Good, C. Edward, *Does Your Resume Wear Apron Strings?*, Blue Jeans Press, Charlottesville, VA (1989).

How to Get a Job in the Federal Government, U.S. Government Printing Office, Washington, D.C. (1981).

Irish, Richard, *Go Hire Yourself an Employer*, Doubleday, New York (1990).

Jackson, Tom, *Guerilla Tactics in the Job Market*, New York (1988).

Lathrop Richard, *Who's Hiring Who?*, Ten Speed Press Berkeley (1990).

Malloy, John, *Dress for Success*, Warner Books, New York (1976).

Malloy John, *The Woman's Dress for Success Book*, Warner Books, New York (1976).

Medley, H. Anthony, *Sweaty Palms - The Neglected Art of Being Interviewed*, Lifetime Learning Publications, Belmont, CA (1978).

Pettus, Theodore, *One-on-One*, Random House, New York (1981).

Raelin, Joseph A., *The Salaried Professional: How to Make the Most of Your Career*, Prager Publishers, New York (1984).

Ryan, Joseph, *Stating Your Case: How to Interview for a Job as a Lawyer*, West, St. Paul, MN (1982).

Stern, Barbara B, *Is Networking for You?*, Prentice Hall, New York (1981).

Yate, John Martin, *Knock 'Em Dead*, Bob Adams, Inc, Boston (1988).

E. Women and Minorities

Couric, Emily, *Women Lawyers: Perspectives on Success*, Prentice Hall, Law and Business, New York (1984).

Espstein, Cynthia Fuchs, *Women in Law*, Andros Press, Doubleday, New York (1983).

Henry, Margaret, and Anne Jordan, *The Managerial Woman*, Doubleday, New York, (1983).

Killoughey, Donna, ed., *Breaking Traditions*, American Bar Association, Law Practice Management Section, Chicago (1992).

Machlowitz, Marilyn, *Advanced Career Strategies for Women*, Career Trade Publications, Boulder, CO (1986).

Nierenberg, Juliet and Irene S. Ross, *Women and the Art of Negotiating*, Simon & Schuster, New York, (1985).

Segal, Geraldine R., *Blacks in the Law*, University of Pennsylvania Press, Philadelphia, PA (1983).

Symposium, *Black Law Journal*, Volume 7, No. 1 (1980).

Williams, Marshall L., *National Directory of Black Law Firms*, McWilliams Publishing, Philadelphia, PA (1983).

F. Legal Career Options

Aron, Nan, *Liberty and Justice for All: Public Interest Law in the 1980's and Beyond*, Westview Press, Boulder, CO (1988).

BAR/BRI DIGEST, BAR/BRI (annual).

Becoming an Environmental Professional, CEIP, Inc., Washington, D.C. (1989).

Boyer, Richard, and David Savageau, *The Peaces Rated Almanac,* Prentice Hall, New York (1989).

CEIP Fund, *The Complete Guide to Environmental Careers,* Ireland Press, Washington, D.C. (1989).

DeBroff, Stacy M, *Public Interest Job Search Guide,* Harvard Law School Cambridge, MA (1991).

Employment Report and Salary Survey, National Association for Law Placement, Washington, D.C., (annual).

Guide to Law Specialties, Law Placement Association of Cleveland, Cleveland (1990).

"Judicial Clerkships: A Symposium on the Institution," 26 Vanderbilt Law Review (Nov. 1973).

Kocher, Eric, *International Jobs: Where They Are and How to Get Them,* Addison Wesley Publishing, Reading MA (1983).

Konen, James S., *How Can You Defend Those People?: The Making of a Criminal Lawyer,* McGraw-Hill, New York (1983).

Law Clerk Handbook, Federal Judicial Center, Washington, D.C. (1989).

McAdams, Terry W. *Careers in the Nonprofit Sector: Doing Well by Doing Good,* The Tact Group, Washington, D.C. (1986).

Munneke, Gary A., *Careers in Law,* VGM Professional Careers Series, Lincolnwood IL (1992).

Occupational Outlook Handbook, U.S. Department of Labor, Bureau of Labor Statistics, Washington, D.C., (annual).

Openchowski, Charles, *Guide to Environmental Law in Washington, D.C.,* Environmental Law Institute, Washington, D.C. (1990).

Opportunities in Public Interest Law, Access, Boston (quarterly).

Powers, Linda, ed., *Careers in International Affairs,* School of Foreign Service, Georgetown University, Washington, D.C. (1988).

Peters, Thomas and Waterman, Robert H., *In Search of Excellence,* Harper & Row, New York (1982).

Stewart, James B., *The Prosecutors: Inside the Offices of the Governments' Most Powerful lawyers*, Simon & Schuster, New York (1987).

Vogt, Leona, *From Law School to Career: Where Do Graduates Go and What Do They Do?*, Harvard Law School, Cambridge, MA (1986).

Williams John W., ed., *Career Preparation and Opportunities in International Law*, American Bar Association, Chicago (1984).

Zehring, John W. *Careers in State and Local Government*, Garrett Park Press, Garrett, MD (1980).

1990 U.S. Census, U.S. Department of Labor, Bureau of the Census.

G. The Legal Press

ABA Journal

American Lawyer

Lawyers Alert

Student Lawyer

National Law Journal

Newsletters
> *Law Office Management and Administration Report*
> *Of Counsel*
> *The Lawyer's PC*

Regional Legal Newspapers (various cities)
State and local bar journals of each state, some cities

H. ABA Career Series

Bay, Monica, *Careers in Civil Litigation* (1990).
Henslee, William, *Careers in Entertainment Law* (1990).
Shropshire, Kenneth L, *Careers in Sports Law* (1990).
Thorner, Abbie W., *Now Hiring: Government Jobs for Lawyers* (1988).
Luney, Percy, R., Jr, *Careers in Natural Resource and Environmental Law* (1987).
Utley, Francis, with Gary A. Munneke, *Nonlegal Careers for Lawyers: In the Private Sector* (1984).
Wayne, Ellen, *Careers in Labor Law* (1985).

I. NonLegal Careers

Anderson, Evelyn, and Elaine Duskoff, *Legal Careers - Choices and options - Volume II*, NALP, Washington, D.C., (1984).

Grant, Kathleen, and Wendy Werner, *The Road Not Taken: A Practical Guide to Exploring Non-Legal Career Options*, NALP Washington, D.C., (1991).

Parker, Penny, ed., *Legal Careers in Business, Volume III*, NALP, Washington, D.C., (1984).

Wayne, Ellen, and Betsy McCombs, *Legal Careers Choices and Options*, NALP, Washington, D.C. (1983).

J. Solo Practice

Foonberg, Jay G, *How to Start and Build a Law Practice*, 3rd edition, American Bar Association.

Killoughey, Donna, ed., *Flying Solo: A Survival Guide for the Solo Practitioner*, American Bar Association, Section of Law Practice Management, Chicago (1984).

Singer, Gerald, *How to Go Directly into Computerized Law Practice Without Missing a Meal (or a Byte)*, Lawyer's Co-op-Bancroft Whitney, Rochester, N.Y., (1986).

K. Directories and Lists

American Bank Directory, vols. I and II, McFadden Business Publications (1987).

American Lawyer 500, The American Lawyer, New York (annual).

Anzalone, Joan, ed., *Good Works: A Guide to Careers in Social Change, Dembner Books*, 3rd edition, New York (1985).

Association of American Law Schools, *Placement Bulletin*, Washington, D.C. (quarterly).

Attorneys & Agents Registered to Practice Before the U.S. Patent and Trademark Office, Department of Commmerce Washington, D.C. (1987).

Best's Directory of Recommended Insurance Attorneys, A.M. Best Company, Oldwick, NJ (1987).

Broadcasting Yearbook, Broadcasting Publication, Inc. (annual).

Book of the States, Council of State Governments, Lexington, KY (annual).

Brownson, Charles B., and Anna Brownson, *Congressional Staff Directory*, Congressional Staff Directory Ltd. Mt. Vernon, VA (1988).

Burek, Deborah M., ed., *Encyclopedia of Associations*, 26th edition, Gale Research Co. (1991).

Directory of Graduate Law Degree Programs, Federal Reports, Washington, D.C. (1990).

Cherovsky, Erwin, *The Guide to New York Law Firms*, St. Martins Press, New York, (1991).

Clearinghouse Review, National Clearinghouse for Legal Services, Inc., Chicago, IL (periodical).

Congressional Directory, U.S. Government Printing Office, Washington, D.C. (annual).

Congressional Yellow Pages, Monitor Publishing Co., Washington, D.C. (annual).

Congressional Yellow Book, Monitor Publishing Co., New York (annual).

Conservation Directory, National Wildlife Federation, Washington, D.C (1983).

Directory of Environmental Attorneys, Prentice Hall, Law & Business, New York (1992).

Directory of Foreign Firms Operating in the United States, 5th Edition. Uniworld Business Publications, Inc. New York (1986).

Directory of Occupational Titles, U.S. Department of Labor, Washington, D.C., 4th ed. (1977); supplement (1986).

Directory of Public Interest Law Centers, Alliance for Justice, Washington, D.C. (1986).

Directory of State and Local Judges, National College of the State Judiciary (annual).

Dubaugh, Kerry, and Gary Serota, *Capitol Jobs: An Insider's Guide to Finding a Job in Congress*, Tilden Press, Washington, D.C. (June 1983).

DuChez, Jo-Anne, ed., *The National Directory of State Agencies*, NSA Directories, Bethesda, MD (1987).

Guide to American Directories, B. Klein Publications, Inc, Coral Springs, FL. (triennial).

Federal and State Judicial Clerkship Survey, NALP, Washington, D.C. (annual).

Federal Law Related Careers, Federal Reports, Washington, D.C. (1990).

Federal Yellow Book, Monitor Bublishing, New York (annual).

Hill, Howard B. and, James Silkenat, *Guide to Foreign Law Firms*, American Bar Association, Section of International Law (1989).

Jessup, Deborah Hitchcock, *Guide to State Environmental Programs*, 2nd ed., Bureau of National Affairs, Washington, D.C. (1990).

Judicial Staff Directory, Staff Directories, Ltd., Mt. Vernon, PA (annual).

Kaiser, Geoffrey & Barbara Mule, *The Public Interest Handbook: A Guide to Legal Careers in Public Interest Organizations*, Locust Hill Press, West Cornwall, CT (1987).

Law and Business Directory of Corporate Counsel, Prentice Hall Law and Business, New York (annual).

Law Firms Yellow Book: Who's Who In The Management of The Leading U.S. Law Firms, Monitor Pub. Co., New York (Semiannual).

Levering, Robert, Milton Moscowitz, and Michael Katz, *The 100 Best Companies to Work for in America*, Addison Wesley Publishing, Reading, MA (1984).

LoPucki, Lynn M., *Directory of Bankruptcy Attorneys*, Prentice-Hall, New York (1988).

Markham's Negligence Council, Markham Publishing Corporation.

Martindale-Hubbell Legal Directory (annual).

College Placement Annual, College Placement Council, Bethlehem, PA (annual).

McLean, Janice, ed., *The Consultants and Consulting Organization Directory*, 8th Edition, Gale Research Co., Detroit, MI (1988).

Moody's Manuals (various), Moody's Industrial Services Inc. (annual).

NALP Directory of Public Interest Internships, National Association of Public Interest Law, Washington, D.C. (annual).

NAPIL Fellowship Guide, National Association for Public Interest Law, Washington, D.C. (annual).

Directory of Graduate Law Degree Programs, Federal Reports, Washington, D.C. (annual).

NLADA Directory, National Legal Aid and Defender Association Clearinghouse Review, Washington, D.C. (annual).

Program Directory, Legal Services Corporation, Washington, D.C. (1984).

Renz, Loren, ed., *The Foundation Directory*, 11th Edition, The Foundation Center, New York (1987).

Russell, John J., ed., *Directory of National Trade and Professional Associations of the United States*, Columbia books, 23rd edition Washington, D.C. (1988).

Standard and Poor Directory of Corporations Directory of Legal Employers, NALP, Washington, D.C. (annual)

State Administrative Officials Classified by Functions, Council of State Governments, Lexington, KY (1984).

State Administrative Officials Classified by Function, The Council of State Governments Lexington, KY (annual).

Summer Legal Employment Guide, Federal Reports, Washington, D.C. (annual).

The Lawyers Almanac, Prentice Hall Law and Business, New York (annual).

The Lawyers Register of Specialties and Fields of Law, Lawyer to Lawyer Consultation Panel, Cleveland, OH (annual).

The National Directory of Prosecuting Attorneys, The National District Attorneys Association, Chicago, IL (annual).

The National and Federal Legal Employment Report, Federal Reports, Inc., Washington, D.C. (monthly).

United States Court Directory, Administrative office of the United States Courts, Washington, D.C. (annual).

U.S. Government Manual, U.S. Government Printing Office, Washington, D.C. (annual).

United States Lawyers Reference Directory, Legal Directories Publishing, Los Angeles, CA (annual).

Zarozny, Sharon, ed., *The Federal Database Finder*, Information, U.S.A., (1987).

Class of 1990 — National Salary Summary Figures — Medians and Means

General Category	National Median	National Mean	Interquartile Range for Group*
Academic	$35,000	$37,400	$27,000-$45,000 ($18K)
Business	$42,000	$46,260	$33,000-$54,300 ($21.3K)
Clerkship	$29,890	$28,740	$27,000-$30,000 ($3K)
Government	$30,000	$31,100	$26,000-$34,800 ($8.8K)**
Law Firm	$50,000	$50,960	$36,000-$65,000 ($29K)
Public Interest	$25,900	$27,070	$21,500-$30,000 ($8.5K)**
All Categories	**$40,000**	**$44,290**	**$29,900-$57,500 ($27.6K)**

* The Interquartile range is the range from the 25th to the 75th percentile, that is, the middle half of all salaries.

** Public defender positions, which were categorized as public interest positions in prior ERSS surveys, were reclassified as government jobs in 1990. The 1990 national median salary for public defenders was $28,000.

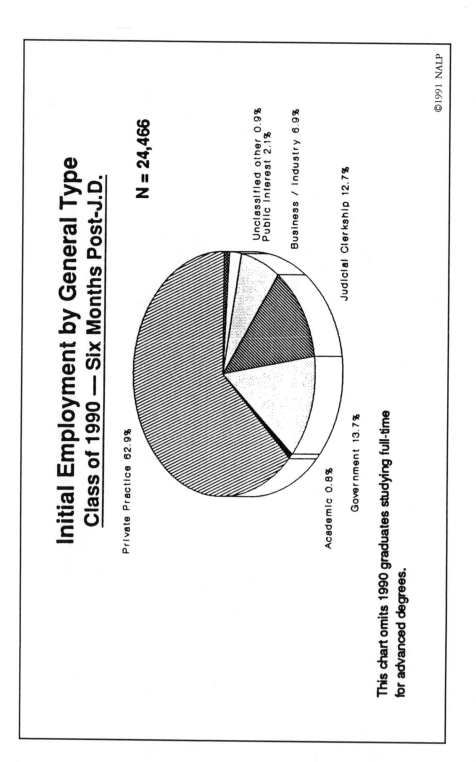

Initial Employment by General Type
Class of 1990 — Six Months Post-J.D.

N = 24,466

Private Practice 62.9%

Unclassified other 0.9%
Public Interest 2.1%

Business / Industry 6.9%

Judicial Clerkship 12.7%

Academic 0.8%

Government 13.7%

This chart omits 1990 graduates studying full-time
for advanced degrees.

INTRODUCTION

The National Association for Law Placement (NALP) was organized in 1971 to promote the exchange of information and cooperation between law schools and employers. In order to advance those interests, the Association has developed, and its members have agreed to abide by, these "Principles and Standards for Law Placement and Recruitment Activities."

The NALP "Principles and Standards for Law Placement and Recruitment Activities" were first adopted in 1978. Part V, "Standards for the Timing of Offers and Acceptances," was derived from "Interviewing Procedures for Law Students and Prospective Employers," a set of guidelines originally adopted in the early 1960s by a group of law schools meeting under the auspices of the Association of the Bar of the City of New York. A second edition was approved by NALP at its 1984 Annual Meeting for a provisional period of one year and then adopted without changes at the 1985 Annual Business Meeting. Following a series of discussions of the proposed changes at NALP's 1988 regional meetings and through subsequent refinements, the current version was adopted at the 1988 Annual Business Meeting.

The "Principles and Standards for Law Placement and Recruitment Activities" are organized as follows:

I. **General Principles**

II. **Principles for Law Schools**

III. **Principles for Candidates**

IV. **Principles for Employers**

V. **General Standards for the Timing of Offers and Acceptances**

NALP encourages law schools and legal employers to educate all participants in the law placement and recruitment process about the spirit and the letter of these "Principles and Standards."

PART I. GENERAL PRINCIPLES

Successful recruitment and placement of law students requires cooperation and good judgment from three groups — law schools, candidates, and employers. These "Principles and Standards" provide concrete guidelines for each group.

Activities related to the placement and hiring of law students should be conducted on the highest professional level. Timely exchange of accurate information is essential.

Recruitment activities should be scheduled so as to minimize interference with students' academic work.

Underlying these guidelines for ethical behavior is NALP's fundamental commitment to the accessibility of the legal profession to all individuals of competence and requisite moral character. NALP is strongly opposed to discrimination which is based upon gender, age, race, color, religious creed, national origin, physical disability, marital, parental or veteran status, sexual orientation, or the prejudice of clients.

In addition to abiding by these guidelines, all parties concerned with placement and hiring should observe strictly all relevant laws, accreditation standards and institutional policies.

If unusual circumstances or particular organizational constraints require a law school, a candidate, or an employer to modify any provision herein, every effort should be made to find an alternative acceptable to all parties concerned.

PART II. PRINCIPLES FOR LAW SCHOOLS

Law schools should make career planning and placement services available to all students.

Career planning and placement are integral parts of legal education. Law schools should dedicate to them adequate physical space, equipment, financial support, and staff.

The professional services of a career planning and placement office should be available to students without charge.

- 1 -

Law schools should strive to meet the placement needs and interests of all students. Preferential treatment should not be extended to any student or employer.

Law schools should establish and implement practices to ensure the fair and accurate representation of students and the institution in the placement process.

Law schools should provide to employers and other interested parties comprehensive information on grade standards and distribution, curriculum, degree requirements, admissions and enrollment profiles, academic awards criteria, and placement office policies and procedures.

Law schools should adopt and enforce policies which prohibit misrepresentation and other student abuses of the employment search process, such as engaging in interviews for practice, failing to decline offers in which there is no longer interest, or continuing to interview after acceptance of employment.

NALP Employment and Salary Survey information should be collected by law schools and the survey results made available to employers, prospective students, and all other interested parties.

Law schools should subscribe to and promote practices that protect their students' legal rights.

Students' privacy should be protected against illegal or inappropriate dissemination of personal information. Information protected by federal, state, or municipal law must not be disclosed without proper consent. Institutional policies conforming to prevailing laws should be formulated and published to the attention of both students and employers.

Law schools should articulate and publish meaningful policies prohibiting discriminatory hiring practices. Procedures should be developed and published whereby claims of violations can be investigated and resolved promptly and fairly.

Law schools should educate students as to proper career investigation techniques and protocol.

Publications and counseling provided by law schools should be designed to afford students adequate information about the variety of opportunities available to persons with legal training and proper methods for exploring such opportunities. Students should be counseled to focus their career choices based on their aptitudes and career goals.

Law schools should work actively to develop employment opportunities for students and graduates. All employment opportunity notices should be publicized to all students.

Students' freedom of choice in career decisions should be protected from undue influences.

In counseling students, placement officers and others within the law school community should avoid interposing either their own values or institutional interests.

Law schools should develop and publish for students and employers clear policies concerning the timing of offers and acceptances.

Law schools should establish adequate procedures to facilitate recruitment by a broad range of potential employers.

To enhance student learning and increase career development opportunities, placement offices should maintain good working relationships with students, faculty, alumnae/i, and other elements of the legal community.

Procedures to enable employers to conduct on-campus interviews, solicit direct applications or collect student resumes should be designed for maximum efficiency and fairness. Those procedures should be clearly articulated and available in writing to students and employers.

Law schools should maintain productive working relationships with employers.

In dealing with employers, law schools should make maximum use of standardized forms and procedures.

Law schools should not disseminate information learned in confidence from employers.

In order to ensure maximum information-sharing and efficiency in the placement process, law schools should cooperate with one another to the fullest extent possible in gathering employer information and providing interview services.

Law schools should not offer placement services to first semester first year students prior to November 1.

The first year of law school demands the student's closest attention. Sound education policy requires that law schools provide an environment as free as is feasible of external distraction so that entering students have the maximum attainable opportunity to devote themselves to their studies.

Law schools should normally not schedule on-campus interviewing of first year students until after semester examinations have ended.

PART III. PRINCIPLES FOR CANDIDATES

Candidates should prepare thoroughly for the employment search process.

Candidates should comply with the placement policies and procedures of law schools whose services they use.

Before beginning an employment search, candidates should engage in thorough self-examination. Work skills, vocational aptitudes and interests, lifestyle and geographic preferences, academic performance, career expectations and life experiences should be carefully evaluated so that informed choices can be made. General instruction should be obtained on employment search skills, particularly those relating to the interview process.

Prior to making employment inquiries, candidates should learn as much as possible about target employers and the nature of their positions. Candidates should interview only with employers in whom they have a genuine interest.

Throughout the employment search process candidates should represent their qualifications and interests fully and accurately.

Candidates should be prepared to provide, at employers' request, copies of all academic transcripts. Under no circumstances should academic biographical data be falsified, misrepresented, or distorted either in writing or orally. Candidates who engage in such conduct may be subject to elimination from consideration for employment by the employer, suspension or other academic discipline by the law school, and disqualification from admission to practice by bar admission authorities.

Candidates should be prepared to advise prospective employers of the nature and extent of their training in legal writing. Writing samples submitted as evidence of a candidate's legal skills should be wholly original work. Where the writing was done with others, the candidate's contribution should be clearly identified. Writing samples from law-related employment must be masked adequately to preserve client confidentiality and used only with the permission of the supervising attorney.

Throughout the employment search process students should conduct themselves in a professional manner.

Candidates who participate in the on-campus interview process should adhere to all scheduling commitments. Cancellations should occur only for good cause and should be promptly communicated to the placement office or the employer.

Invitations for in-office interviews should be acknowledged promptly and accepted only if the candidate has a genuine interest in the employer.

Candidates invited to interview at employer offices should request reimbursement only for ordinary and necessary expenses which are directly related to the interview and incurred in good faith. Failure to observe this policy, or falsification or misrepresentation of travel expenses, may result in elimination from consideration for employment or the revocation of offers by an employer.

Candidates expecting reimbursement for travel expenses should reach an understanding with the employer prior to the trip. Expenses for trips during which interviews with more than one employer occur should be prorated in accordance with those employers' policies.

First semester first year students shall not initiate contact with prospective employers before December 1.

Candidates should notify employers and their placement offices of their acceptance or rejection of employment offers by the earliest possible time, and no later than the time established by rule, custom, or agreement.

Candidates should expect and request offers to be confirmed in writing. Candidates should abide by the standards for student responses set out in Part V and should in any event respond in writing to offers as soon as their decision is made, even if that decision is made in advance of the prevailing deadline date.

In fairness to both employers and peers, students should act in good faith to decline promptly offers for interviews and employment which are no longer being seriously considered. In order for law schools to comply with federal and institutional reporting requirements, students should notify the placement office upon acceptance of an employment offer, whether or not the employment was obtained through the office.

Candidates seeking or preparing to accept fellowships, judicial clerkships, or other limited term professional employment should apprise prospective employers of their intentions and obtain a clear understanding of their offer deferral policies.

Candidates should consider the acceptance of an offer a binding obligation.

Candidates should, upon acceptance of an offer of employment, immediately withdraw from consideration with all other employers.

If, because of unforeseen circumstances, it becomes necessary for a candidate to request release from or modification of his or her acceptance, both the employer and the placement office should be notified promptly.

Students who engage in law-related employment should adhere to the same standards of conduct as lawyers.

In matters arising out of law-related employment, students should be guided by the standards for professional conduct which are applicable in the employer's state. When acting on behalf of employers in a recruitment capacity, students should be guided by the employer principles in Part IV.

Students should exercise care to provide full and fair information when advising peers about former employers.

Candidates should promptly report to the placement office any misrepresentation, discrimination or other abuse by employers in the employment process.

PART IV. PRINCIPLES FOR EMPLOYERS

Employers should respect the policies, procedures and legal obligations of individual law schools and should request only services or information which are consistent therewith.

Employers should not expect or request preferential services from law schools.

Employers should not solicit information received by law schools in confidence from candidates or other employers.

Employer organizations are responsible for the conduct of their recruiters and for any representation made by them.

Hiring decisions must be based solely on bona fide occupational qualifications. Employers should carefully avoid conduct of any kind during the interview and selection process that acts or appears to act to discriminate unlawfully or in a way contrary to the policies of a particular institution.

Factors in candidates' backgrounds which have no predictive value with respect to employment performance, such as scores on examinations required for admission to academic institutions, should not be relied upon by employers in the hiring process.

Candidates' personal privacy should be safeguarded. Information about candidates which is protected by law should not be disclosed by an employer to any third party without specific permission.

An employer should honor all commitments made on its behalf. Offers of employment should be made in writing, with all terms clearly expressed.

Employers should designate recruiters who are both skilled and knowledgeable about the employing organization. Employers should instruct interviewers not to make any unauthorized commitments.

Employers should refrain from any activity which may adversely affect the ability of candidates to make an independent and considered decision.

Appointments with candidates for in-house interviews should be established for a mutually convenient time.

Employers should give candidates a reasonable period of time to consider offers of employment and should avoid conduct which subjects candidates to undue pressure to accept.

Response deadlines should be established when the offer of employment is made. Employers who extend offers in the Fall should abide by the timetable for student response set out in Part V and must abide by it with respect to students enrolled in law schools which have adopted it as an employer requirement.

Employers should not offer special inducements to persuade candidates to accept offers of employment earlier than is customary or prescribed under the circumstances.

Employers shall not initiate contact with, interview, or make offers to first semester first year students prior to December 15.

When evaluating second and third year applicants, employers should not place undue emphasis on the nature of a first year summer job experience or on a student's decision not to work after the first year.

There has been a long-standing tradition that the first year summer be used to engage in public service work or to take time away from the law.

Employers should avoid the preconception that students who choose to take time away from the law altogether during the summer following their first year of law school are less motivated or less dedicated to their legal careers.

First year students need freedom to experiment with various career options.

The recent practice of having first year students work in private law firms provides additional employment opportunities to some students, but such experiences should not be valued or emphasized inordinately.

Employers should provide full and accurate information about the organization and the positions for which recruitment is being conducted.

Employers should provide to law schools complete organizational information as contained in the NALP Employer Questionnaire, well in advance of any recruitment activities. Position descriptions should include information about the qualifications sought in candidates, the hiring timetable, nature of the work, the number of available positions, and, if known at the time, the starting salary to be offered.

Invitations for in-office interviews should include a clear explanation of all expense reimbursement policies and procedures.

Employers should maintain productive working relationships with law schools.

Employers should inform law school placement offices in advance of any recruiting activities involving their students, whether conducted on- or off-campus, and

- 4 -

should, at the conclusion of those activities, inform the placement offices of the results obtained.

Employers who conduct on-campus interviews should refrain from making unnecessary schedule change requests.

Employers should promptly report to the placement office any misrepresentation or other abuse by students of the employment search process.

Employers without formal recruiting programs or whose hiring activities are sporadic in nature should notify law school placement offices as far in advance as possible of planned recruiting activities in order that appropriate assistance might be arranged.

PART V. GENERAL STANDARDS FOR THE TIMING OF OFFERS AND ACCEPTANCES

In order to foster an orderly interviewing, selection and decision-making process, the following employment offer and acceptance dates should be adhered to:

1. All offers to law students shall remain open for at least two weeks after the date made. This provision shall be construed for students covered by paragraphs 3 and 4 below so that the later response date is applied.

2. Prospective employers shall not initiate contact with, interview, or make offers to first semester first year students before December 15. First semester first year students shall not initiate contact with prospective employers before December 1.

3. Prospective employers offering positions prior to October 1 to second and third year students employed by them during the preceding summer shall leave those offers open until at least November 15, provided the student reaffirms his/her interest in the offer within 30 days of the date of the offer letter.

Any such students who are unable to complete their interviewing prior to November 15 may request from the offering employers a later date until which an offer should be left open.

4. Prospective employers offering positions in the fall to other students who were not employed by them during the preceding summer, and prospective employers offering positions on or after October 1 to second and third year students employed by them during the preceding summer, shall leave their offers open until at least December 15, provided the student reaffirms his/her interest in the offer within 30 days of the date of the offer letter.

Any such students who are unable to complete their interviewing prior to December 1 may request from the offering employer a later date until which an offer should be left open.

5. Employers having fewer than 25 attorneys may be exempted from the provisions of paragraphs 3 and 4 above.

Employers offering part-time positions for the school term may be exempted from the provisions of paragraphs 3 and 4 above with respect to the part-time offers. Both such employers are subject to the remaining provisions of NALP's Principles and Standards for Law Placement and Recruitment Activities.

6. A law student shall reaffirm his/her interest in an offer within 30 days of the date of the offer letter. Employers may retract offers which are not reaffirmed by students.

After October 1, a law student shall not hold open more than four offers of employment simultaneously, including offers received as a result of previous summer employment. For each offer received that places a student over the limit, the student shall, within one week of receipt of the excess offer, reject an offer. It is recommended that employers provide copies of offer letters to the students' placement directors to assist them in monitoring this standard.

Second and third year students may with the consent of the employer extend only one open offer beyond December 15.

7. An individual school may set offer response dates other than those established above. A school will do so only if it sees no reasonable alternative which will be fair to all employers who adhere to the school's rules for interviewing on campus and if it provides notice to all employers using its facilities of its special dates.

8. Violations of these standards should be reported to the student's placement director.

9. A law school may deny use of its placement facilities to students and employers who fail to adhere to these principles and standards for law placement and recruitment activities.

- 5 -

Government & Public Interest Organization Questionnaire
1992-93 Academic Year

Date completed _____
NALP member   Y ☐   N ☐
Collective form   Y ☐   N ☐
NALP region _____

National Association for Law Placement

CONTACT INFORMATION (as of 2-1-92)
Organization: _____

Street Address: _____
City: _____ State: _____ Zip: _____ Telephone: _____
Hiring Attorney: _____
ADDRESS INQUIRIES TO:
Name _____
Org. _____
_____
Address _____
_____
Phone (_____) _____

PRIMARY PRACTICE AREAS (as of 2-1-92)

Substantive Practice Areas (see instructions for terms)	% of Atty. Time

as of 2-1-91	Supervising Atty.	Sr./Staff Atty.	Summer 91 Intern	Paralegals	Other Prof.	Support
Men						
Women						
Totals						
Black						
Hispanic						
Am. Ind./Alsk.						
As. & Pac. Isl.						
Disabled						

as of 2-1-92	Supervising Atty.	Sr./Staff Atty.	Summer 92 Intern	Paralegals	Other Prof.	Support
Men						
Women						
Totals						
Black						
Hispanic						
Am. Ind./Alsk.						
As. & Pac. Isl.						
Disabled						

Nature of Work (Check all that apply)
☐ Trial Work   ☐ Legal Research   ☐ Lobbying
☐ Case Referrals   ☐ Appellate Work
Other (explain): _____

DEMOGRAPHICS (as of 2-1-92)
Office Completing Form
Supervising Attys. _____
   Title/Level _____
Senior Attys. _____
   Title/Level _____
Staff Attys. _____
   Title/Level _____
Total Attys. _____
Office size (attys.):   ☐ 2-10   ☐ 11-25   ☐ 26-50
   ☐ 51-100   ☐ 101-250   ☐ 251-500   ☐ 501 +
Organizers/Lobbyists _____ Other Prof. Staff _____
Paralegals _____ Support _____

Other Offices (city, state, no. of lawyers)

_____   _____
_____   _____
Total size (attys.):   ☐ 2-10   ☐ 11-25   ☐ 26-50
   ☐ 51-100   ☐ 101-250   ☐ 251-500   ☐ 501 +

EMPLOYMENT DATA (as of 2-1-92)

		No. Employed 1991	Anticipated Openings 1992	Anticipated Openings 1993
Attorneys	Laterals	( )	( )	( )
Attorneys	Entry-level	( )	( )	( )
Attorneys	LLMs	( )	( )	( )
Attorneys	Foreign LLMs	( )	( )	( )
Summer	Post-3Ls	( )	( )	( )
Summer	2Ls	( )	( )	( )
Summer	1Ls			

( ) number in parens represents former summer clerks
2Ls considered for attorney offers in 1991 _____
   No. offers made _____
Prefer students w/ significant prior experience in area?
   Y ☐   N ☐
For atty. hires, require: Bar admission?   Y ☐   N ☐
   Prior practice experience?   Y ☐   N ☐   No. yrs. _____
Hiring criteria _____
_____
_____

U.S. citizenship required?   Y ☐   N ☐

	1991	1992
Avg. total atty. hrs. worked p.a.	_____	_____
Usual scheduled working day	_____	_____

Organization: _____

EMPLOYMENT DATA, cont'd.　　　　$/week

Summer clerk	1991	1992
Grade/level _____	_____	_____

New atty.
　Grade/level _____　　_____　_____

What % of legal staff has been with the organization
　　for more than two years? _____
　　for more than five years? _____
　　for more than ten years? _____

OTHER DATA (as of 2-1-92)

Work assignments:　Departmentalized?　Y ☐　N ☐
　　Rotation?　Y ☐　N ☐　Length: _____

Alternative Schedules
　　Part-time allowed?　Y ☐　N ☐
　　No. part-time attys.: _____
　　Part-time available to entry level?　Y ☐　N ☐
　　Flex-time allowed?　Y ☐　N ☐

BENEFITS _____
_____
_____

MINORITY RECRUITMENT _____
_____
_____

Fellowships

Accept applicants with subsidized salaries?　Y ☐　N ☐
☐ Work study　☐ Student-funded　☐ Law firm funded
☐ Grants　☐ Externships for academic credit
Outside funding required for employment　Y ☐　N ☐
Match outside funding source?　Y ☐　N ☐
Willing to consider fellowship affiliations?　Y ☐　N ☐
　　Explain _____
_____

List prior fellowship affiliations _____
_____

Sponsor your own fellowship program?　Y ☐　N ☐

APPLICATION PROCESS　　　Summer　　　Atty.

	Summer	Atty.
Date appls. first accepted	_____	_____
Deadline for appls.	_____	_____
Av. length of hiring process (mos.)	_____	_____
Most hiring done in (month)	_____	_____

1Ls hired?　Y ☐　N ☐　Other _____
When after 12/1 should 1Ls apply? _____

CAMPUS INTERVIEWS (as of 2-1-92)

_____	_____	_____
_____	_____	_____
_____	_____	_____

NARRATIVE (*no attachments, please*):

NALP • Suite 450, 1666 Connecticut Ave., Washington, DC 20009 • (202) 667-1666

CORPORATE Questionnaire
1992-93 Academic Year

Date completed _____
NALP member Y ☐ N ☐
Collective form Y ☐ N ☐
NALP region _____

**National
Association
for Law
Placement**

CONTACT INFORMATION (as of 2-1-92)
Organization: _____
Street Address: _____
City: _____ State: _____ Zip: _____ Telephone: _____
Hiring Attorney: _____

ADDRESS INQUIRIES TO:
Name _____
Title _____
Org. _____
Address _____

Phone (_____) _____

DEMOGRAPHICS (as of 2-1-92)
Size of Office Completing Form

Counsel/		Paralegals	_____
Senior Attys.	_____	Other Prof.	_____
Staff Attys.	_____	Support	_____
Total Attys.	_____		

Office size (attys): ☐ 2-10 ☐ 11-25 ☐ 26-50
☐ 51-100 ☐ 101-250 ☐ 251-500 ☐ 501 +

Other Offices

City	No. Attys
_____	_____
_____	_____
_____	_____
_____	_____

Total size (attys): ☐ 2-10 ☐ 11-25 ☐ 26-50
☐ 51-100 ☐ 101-250 ☐ 251-500 ☐ 501 +

	2-1-91			2-1-92		
	Counsel	Attorneys	Summer 91 Interns	Counsel	Attorneys	Summer 92 Interns
Men						
Women						
Totals						
Black						
Hispanic						
Am. Ind./Alsk.						
As. & Pac. Isl.						
Disabled						

CAREER DEVELOPMENT

	81	82	83	84	85	86
Entering class size:						
Laterals hired:						
Considered for promotion:						
Counsel made:						
No. remaining (unpromoted):						

Counsel track (yrs.): _____
Notes: _____
_____
_____

PRIMARY PRACTICE AREAS (as of 2-1-92)

Practice areas over 5% of practice (see instructions for terms)	No. Counsel/ Sr. Attys.	No. Attorneys

EMPLOYMENT DATA (as of 2-1-92)

		No. Employed	Anticipated Openings	
		1991	1992	1993
Attorneys	Laterals	( )	( )	( )
	Entry-level	( )	( )	( )
	LLMs	( )	( )	( )
	Foreign LLMs	( )	( )	( )
Summer	Post-3Ls	( )	( )	( )
	2Ls	( )	( )	( )
	1Ls			

( ) number in parens represents former summer clerks
2Ls considered for attorney offers in 1991 _____
No. offers made _____
Split summers allowed? Y ☐ N ☐ Min. weeks: _____
1Ls hired? Y ☐ N ☐ Other _____
When after 12/1 should 1Ls apply? _____
Accept applications for 1993 summer program from:
1996 joint degree candidates? Y ☐ N ☐
Judicial clerks? Y ☐ N ☐
Students at foreign law schools? Y ☐ N ☐
Hiring criteria _____
_____
_____

	1991	1992
Avg. total atty. hrs. worked p.a.	_____	
Min. no. atty. hrs. required p.a.	_____	_____
Summer Intern $/week	$ _____	$ _____
New Attorney $/year	$ _____	$ _____

Other compensation _____

Organization: _____

OTHER DATA (as of 2-1-92)

Work assignments: Departmentalized? Y ☐   N ☐
    Rotation? Y ☐   N ☐ Length: _____
    Part-time allowed? Y ☐   N ☐
    No. part-time attys.: _____
    Part-time available to entry level? Y ☐   N ☐

CAMPUS INTERVIEWS (as of 2-1-92)

_____ _____ _____
_____ _____ _____
_____ _____ _____
_____ _____

BENEFITS _____
_____
_____

PRO BONO _____
_____
_____

PUBLIC INTEREST FELLOWSHIPS _____
_____

MINORITY RECRUITMENT EFFORTS _____
_____
_____

NARRATIVE (*no attachments, please*):

NALP • Suite 450, 1666 Connecticut Ave., Washington, DC 20009 • (202) 667-1666

LAW FIRM Questionnaire
1992-93 Academic Year

Date completed _____
NALP member Y ☐ N ☐
Collective form Y ☐ N ☐
NALP region _____

National Association for Law Placement

Please refer to instructions before completing this form.

CONTACT INFORMATION (as of 2-1-92)

Firm: _____
Street Address: _____
City: _____ State: _____ Zip: _____ Telephone: _____
Hiring Attorney: _____

ADDRESS INQUIRIES TO:
Name _____
Title _____
Firm _____
Address _____

Phone (___) _____

DEMOGRAPHICS (as of 2-1-92)
Size of Office Completing Form

Partners _____   Paralegals _____
Counsel _____   Other Prof. _____
Associates _____   Support _____
Senior Attys. _____
Staff Attys. _____
Total Attys. _____

Office size (attys): ☐ 2-10 ☐ 11-25 ☐ 26-50
☐ 51-100 ☐ 101-250 ☐ 251-500 ☐ 501+

Other Offices

City	No. Attys
_____	_____
_____	_____
_____	_____
_____	_____
_____	_____

Total firm size (attys): ☐ 2-10 ☐ 11-25 ☐ 26-50
☐ 51-100 ☐ 101-250 ☐ 251-500 ☐ 501+

as of 2-1-91

	Partners	Counsel	Assocs.	Senior Attys.	Staff Attys.	Summer 91
Men						
Women						
Totals						
Black						
Hispanic						
Am. Ind./Alsk.						
As. & Pac. Isl.						
Disabled						

as of 2-1-92

	Partners	Counsel	Assocs.	Senior Attys.	Staff Attys.	Summer 92
Men						
Women						
Totals						
Black						
Hispanic						
Am. Ind./Alsk.						
As & Pac. Isl.						
Disabled						

PRIMARY PRACTICE AREAS (as of 2-1-92)

Practice areas over 5% of practice (see instructions for terms)	No. Partners/ Counsel	No. Other Lawyers

EMPLOYMENT DATA (as of 2-1-92)

		No. Employed	Anticipated Openings	
		1991	1992	1993
Attorneys	Laterals	( )	( )	( )
	Entry-level	( )	( )	( )
	LLMs	( )	( )	( )
	Foreign LLMs	( )	( )	( )
Summer	Post-3Ls	( )	( )	( )
	2Ls	( )	( )	( )
	1Ls			

( ) number in parens represents former summer associates
2Ls considered for associate offers in 1991 _____
   No. offers made _____
Split summers allowed? Y ☐ N ☐ Min. weeks: _____
1Ls hired? Y ☐ N ☐ Other _____
When after 12/1 should 1Ls apply? _____
Accept applications for 1993 summer program from:
   1996 joint degree candidates? Y ☐ N ☐
   Judicial clerks? Y ☐ N ☐
   Students at foreign law schools? Y ☐ N ☐
Hiring criteria _____
_____

	1991	1992
Avg. total assoc. hrs. worked p.a.	_____	
Avg. total assoc. billable hrs. p.a.	_____	
Min. assoc. billable hrs.	_____	_____
1L summer $/week	$ _____	$ _____
2L summer $/week	$ _____	$ _____
Post- 3L summer $/week	$ _____	$ _____
New associate $/year	$ _____	$ _____

Other compensation _____
_____

Firm: _____

PARTNERSHIP DATA	81	82	83	84	85	86
Entering class size	___	___	___	___	___	___
Laterals hired	___	___	___	___	___	___
Considered for ptrship.	___	___	___	___	___	___
Partners made	___	___	___	___	___	___
Remaining (non-ptrs.)	___	___	___	___	___	___

Two or more tiers of partners? Y ☐ N ☐
Partnership track (yrs.): _____
Notes: _____
_____
_____

BENEFITS _____
_____
_____

PRO BONO _____
_____

PUBLIC INTEREST FELLOWSHIPS _____
_____

MINORITY RECRUITMENT EFFORTS _____
_____
_____

OTHER DATA (as of 2-1-92)
Work assignments: Departmentalized? Y ☐ N ☐
    Rotation? Y ☐ N ☐ Length: _____
Part-time allowed? Y ☐ N ☐ No. part-time attys.: _____
Part-time available to entry level? Y ☐ N ☐

CAMPUS INTERVIEWS (as of 2-1-92)
_____ _____ _____
_____ _____ _____
_____ _____ _____
_____ _____ _____

NARRATIVE (*no attachments, please*):

NALP • Suite 450, 1666 Connecticut Ave.,
Washington, DC 20009 • (202) 667-1666

Action Verb List

Accelerated	Documented	Pledged
Accepted	Donated	Predicted
Acquitted	Drafted	Prepared
Addressed	Edited	Presented
Advocated	Effected	Produced
Allocated	Enforced	Proposed
Amended	Engaged	Prosecuted
Analyzed	Enhanced	Protected
Applied	Enlarged	Provided
Arbitrated	Entered	Pursued
Argued	Established	Recommended
Arranged	Executed	Recruited
Assembled	Exercised	Refined
Assisted	Expanded	Represented
Attracted	Expedited	Renewed
Authored	Explored	Reorganized
Backed	Exposed	Reported
Brought	Facilitated	Researched
Budgeted	Filed	Resolved
Built	Formulated	Restructured
Chaired	Fought	Revealed
Challenged	Handled	Revised
Charted	Implemented	Revitalized
Collected	Improved	Served
Compiled	Increased	Settled
Completed	Initiated	Simplified
Conceived	Innovated	Solved
Conducted	Inquired	Sponsored
Constructed	Instituted	Started
Contracted	Instructed	Stimulated
Contributed	Interviewed	Strengthened
Controlled	Introduced	Studied
Convicted	Investigated	Suggested
Corrected	Litigated	Summarized
Coordinated	Managed	Supervised
Counseled	Maximized	Supported
Created	Mobilized	Systematized
Cross Examined	Motivated	Took Charge
Defended	Negotiated	Took Over
Demonstrated	Noted	Trained
Designed	Obtained	Transacted
Determined	Operated	Tried
Developed	Organized	Upgraded
Devised	Originated	Upset
Devoted	Persuaded	Won
Directed	Planned	Wrote
Disseminated